DANIEL MORGAN

Revolutionary Rifleman

The Institute of Early American History and Culture is sponsored jointly by the College of William and Mary and Colonial Williamsburg, Incorporated. Publication of this book was assisted by a grant from the Lilly Endowment, Inc.

DANIEL MORGAN. Portrait by Charles Willson Peale.

DANIEL MORGAN

Revolutionary Rifleman

by DON HIGGINBOTHAM

PUBLISHED FOR THE
*Institute of Early American History and Culture
at Williamsburg, Virginia*

by The University of North Carolina Press   ·   Chapel Hill

TO MARY

Preface

THIS is not the first biography of Daniel Morgan. Previously James Graham wrote *The Life of General Daniel Morgan* ... (1856), based in part on the General's papers now preserved in the New York Public Library. Graham's study, though having considerable merit, largely ignores Morgan's domestic activities and certain significant aspects of his military career. At the same time, it contains so many digressions of dubious pertinence that the man is often obscured by his "times." More important, a host of manuscripts and printed sources with direct bearing upon Morgan have become available since Graham's book appeared. Certainly a new biography of Morgan is in order.

Morgan's life was a varied and notable one. It sheds light on frontier conditions in colonial Virginia. It affords an opportunity to study the hit-and-run backwoods fighting that American Revolutionary soldiers knew best. It presents a vantage point from which to view such prominent patriot military figures as Benedict Arnold, Horatio Gates, and Nathanael Greene—to see them as their subordinate, Morgan, saw them. It gives new information about the suppression of the Whisky Rebellion. And it offers some sidelights on Federalist politics in the 1790's.

Essentially, though, this is a book about Morgan, not an account of his "times." It was a vigorous, zestful life that embraced the last six and one-half decades of the eighteenth century, a formative period in the history of the United States. Morgan

vii

joked, clowned, loved rum, enjoyed cards, took a common-law wife, and liked Indian attire. Without formal education, he spelled atrociously and lacked the prose style of "pope, Voltiere, or Shakespear." Preferring nicknames, he designated Washington as the "old horse" and Cornwallis as the "old Fox." He himself was the "old wagoner" or "old Morgan." His friends were "dear boys"; his enemies, "raskels" and "scoundrels." He could be kind and tender. He could be pugnacious—his fiery temper and sensitivity to criticism involved him in innumerable brawls and lawsuits. If this man had his share of faults, mostly of temperament, they paled against his greatest virtue: loyalty—loyalty to his soldiers, his friends, and his country. In Morgan's leathery face, with its prominent nose and forehead, firm mouth, and square chin, there was the appearance of rugged solidarity. Once he made a decision, he could be expected to stick to it. One had only to ask to determine his views on any issue. The American frontier movement produced few individuals as picturesque as Daniel Morgan.

A teamster and farmer before the Revolution, Morgan also fought in two Indian wars. He was with Braddock in 1755 and was severely beaten for striking a British soldier. He was wounded and almost tomahawked. He went on several grueling marches. He learned to fight in Indian fashion. Tall and muscular, he was well equipped for these activities, well equipped too for the strenuous duties of a combat officer of his day. And as a Revolutionary combat officer Morgan deserves to be remembered most. An excellent tactician, a superb leader of men, an outstanding light infantry commander, Morgan found his background for these accomplishments in his frontier experience. Only a handful of American officers performed on as many battlefields as he. His services ranged from Quebec in Canada to the Cowpens in South Carolina. Leading his famous rifle corps, he played a decisive role in the defeat of General John

Burgoyne's Anglo-German army which had marched southward from Canada in the hope of sealing off New England from the other American states. But Morgan's greatest personal triumph came at the Cowpens, where he gave Banastre Tarleton's hated Tory Legion "a whale of a licking," an action often called the tactical masterpiece of the War for Independence.

Though later serving in the army that put down the Whisky Rebellion and in the United States House of Representatives, Morgan was foremost a Revolutionary soldier; for this reason nine of thirteen chapters cover his performance in the Continental Army.

I am in debt, first, to my wife, Mary S. Higginbotham, who shared in this project from an early stage. Her challenging criticism and constant editorial assistance have added greatly to whatever merits this book may have. I owe much to Professor John R. Alden, who suggested to me the need of a new Morgan biography: under his steady guidance the early drafts were written. My thanks are due to Mr. Frederick A. Hetzel of the Institute of Early American History and Culture for his interest and wholehearted co-operation. Professors Jack P. Greene, Clyde R. Ferguson, Keith B. Berwick, and Jay Luvaas gave friendly advice on a number of matters. I am grateful to Mrs. Clifton Price, who lives in one of Morgan's fine old homes, "Soldier's Rest," near Berryville, Virginia. While on research trips in Clarke and Frederick counties, I had the pleasure of making "Soldier's Rest" my headquarters. The hospitality accorded me there was in keeping with the best of Morgan traditions.

Don Higginbotham
Baton Rouge, Louisiana

Contents

Illustrations

DANIEL MORGAN

Revolutionary Rifleman

CHAPTER I

The Frontiersman

D ANIEL MORGAN spent most of his life near Winchester in the Valley of Virginia. Only a village in 1753, with tall forests crowding round it, Winchester, seat of Frederick County, consisted of sixty crudely built dwellings, stores, and taverns. What it lacked in size, it made up for in noise. Cursing, drunkenness, quarreling, and fighting were so prevalent that Moravian missionaries and other pious souls skirted it during their travels through the back country. Local constables, though quick to arraign the lawbreakers before the justices in the small log courthouse, found that fines and jail sentences failed to temper unruly behavior for long. Yet all was not disorder. Up one narrow, dusty street stood a stone Anglican church on land donated by Lord Thomas Fairfax, who just beyond the village limits had also given plots for two dissenters' meetinghouses. To the churches, stores, taverns, and courthouse in Winchester came the farming folk of Frederick County; it was their center of civilization.

There too came Daniel Morgan in the spring of 1753. The youth of about eighteen years drew scant attention as he wandered in and out of the stores and taverns. Like the residents, he spoke awkwardly and wore simple homespuns. He was "so poor" that he had scarcely any personal belongings.[1]

1. "Notes from ... Benjamin Berry ... in Relation to General Daniel Morgan," Ludwell-Lee Papers, Va. Hist. Soc. (hereafter Berry's Notes).

Morgan was reluctant to talk about his past. Indeed, he told few if any of his friends the identity of his parents, the place of his birth, and the location of his home before reaching Frederick County. Even his own children and their descendants had little authoritative knowledge. They believed Daniel to be the son of Welsh immigrants—his father a farm laborer—who lived in New Jersey when Daniel was born, probably in 1735.[2] The size and fortunes of the family are shrouded in mystery.[3]

Daniel emerges from obscurity in the winter of 1752-53. Soon after a bitter argument with his father, he journeyed westward through Pennsylvania, stopping at Carlisle to work at odd jobs until the snows melted. Then he made his way southward and entered the Great Wagon Road.[4] As he moved through Maryland, across the Potomac, and into northwestern Virginia, he

2. Early in Jan. 1776, Morgan gave his age as 40. "... Return of the Rebel Prisoners Taken at Quebec," British Public Record Office Transcripts, Ser. Q, XIII, Public Archives of Canada.

3. James Graham, *The Life of General Daniel Morgan* ... (New York, 1856), 18-20; interview of Lyman C. Draper with Mrs. Winifred Kouns, a granddaughter of Morgan, [1850's], Draper Papers, 22S215-19, State Hist. Soc. of Wis.; Morgan biographical notes compiled by Reverend William Hill, Ludwell-Lee Papers, Va. Hist. Soc. (hereafter Hill's Notes). Hill, pastor of the Presbyterian church in Winchester, Virginia, and a friend of Morgan, at one time planned to do a life of the General, the outline of which is in the Union Theological Seminary Library, Richmond. In addition to the notes and outline, Hill wrote a brief sketch of Morgan which no longer exists, although Graham used it in preparing his study.

The lack of conclusive evidence concerning Morgan's family and birthplace has resulted in a good deal of idle speculation. In addition to New Jersey, both Pennsylvania and Virginia have claimed him as a native son. See Joseph F. Folsom, "General Daniel Morgan's Birthplace and Life," New Jersey Historical Society, *Proceedings*, New Ser., 14 (1929), 277-92.

4. The road began at Philadelphia, passed through Lancaster, turned southward to Frederick, Maryland, ran through Winchester, traversed the eastern and middle parts of the Valley of Virginia, and ended at the Yadkin River in North Carolina.

doubtless encountered motley processions of people, for over this winding route passed thousands of newcomers in the mid-eighteenth century. They migrated to the back country to preserve their national traits, to avoid paying high prices for land in Pennsylvania, or to acquire farms where acreage was cheap. Still others, having no homes or close ties, were merely caught up in the movement, following the rest and trusting to luck. Morgan, without family or friends in the hinterland, must have belonged in this last category.

Though many of the footsore travelers were going on to Augusta in the south Valley or to the North Carolina Piedmont, Morgan decided to seek his fortune in Winchester. Small as it was, its English, Scotch-Irish, and German inhabitants formed the largest inland settlement below Lancaster, Pennsylvania. But since the town did not afford Morgan his best opportunity for work, he accepted a job with a farmer named Roberts in eastern Frederick County. Morgan performed his tasks so well that Roberts made him foreman of his sawmill. He had scarcely gotten started at this new assignment when Robert Burwell, who owned extensive lands in the Valley, induced him to drive a wagon at a higher salary. A restless, high-spirited youth, Morgan enjoyed the freedom of wagoning and he also liked the company of Burwell's overseer, John Ashby, a skilled horseman, marksman, pugilist, and rum-drinker. Despite good times with Ashby, Morgan saved most of his salary, so that within a year he was able to purchase a team and enter the hauling business for himself.[5]

His career as an independent wagoner was cut short. In 1754 French troops pressing down from Canada erected Fort Duquesne at the forks of the Ohio and then defeated George Washington's Virginia militiamen, who had hoped to drive them away. With France making good her claim to the disputed Ohio Valley, the sluggish British lion began to stir. Major General Edward Braddock, his instructions to roll the French tide back, landed in

5. Hill's Notes; Berry's Notes; Graham, *Morgan*, 20-21.

Virginia with two regiments of regulars early in 1755. Morgan heard that Virginia's Lieutenant-Governor Robert Dinwiddie had issued an appeal to Valley teamsters to transport provisions to Braddock's advance base at Fort Cumberland, Maryland. Morgan responded; there would be handsome wages and adventure. That spring he made repeated trips from Winchester to Fort Cumberland, his wagon bearing flour, salt, and other stores over a hastily cut road through the wilderness. Braddock arrived at the fort in May and discovered a shortage of army wagons to carry his supplies. He therefore engaged Morgan and additional frontier teamsters to accompany his army. Actually, they had no choice; the General, desperate for drivers, wagons, and horses, impressed all within reach.[6]

British officers, accustomed to strict obedience from their own troops, considered the Valley wagoners a troublesome group. The Virginians seldom had experienced restraint and refused to accept it here. They fought among themselves and with redcoat enlisted men; they gambled and drank; they flirted lustily with Indian women who came to the fort and rendezvoused with them in nearby woods. In short, the men made life unpleasant for royal officers, whose opinion of provincials had never been marked by admiration. Ill-feeling between Britons and Americans increased as did penalties for breach of camp regulations. Some offenders got sentences of as many as a thousand lashes laid on by a drummer at the camp whipping post.

Morgan himself felt the sting of a drummer's whip, either before or during Braddock's march to Fort Duquesne. The details are vague, but it is clear that a British officer or enlisted man angered Morgan, that the husky frontiersman knocked the Briton down, and that a drum-head court-martial sentenced Morgan to receive four or five hundred lashes. Before the ordeal ended, his back was bathed in blood and his flesh hung down in

6. *Ibid.*, 23.

ribbons. And yet Morgan claimed to have retained conscious-
ness throughout. In fact, counting with the drummer, Morgan
heard him miscount but "did not think it worthwhile to tell
him of his mistake, and let it go so!" If Morgan did keep his
senses, it was a tribute to his superb physique. Standing six
feet tall, with broad shoulders and massive arms, he was certainly capable of enduring great punishment. Once the pain
and bitterness were gone, "old Morgan" would not have taken
anything for that whipping; it gave him a story that never grew
old.[7]

On the morning of June 7, Morgan guided his heavily loaded
wagon into line as Braddock's column set out to attack distant
Fort Duquesne. By June 18, the column had progressed only
twenty-three miles beyond Fort Cumberland. The next day,
leaving behind 1,100 troops and most of the wagons, including
Morgan's, Braddock pushed ahead with 1,300 picked men;
Colonel Thomas Dunbar followed with the rear echelon. After
crossing the Monongahela on July 9, Braddock encountered a
French and Indian force which in the ensuing battle fought from
behind rocks, trees, and bushes. In vain, redcoats fired at their
unseen assailants. In vain, Braddock's officers tried to preserve
order among their confused and frightened men. The British
General who had placed full confidence in his regulars and who
had prepared no alternative to line fire in wooded country met a
humiliating defeat. It was a case of New World fighting methods
prevailing over those of the Old.

Morgan, back with Dunbar, witnessed the dramatic events
after the disaster: fugitives trickling in from the battlefield,
George Washington galloping up with orders for Dunbar, and

7. [Joseph Graham], "A Recollection of the American Revolutionary
War," *Virginia Historical Register*, 6 (1853), 211; Berry's Notes;
Graham, *Morgan*, 29-30, errs in saying the event took place after Brad-
dock's campaign.

finally, on July 11, the mortally wounded Braddock appearing with the remnant of the advance force. Before the retreat began, Morgan assisted in destroying enough ammunition, powder, and flour to provide wagon space for the wounded.[8]

Several weeks later, once again in Frederick County, Morgan saw his friend John Ashby, recently commissioned a captain in the Virginia rangers. Ashby, recruiting one of three ranger companies authorized by the colonial assembly to assist in protecting the frontier, had to work quickly: France's Indian allies, emboldened by Braddock's catastrophe, were making incursions into the Valley. Morgan agreed to join Ashby's company, which marched to the South Branch of the Potomac in September 1755. That fall, while Morgan helped build blockhouses and escort supplies to Fort Cumberland, the frontier people experienced the worst Indian raids ever seen in the Valley. Sweeping down in small parties, the savages cut off communications with Fort Cumberland and extended their swath of murder and destruction to within a few miles of Winchester. As commander in chief of Virginia's western defenses, Washington heard rumors at Winchester that the troops near the South Branch were under siege in stockades; but if Ashby suffered any casualties, he failed to report them.

In December, Ashby occupied a small blockhouse on Patterson's Creek, just east of the South Branch. For the moment Indian raids had ceased, and monotony reigned. The most exciting event of the winter seems to have been the arrival of Joseph Coombs, one of Morgan's teamster friends, with a wagonload of rum. Ashby bought several barrels for his little garrison, and the rangers imbibed heavily; until the pleasing effects wore off, no one bothered to perform the routine duties of the post.[9]

8. *Ibid.*, 24-26.
9. "...Return of the 2nd Company of Rangers," Oct. 21, 1755, George Washington Papers, Lib. Cong.; John C. Fitzpatrick, ed., *The Writings*

In April 1756, Morgan guided a militia contingent from Fort Ashby to Fort Edwards, twenty miles north of Winchester. He and another ranger started back to Fort Ashby on the 16th. Fourteen miles out, seven Indians sprang from ambush and opened fire, killing Morgan's companion. A musket ball tore into Morgan's neck and passed out through the cheek, dislodging several teeth. Morgan wheeled his horse about and spurred back toward Fort Edwards. Six of the Indians stopped to scalp the dead man, leaving the seventh to overtake the fleeing Morgan. But Morgan had the faster mount; as he widened the distance between them, his pursuer threw his tomahawk but missed. Delirious from pain and shock, Morgan was still astride his animal on entering the fort. The wound, though not serious, left a permanent scar on his face.[10]

Morgan remained in Ashby's unit until Washington disbanded the ranger companies in October. Never at maximum strength, they had received mediocre leadership from their officers, especially Ashby. Poor Ashby even had trouble controlling his wife; Washington said she had been guilty of "irregular Behaviour" with her husband's troops.[11]

It is impossible to determine exactly what Morgan did after leaving the rangers. One source has him serving as a militiaman in the vicinity of Winchester; another maintains that he hunted wild game, once staying outside human habitation for

of *George Washington* (Washington, 1931-1944), I, 193, 204-5, 210, 264-65.

10. Graham, *Morgan*, 33-34. Graham, unaware of Morgan's service with Ashby's rangers, confuses the time and place of the event. Correct information on these points appears in a letter from Fort Edwards. John Mercer to Washington, Apr. 17, 1756, Washington Papers, Lib. Cong.

11. Fitzpatrick, ed., *Writings of Washington*, I, 422, 462, 470, 475, 485, 495.

four months.[12] At least by 1758, when the British capture of
Fort Duquesne erased the threat of further Indian encroach-
ments, Morgan resumed his wagoning. By then Frederick County
farmers were growing wheat, flax, tobacco, and hemp for shipment beyond the Valley. Loading this produce in his wagon,
Morgan drove eastward, ferried the murky waters of the Shenandoah, reached the towering Blue Ridge, passed through one of
its narrow gaps, and headed toward Alexandria, Dumfries, Fredericksburg, or Falmouth. He is known to have traded with
several prominent merchants: Francis Triplett of Dumfries, later
a Revolutionary officer; Fielding Lewis of Fredericksburg, a
relative of Martha Washington; and William Allason of Falmouth, a Scotsman who did a thriving business with Frederick
County farmers. On return trips Morgan carried grindstones,
tar, nails, salt, sugar, rum, and other freight to the frontier
people. Truly he was "as well acquainted with the roads as any
man" in Virginia.[13]

In Winchester after a tiresome journey, Morgan could likely
be found playing cards with other teamsters at the Shenandoah
Store, owned by William Allason but managed by his brother
David. Seated toward the rear, in an atmosphere laden with
smoke and rum, the players were intent on their game, for
David Allason usually advanced the liquor provided the losers
agreed to pay for it. He kept a sharp eye on these rough, hearty
men; past experience had shown that they did not always acknowledge their debts. Yet Allason tolerated them because
he profited from their trade—Morgan was a particularly valuable

12. Graham, *Morgan*, 30-31; Charles Carter Lee Notes, Lib. Cong.
13. Miles Malone, "Falmouth and the Shenandoah: Trade Before the
Revolution," *American Historical Review*, 40 (1935), 693-703; Edith E.
Thompson, "A Scottish Merchant in Falmouth in the Eighteenth Century," *Virginia Magazine of History and Biography*, 39 (1931), 108-17,
230-38; Morgan to Horatio Gates, June 24, 1780, Gates Papers, N. Y.
Hist. Soc.

customer during the Christmas seasons of 1761 and 1762, buying large quantities of rum.[14]

The Shenandoah Store, a satisfactory loitering place in Winchester, did not in Morgan's estimation compare with the Battletown [15] settlement in eastern Frederick County. At Battletown or close by Morgan stayed when not on a hauling venture. He met young frontiersmen for drink, horse racing, and other activities, especially on idle Saturday afternoons in spring and summer. His great strength and vigor made him the recognized leader of the group. No one could ride better than he or outdistance him in footracing. (Even in his fortieth year he outran sturdy men half his age.) In wrestling he excelled, displaying remarkable agility for his size. Although Morgan could joke with a vanquished opponent, slapping him on the back and saying their struggle was close, he could also burn inwardly on the few occasions he lost a physical contest. Underneath his usually jovial exterior, he possessed a fierce temper; and he was proud, far more so than most men. Woe to the onlooker who, in jest or otherwise, cast reflection on his skill or prowess!

Outsiders in particular found Morgan a dangerous man when crossed. For some time there had been friction between Morgan and Bill Davis, a muscular pugilist from nearby Bullskin Creek whom Morgan considered a threat to his domination of the Battletown games. According to a story recorded long afterward, one afternoon the two men had a bitter argument that erupted in a fight. Though Morgan won after a lengthy struggle, Davis and his relatives vowed to return and square accounts with him and any who stood with him. When the Davises reappeared, Morgan's "gang" overpowered them in a mass brawl, both sides resorting to kicking, biting, and gouging. Morgan planted a

14. William Allason's Shenandoah Store Account Books, Ledgers A and B, and his Shenandoah Day Book, Va. State Lib.

15. Now Berryville, Va.

foot in Bill's back and found it none too resilient; he broke a toe which never healed properly.[16]

Morgan repaid his comrades by supporting them in court against misdemeanor charges. Joseph Coombs, who had brought the liquor to Fort Ashby, called on him: first accused of breaking the peace, Coombs then was arraigned for supposedly "living in sin" with a fallen woman. Morgan, however, needed his friends' aid at the courthouse more than they required his between 1758 and 1763. Thomas Cresap, presumably the celebrated Indian fighter, gave information convicting Morgan of taking his bay horse. Morgan was tried for "Feloniously" burning a tobacco storehouse, but the case was dismissed for want of conclusive testimony. From time to time men swore before the justices that Morgan "did wound and evilly treat" them. How did he react to these assault and battery charges? Though twice taking to arms and successfully defying a deputy sheriff with orders to bring him to Winchester, he may well have had good reason to think those specific accusations unfair; usually he complied with each summons except when out of the county. Moreover, his antagonists often failed to show up in court to present their proof. Very possibly their claims grew out of drunken brawls; guilt in such instances would have been hard to prove.[17]

Morgan did not spend all his free time carousing. David Allason's musty, faded ledgers give a clue to a different activity: courtship. The store records reveal that by November 1761 Morgan was taking considerable interest in his personal appear-

16. Hill's Notes; Berry's Notes; Graham, *Morgan*, 36-38.
17. Order Books, X, 404, XI, 89; Daniel Morgan Suit Papers, Packets 1, 32, 38. These records as well as all subsequent Order Books, Suit Papers, and Deed Books are for Frederick County and are located in the County Clerk's Office, Winchester, Va. (all of which hereafter cited without reference to county or repository). Some years ago all the Suit Papers relating to Morgan and his friends were arranged topically in small packets.

ance by purchasing a "gentleman's" hat, a watch, several combs, and sleeve buttons. He also bought feminine items: a handkerchief, silk cloth, strips of ribbon, and, once, a pair of shoes. Imagine Morgan unhitching his wagon after a hauling trip, changing from his linsey hunting shirt and Indian leggins into more appropriate clothing, and carrying a gift to his young woman. She was Abigail Curry, in her late teens, and the daughter of a relatively prosperous Frederick County farmer. Morgan was persistent. Handsome and imposing in physique, witty and good-natured except when angered, he eventually won Abigail's heart.[18]

By 1763 Morgan and Abigail had made a home together out of wedlock. Was he simply a "confirmed Libertine" seeking the "virtue of everything within his reach," as some Winchester gossips were saying years after his death? Such a charge seems unfair. Informal unions were not uncommon on the Virginia frontier, and the alliance of Morgan and Abigail Curry was permanent. Evidently she was not the kind of woman to tolerate any other relationship. "Plain, sensible, and pious," she possessed some education and an interest in religion, both of which she reputedly passed on to Morgan. In the 1760's she bore him two daughters, Nancy and Betsy, whom she educated herself until Morgan employed a tutor.[19]

With family responsibilities and a permanent roof over his head, Morgan made a turn for the better. In the next few years

18. Shenandoah Store Account Books, Ledgers A and B, and Shenandoah Day Book, Va. State Lib.

19. As early as June 25, 1763, David Allason recorded under Morgan's account: "Abbie Currie [sic] for sundries by her." Shenandoah Account Books, Ledger B, *ibid.*; Samuel H. Davis to Jared Sparks, Dec. 18, 1826, and Lemuel Brent to Sparks, Sept. 3, 1827, Sparks Papers, Harvard College Lib.; William Hill, "MM [MS] about Gen. Morgan, of the Revoln. who died and was buried in Winch.—in membership of the Pn [Presbyterian] church," Union Theological Seminary Lib., Richmond.

only two assault and battery cases were aimed at him, and both were dropped by the plaintiffs. He lodged the same complaint against three of the Davises, but this too failed to result in court action, "the matter being agreed by the parties." [20]

Mostly at home after 1763, Morgan rented some land and became a farmer. At first he concentrated on marketable tobacco crops, which he sold at Falmouth in 1764 and 1765. He also grew hemp by 1767, the year the colony awarded him two premiums for his "Bright and Clean" harvest. Indeed, his crops, his garden which he personally attended, and his routine farm duties so consumed his energies that he ceased to deliver freight. Accordingly, in 1769 he leased his wagon and provided a driver to Isaac Zane, an ex-Quaker who, like himself, dwelled with a woman without sanction of church and state. Zane had constructed one of the first iron works in the Valley at Marlboro,

20. Order Books, XIII, 569, XIV, 486, XV, 308; Suit Papers, Packet 2. Stories of Morgan's pugilism adorn local Virginia histories and other works, almost all of which, alas, are apocryphal or cannot be verified. Illustrative of these anecdotes is one related by a former governor of Virginia, whose grandmother supposedly knew Morgan. Regarding the fights at Battletown: "On one of these occasions he was badly worsted by a powerful young fellow from the Blue Ridge Mountains; reaching home very much mortified over his defeat, his wife, who was a lady of culture and refinement, upbraided him severely, as she had done before, for his 'rowdyism,' and begged him for her sake to change his ways. He promised her solemnly he would do so, after he had whipped the young mountaineer. When the next law day came he told his wife he could not succeed in his coming combat, with his long hair, and asked her to clip it short.

"His wife admired his long flowing locks and declined to clip them, but told him she would 'fix' his hair for him, and this she proceeded to do. She dexterously wove pins and needles all through his hair, and he left for Battletown, where he found his antagonist ready and waiting for him.

"He returned that evening a victor and a happy man. His wife's ingenuity had won the fight for him. He kept his promise to his wife and never engaged in another fistic encounter at Battletown." Charles T. O'Ferrall, *Forty Years of Active Service* (New York, 1904), 358-59.

his estate near Winchester, and he used Morgan's teamster to transport his iron products to Falmouth and other points eastward.[21]

Sometime between 1769 and 1772, Morgan purchased a 255-acre tract from Abigail's uncle, Samuel Blackburn. Situated three miles north of Battletown and eleven miles east of Winchester, it was near the land Morgan had previously rented and not far from the home of Abigail's father, Daniel Curry. The transaction caused him some difficulty, Morgan confided to Francis Triplett in a letter that gives the flavor of his vocabulary.

Dear Frank

Mr. Tibs showd me an order from you which I should be very glad to have settled if it lay in my power. but if it was to a savd my life I could not a paid five pound, [which is] the cash I ow [you] and will pay . . . as soon as it lays in my power. you should not a lay out of your money so long only I was obligd to lay out money for land and then to lay out to improve it . . . and I intend Down after harvest and try if I can settle it—I have often Inquired of you[r] . . . [activities] and always has had pleasue to hear you shine—which gives infinite satisfaction.[22]

Other expenditures were necessary. Revitalizing the soil, experimenting with new crops, acquiring livestock—all proved a drain on Morgan's limited resources. Furthermore, there were one or more years when Morgan's crops failed because of droughts, torrential rains, or insect pests. Though accused in court of indebtedness at least twenty-two times between 1767

21. Order Books, XIV, 57-58, XVI, 218; Suit Papers, Packet 3.
22. Deed Book, 1771-1772; "The George Carter Tract," Clarke County Historical Society, *Proceedings*, 3 (1943), 18-19; Morgan to Triplett, May 25, 1769, Morgan Papers, Va. State Lib. Confusion arises because Morgan's deed was not recorded until 1772, although he claimed in 1769 to have already purchased the land. It is just possible that the date on Morgan's letter was added later by an officious editor or collector.

and 1774, he usually reached an agreement with the plaintiffs before the justices took action.

The dearth of specie in the agricultural Valley complicated Morgan's financial problems, since he was forced to contract many of his obligations through barter, a system made hazardous by fluctuating prices. For example, it seems that not infrequently he secured items from merchants and traders by promising to pay for them in tobacco. But tobacco prices sometimes fell before Morgan wiped out his debts, raising the question of whether settlement should be based on past or present market values. Recognized as a shrewd businessman capable of driving a hard bargain, Morgan attempted to turn over as little produce as possible, just as his creditors asked for the current selling price. If compromise proved impossible, the issue was generally dropped in the laps of the justices, who usually ordered Morgan to award his creditors a sum between their contention and his.[23]

Indebtedness, though aggravating to debtor and creditor alike, was an accepted fact of life in the Valley and did not necessarily damage one's reputation. A neighbor more than once called Morgan into court, only to post bond for him later. Even the justices considered Morgan stable enough to give bond for a county surveyor and a deputy sheriff, and they called on him for occasional jury service. These county officials secured his appointment as a militia captain in 1771, for which he took the customary oath to support the King and his government. Another job for Morgan was to supervise the maintenance of a county road, a position accorded him three different times, the court instructing him to work all citizens for three miles on each side of the road. The most important route under his supervision extended from Cunningham's Chapel, near his farm, to Green-

23. Morgan's debts are in Order Books, XII-XVI; Suit Papers, Packets 2-3.

way Court, home of Lord Fairfax, Virginia's only resident officially a lord.[24]

Morgan had come far by 1774. Adding three more slaves in March of that year, he had a total of ten, an impressive number for a yeoman farmer. That same month he took a complete outlay of furniture as compensation for money owed him. He was energetic and enterprising. Despite his tumultuous youth, his abilities were recognized and put to use in county affairs, an indication that in frontier Virginia a man's worth was measured more in terms of his present status and potential than in light of his past. He had the respect of three important county leaders: Isaac Zane, Major Angus McDonald, and Charles Mynn Thruston. Zane, the iron manufacturer, was a justice and later a Valley delegate to the Virginia convention of 1776; McDonald, also a justice, had been Morgan's immediate superior in the militia; Thruston was the rector of Frederick Parish and an active participant in local politics. Perhaps it was Thruston who persuaded Morgan and Abigail to be married in 1773, a step which Abigail may well have advocated for some time.[25]

24. George C. Chumbly, *Colonial Justice in Virginia* (Richmond, 1938), 99; Order Books, XIII, 19, 84, 250, XIV, 354, XV, 42, 211, 240, XVI, 329; Suit Papers, Packet 5; Clarke County Hist. Soc., *Proceedings*, 2 (1942), 27; Graham, *Morgan*, 42-43.
25. Suit Papers, Packet 4; the author's typescript of the Morgan-Curry marriage bond was obtained through the courtesy of Mr. George F. Scheer, Chapel Hill, N. C.

CHAPTER II

Appeal to Arms

WHILE Morgan sought prosperity and stability in the decade before Lexington and Concord, many of his Valley neighbors tramped through Allegheny passes and entered the fertile Ohio country, a region forbidden to white settlement by the Proclamation of 1763. Originating primarily from the London government's desire to ward off Indian wars, the proclamation aggravated pioneers searching for new homes or trading opportunities. Not only did westerners ignore it; they disregarded Shawnee claims to traditional hunting grounds. Bloodshed resulted: settlers raided tribal villages in retaliation for Indian forays into the Valley. And as the frontier girded itself for the prospect of war, Morgan found an increasing amount of his time taken up with militia duties. With 2,200 men under arms by 1772, the Frederick County militia erected stockades and patrolled remote areas.

Finally, in June 1774, Lord Dunmore, governor of Virginia and advocate of the colony's expansion, took action by ordering Major Angus McDonald to secure control of the Ohio River around Wheeling. McDonald, raising a volunteer unit, persuaded Morgan to enlist a company of fifty or sixty "good" men. Accomplishing this by early July, Morgan advanced with McDonald to Wheeling, where they encountered no opposition. The Scotsman then moved twenty-four miles downstream and began a ninety-mile march into the Ohio country to destroy

16

Shawnee villages on the Muskingum River. After wearisome days on foot, as the expedition entered a dense swamp near the Muskingum, Indians fired from ambush on the lead company commanded by Captain James Wood. Morgan, close behind, rushed his troops to Wood's assistance. A sharp, thirty-minute contest ensued, ending when the Indians withdrew, leaving five of their number dead as against the loss of two Virginians. The next morning McDonald crossed the Muskingum to discover that the Indians had abandoned their villages. He ordered Morgan and Wood to raze the dwellings and crops, then grew apprehensive of further aggressive action: he was deep in enemy country and short of rations. He hastily retired to Wheeling, where Dunmore had assembled a militia army drawn from the north Valley.[1]

Morgan had only a brief respite on reaching Wheeling. Considered a valuable officer by McDonald, who evidently recommended him to the Governor, Morgan was selected by Dunmore to accompany Colonel William Crawford against the villages of the Mingo, allies of the Shawnee, near the Scioto River. A twenty-four hour march brought the Virginians to their objective, and they met little interference as they destroyed and plundered. After their return to Dunmore's base with a number of prisoners, the participating troops received the proceeds from the sale of their spoils, a common practice in Indian wars, and a point that recruiting officers emphasized to lure new men.[2]

Meanwhile, a second Virginia division, formed in the south

1. Freeman Hart, *The Valley of Virginia in the American Revolution* (Chapel Hill, 1942), 77; McDonald to Morgan, June 11, 1774, Graham, *Morgan*, 46; Peter Force, ed., *American Archives*, 4th Ser. (Washington, 1837-1846), I, 682, 684, 722-24; Reuben G. Thwaites and Louise B. Kellogg, eds., *Documentary History of Dunmore's War* (Madison, 1905), 151-56; Draper Papers, 3D5-11, State Hist. Soc. of Wis.

2. Thwaites and Kellogg, eds., *Dunmore's War*, xxv, 303-4; *Journals of the House of Delegates* [1776] (Richmond, 1827-1828), 88.

Valley under Andrew Lewis, repulsed a large party of Indians in the only major engagement of Dunmore's War. Presently the savages sued for peace. Morgan, who described his part in the struggle as "very active and hard," witnessed the signing of a preliminary treaty between Dunmore and the chiefs that ended hostilities.[3]

Even so, a martial spirit hovered over the Valley of Virginia. There the Revolutionary movement was well entrenched under the leadership of Tidewater planters in the House of Burgesses. The absence of serious east-west differences in the Old Dominion helps to explain why the Valley supported the patriot cause so enthusiastically. The Tidewater-controlled Assembly had steadily established counties and roads as the wave of settlement passed beyond the Blue Ridge. Indeed, by 1755 three routes connected Winchester with deepwater ports on the Potomac and Rappahannock, while numerous legislative acts had encouraged the building of bridges and ferries to further communication and trade. In addition to the close economic ties between the Valley and Tidewater (strengthened after 1770 because of western exportation of flour), there was a political alliance. Men of substance and influence, with interests similar to those of Chesapeake planters, usually represented the Valley in the Burgesses at Williamsburg. Of course variations existed: the back country contained fewer men of wealth and fewer Anglicans, more small farmers and more non-English elements. But in general the Valley accepted Eastern rule, probably because of reasonably fair treatment at the hands of Williamsburg's ruling circle.

Thus Valley people harbored no sectional feeling against following other Virginians in opposing British revenue measures in

3. Graham, *Morgan*, 464; "Morgan's Autobiography," *Historical Magazine*, 2d Ser., 9 (1871), 379. Morgan received pay for 167 days' service. "List of the Militia Paid at Romney," Va. State Lib.

the 1760's and 1770's. With expanding business activity in the Valley, accompanied by an increase in legal transactions, both the Stamp tax and Townshend duties, if enforced, would have been felt in some degree by frontier Virginians. (How Morgan, always short of cash, would have complained at paying for the stamps designated for playing cards!)

Patriot resistance throughout the colonies stiffened in 1774. On June 8, prominent citizens of Frederick County issued a ringing declaration against the Boston Port Act, first of the "Intolerable Acts" resulting from the Boston Tea Party. Any attempt to uphold the Port Act, they warned, would "raise a civil War" and dissolve the colonies' union with Britain.[4] Equally strong was a resolution adopted during Dunmore's War by Morgan and scores of his fellow militiamen, who pledged to assist with force their "brethren in Boston" in the event of hostilities there. Morgan doubtless hoped that open conflict could be avoided, for in the spring of 1775 he planted his crops as usual, even hiring two extra field hands.[5]

Although western Virginians went about their daily labors, they would take the field at a moment's notice, reported Richard Henry Lee. The colony's six frontier counties, he announced, could produce 6,000 men known for their "amazing hardihood" gained through "living so long in the woods." These veteran hunters and Indian fighters had traveled long distances without provisions and displayed remarkable "dexterity" with the rifle. In shooting matches they desired targets at least 200 yards distant, preferably no larger than an orange.[6]

4. Force, ed., *American Archives*, 4th Ser., I, 392-93.

5. Graham, *Morgan*, 464; "Morgan's Autobiography," *Historical Magazine*, 2d Ser., 9 (1871), 379; depositions of William Greenway and William Flud, Revolutionary War Pension Files, National Archives.

6. James C. Ballagh, ed., *Letters of Richard Henry Lee* (New York, 1912-1914), I, 130-31.

Contemporary accounts indicate that Lee did not exaggerate their marksmanship. Some observers even credited the frontiersmen with hitting objects at 250 or more yards. (A musket ball fell harmlessly to the ground at half that distance.) Whatever the truth, the Kentucky rifle, as it was called, was a deadly weapon in the hands of an expert. Spiral grooves inside the barrel, making the bullet rotate in flight, gave it range and accuracy. Despite the advantages of the long, slender rifle, it did have serious limitations. While muskets could be fired four or five times a minute, riflemen were fortunate to deliver two shots in that time. Thus they found it difficult to stop a determined attack by their firepower, and they had not learned how to attach bayonets to their guns. Though unable to stand against a bayonet charge in open fields, they would be valuable as snipers and wood-fighters if the growing friction between the colonies and mother country culminated in war. America was mostly a dense wilderness, and riflemen, wearing their traditional hunting shirts —the color of a dry leaf—would blend superbly into this landscape.

Lee had not underestimated their determination. When, in April 1775, Governor Dunmore seized twenty kegs of powder from the provincial magazine in Williamsburg and placed it on a British ship lying in the James River, hundreds of backwoodsmen rapidly assembled at Fredericksburg, ready to move upon Williamsburg. An eye-witness declared there were "1,000 men . . . among which was 600 good Rifle men. There was a Council of War held three days . . . if we had continued there one or two days longer we should have had upwards of ten thousand men. All the frontier counties were in motion. . . . Fredericksburge never was so honour'd with so many brave hearty men since it was a town[,] every man Rich and poor with their hunting Shirts[,] Belts and Tomahawks fixed . . . in the best manner." These angry patriots were persuaded not to march by Washington and other leaders of the Burgesses, who also convinced Dunmore to pay the colony for the powder.[7]

Frederick County stayed alert. Perhaps Morgan and his militiamen were in Winchester on June 6, when a young preacher named Philip Fithian visited there and recorded his observations:

Mars, the great God of Battle, is now honoured in every Part of this spacious Colony, but here every Presence is warlike, every Sound is martial! Drums beating, Fifes & Bag-Pipes playing, & only sonorous & heroic Tunes—Every Man has a hunting-Shirt, which is the Uniform of each Company—Almost all have a Cockade, & Bucks-Tale in their Hats, to represent that they are hardy, resolute, & invincible Natives of the Woods of America—

The County Committee sat. Among other Resolves they passed this resolute & trying Determination—

That every Member of this County, between sixteen, & sixty years of Age, shall appear once every Month, at least, in the Field under Arms; & it is recommended to all to muster weekly for their Improvement.

Obviously impressed, he returned thirteen days later and found the men still in arms—to the youthful minister, they made "a grand Figure." Another minister, Morgan's friend the Reverend Charles Mynn Thruston, who was chairman of the local Revolutionary committee, used parish funds to purchase military stores.[8]

At first, in spite of preparations in the Middle and Southern colonies, the war that began on Lexington green was mainly New England's concern. But after the Second Continental Congress "adopted" the besieging forces, the legislators realized the need for additional troops, including marksmen to snipe at the enemy

7. Michael Wallace to Gustavius Wallace, May 14, 1775, Wallace Family Papers, Alderman Lib., Univ. of Va.; Hamilton J. Eckenrode, *The Revolution in Virginia* (New York, 1916), 49-52.

8. "Charles Mynn Thruston," Clarke County Hist. Soc., *Proceedings*, 2 (1942), 31-34; R. G. Albion and L. Dodson, eds., *Journal of Philip Vickers Fithian, 1775-1776* (Princeton, 1924), 24-25, 31.

behind their Boston entrenchments. Since the rifle was almost unknown in New England, delegates from that region asked their colleagues to the south to describe its performance. John Adams was impressed by what he learned about this "peculiar kind of musket." John Hancock, who also heard favorable reports, informed Elbridge Gerry that riflemen were "clever fellows," and he told James Warren that they were the "finest Marksmen in the world." With the support of Adams, Hancock, and other New Englanders, Congress voted on June 14, 1775, to raise ten companies of "expert rifflemen": six from Pennsylvania, two from Maryland, and two from Virginia.[9]

When the lawmakers called on Frederick County to provide one Virginia company, the patriot committee wholeheartedly agreed. Composed of Thruston, Zane, McDonald, and three others, the group "unanimously" elected Morgan captain of the unit and informed him that his "courage, conduct, and reverence for liberty" made him the best man for the job. Echoing this opinion was Horatio Gates of nearby Berkeley County, soon to become a general in the Continental Army, who wrote George Washington that Morgan and Hugh Stephenson (commander of Virginia's second company, raised in Berkeley) would be "excellent for the service." His selection was a singular honor for Morgan, and he knew it. Frederick County could boast of several able men with military experience, one of them James Wood, afterward a Revolutionary colonel and governor of Virginia. Though Morgan disliked leaving his family and farm to the uncertainties of wartime, he nevertheless relished his appointment. The excitement and adventure of a military life

9. Charles F. Adams, ed., *Familiar Letters of John Adams and His Wife Abigail Adams during the Revolution* (New York, 1876), 67; Edmund C. Burnett, ed., *Letters of Members of the Continental Congress* (Washington, 1921-1936), I, 134-35; Worthington C. Ford, ed., *Journals of the Continental Congress* (Washington, 1904-1937), II, 89.

appealed to this vigorous man, who later maintained that his most satisfying years had been spent under arms; and, if Valley tradition be correct, the lined scars on his back reminded him of a desire to settle an old score with the army of George III. In any event, he would make his mark in this war; of that he was certain.[10]

First, the company had to be raised and marched to Boston. The great drive and zeal Morgan displayed throughout the Revolution were noticeable in the way he performed this first assignment. Saddling his horse each morning, he rode about the county, telling of glories to be won and American rights to be upheld. His appeal brought an enthusiastic reception. Twenty-two-year-old Peter Bruin, serving as Morgan's ensign, always remembered how scores of men "crowded to the Standard" and how only the most promising among them were taken. Possibly Morgan, like several other rifle captains, held contests to determine which volunteers were the best shots. One captain drew a nose on a flat board one foot square, propped the board against a tree 150 yards away, and announced that he would accept those whose bullets came closest to the target.

So great was the response in Frederick County that Morgan finally accepted ninety-six recruits, twenty-eight more than stipulated by Congress. Mostly in their early twenties, they were tall, rangy men, each equipped with a rifle, tomahawk, and scalping knife, and dressed in a long hunting shirt, leggins, and moccasins. Morgan too wore Indian clothing and carried a new rifle which he had purchased from Fielding Lewis. After three weeks' preparation the company was ready to march. Before leaving Winchester, Morgan paraded his men by the courthouse, the Anglican church, and Philip Bush's popular Golden Buck Tav-

10. Graham, *Morgan*, 53; Stanislaus M. Hamilton, ed., *Letters to George Washington and Accompanying Papers* (Boston and New York, 1896-1902), V, 175-76.

ern amidst fanfare that must have equaled the display described by Fithian.[11]

It is said that Morgan broke a promise to Captain Stephenson to wait a few days and head northward with the Berkeley County company, that he desired the honor of bringing the first Virginia troops to support the Continental Army. Certainly he marched at a phenomenal pace, and Stephenson, sometimes averaging thirty miles a day, tried to overtake him. Morgan had set out by July 15—Stephenson by July 17—and two days afterward his riflemen entered Frederick, Maryland, where people lined the streets to see them pass. One observer exclaimed that "their appearance was truly martial, their spirits amazingly elated, breathing nothing but a desire to join the American army, and to engage the enemies of American liberty." Escorted out of town by local militia, small boys, and barking dogs, the riflemen hurried on over sandy roads scorched by July heat. Now and then a woman came forth with cider; here and there a baker offered fresh bread. An occasional display of marksmanship served to repay local inhabitants for favors. Passing through parts of New Jersey, New York, Connecticut, and Massachusetts, they arrived at Cambridge on August 6. Morgan had won the race; Stephenson appeared five days later.[12]

11. Deposition of Peter Bruin, Revolutionary War Pension Files, National Archives; Frank Moore, ed., *Diary of the American Revolution from Newspapers and Original Documents* (New York, 1865), I, 111; "Diary of John Harrower," *American Historical Review*, 6 (1900), 100; Graham, *Morgan*, 464; "Morgan's Autobiography," *Historical Magazine*, 2d Ser., 9 (1871), 379; Ford, ed., *Journals of Congress*, IV, 114, 168, 292; Suit Papers, Packet 4.

12. Henry Bedinger to —— Findley, n. d., and Bedinger's journal, Danske Dandridge, *Historic Shepherdstown* (Charlottesville, 1910), 79-82, 101; Draper Papers, 1A9, State Hist. Soc. of Wis.; "Extract of a letter from a Gentleman in Frederick town...dated July 19," Williamsburg *Virginia Gazette* (Dixon & Hunter), Aug. 19, Sept. 9, 1775; John W. Jordan, ed., "Bethlehem During the Revolution (diary extracts)," *Penn-*

The speed with which Morgan's company reached Cambridge elicited considerable excitement among the New Englanders, and Morgan, though only a captain, became a well-known officer in the American camp. As the clergyman Ezra Stiles observed, "The Rifle Men commanded by Captain Daniel Morgan of Fredericks [sic] County Virginia, 600 miles from Cambridge, arrived in three weeks." And James Warren, president of the Massachusetts Provincial Congress, remarked that Morgan had a "very fine company." One of the first things Morgan did was to renew acquaintances with Horatio Gates, now adjutant general of the army. Then, after billeting his troops in nearby Roxbury, he gave them the opportunity to display their sharpshooting against the enemy on Boston Neck.[13]

In the beginning Morgan's company and the other rifle units terrorized the British by picking off sentries and stragglers and sending dignified officers scurrying for cover. Since the long-range weapon had not been used during the first three months of the siege, the redcoats had been lax in staying behind protection. Even when it became evident the enemy had learned their lesson, some of the Pennsylvania riflemen were reluctant to cease

---

sylvania Magazine of History and Biography, 12 (1888), 387; Graham, Morgan, 464; "Morgan's Autobiography," Historical Magazine, 2d Ser., 9 (1871), 379.

13. Franklin B. Dexter, ed., The Literary Diary of Ezra Stiles (New York, 1901), I, 601; Warren-Adams Letters (Massachusetts Historical Society, Collections, Vols. 72-73 [1917-25]), I, 100; Gates to Artemas Ward, Aug. 11, 1775, Gates Papers, N. Y. Hist. Soc. There appears to be no evidence for the story told by John Esten Cooke and others that Morgan greeted Washington with the words, "from the south bank of the Potomac," and that the General wept and shook the hand of each rifleman. Such conduct certainly was not characteristic of Washington. Perhaps he did show an interest in them, for they were the first Virginia enlisted men to join his army. Since he had represented Frederick County in the House of Burgesses and had spent considerable time in the county, he may have known some of the families represented.

their sniping, and despite orders to the contrary, the crack-crack of rifles was heard up and down the American lines. Many also wasted ammunition in target practice designed to amuse themselves and impress the Yankee soldiers. Another of their faults was brawling. Washington, Gates, and Charles Lee spoke disapprovingly of their conduct. That men unaccustomed to town life and military regimentation should be discontented with garrison tasks is not surprising. Unfortunately for their restless spirits, there was no second Bunker Hill.

Though Morgan's men seem not to have been among those accused of misconduct, they too must have grumbled at their inactivity. Had they marched 600 miles merely to perform routine duties? Early in September their outlook brightened. Washington, organizing an army to invade Canada by way of Maine, decided to include three rifle companies. Morgan, fired by the prospect of action, offered his company, as did several other rifle commanders. To settle the matter, the captains drew lots, with Morgan and two Pennsylvania officers winning the right to join the expedition.[14]

14. Bedinger's journal, Dandridge, *Historic Shepherdstown*, 105-10; journal of William Hendricks and John Chambers, *Pennsylvania Archives*, 2d Ser., XV, 31; "Daniel McCurtin's Journal . . . of the Siege of Boston," Thomas Balch, ed., *Papers Relating Chiefly to the Maryland Line* (Philadelphia, 1855), 11-13.

CHAPTER III

Maine Wilderness

THIRTY-FOUR-YEAR-OLD Colonel Benedict Arnold, able, zealous, and headstrong, a former apothecary and merchant of New Haven, Connecticut, commanded the expedition from Washington's camp. A second American army, under Major General Philip Schuyler, advanced northward from Lake Champlain to invest the British forts on the Sorel River, take the city of Montreal, and eventually join Arnold's column in attacking the fortress of Quebec. This two-pronged invasion would end with Canada as the fourteenth colony in patriot hands—that was the hope of Washington and Congress. Perhaps the most remarkable fact about the Canadian venture was that Arnold's men ever reached Quebec. The credit for their arrival—after a journey over exhausting portages, swollen streams, and deep swamps— belongs largely to Arnold and, to a less extent, to his subordinate Morgan.

From the first, Arnold recognized Morgan as an officer of promise, for in organizing his army he appointed the Virginia Captain to head the three rifle companies. These units of frontiersmen proved better able to withstand the hardships of the Maine wilderness than the bulk of Arnold's force, composed of ten companies of New England clerks, farmers, and fishermen. Arnold divided the musket-carrying Yankees into two battalions, one led by Lieutenant Colonel Christopher Greene of Rhode Island and Major Timothy Bigelow of Massachusetts; the second, by Lieutenant Colonel Roger Enos of Vermont and Major Return J. Meigs of Connecticut. Several gentlemen volunteers also accompanied Arnold: Christian Febiger, a Dane, became Morgan's intimate friend; two of the others were former students at Princeton College, Aaron Burr, the future vice president, and Matthias Ogden. Strangely enough, two Pennsylvania riflemen brought along their wives, neither woman returning alive. According to one authority, the entire force numbered roughly 1,050.[1]

On September 11, drums rolled, fifes sounded, and, at Morgan's word, the riflemen swung onto the road to Newburyport, where Arnold's entire force assembled five days later. Then they boarded a fleet of eleven small ships which carried them to Gardiner, Maine.

After the army moved to Fort Western (near modern Augusta), Morgan became disturbed when Arnold announced his intention to send a rifle company as part of an advance force under Greene. Morgan considered this arrangement an encroachment upon his authority as leader of the riflemen. Moreover, he and the Pennsylvania rifle captains told Arnold that they refused to serve under Greene or any of the other New England militia officers; since Morgan and Arnold held commissions in the Continental Army, they alone could head the riflemen. When Morgan added that Washington himself had stated this opinion, Arnold chose him to form the advance party with the rifle companies; although Washington disavowed such a view, neither

1. Justin H. Smith, *Arnold's March from Cambridge to Quebec* (New York, 1903), 57. Smith's book, the standard work on the subject, is based mostly on accounts of the participants. These diaries and journals vary as to reliability, many being recorded long after Arnold's trek. The most reliable ones were edited by Kenneth Roberts and are in his *March to Quebec* (New York, 1940). He used them as the basis for his novel *Arundel*.

Arnold nor the militia officers tried to remove Morgan from his position. They, like Morgan's companions at Battletown, had found the muscular Virginian a highly sensitive man; and they had also discerned that frontier troops preferred to stay together under an officer of their own kind.[2]

Supplied with provisions for forty-five days, Morgan and his rifle companies began ascending the Kennebec River on September 25. Their orders from Arnold were to halt at the Great Carrying Place and cut a road to the Dead River. Some of the men walked on the banks; others handled bateaux, heavy boats used almost exclusively on the lower part of the river. As Morgan's troops moved along, they discovered why bateaux were seldom found on the upper region of the Kennebec. The stream contained numerous waterfalls large enough to force the men to maneuver their boats between rocks or to portage them. At the first major obstacle, Ticonic Falls, they carried their supplies around the rushing waters—then, sweating and straining, brought the bateaux forward. Morgan had been afloat again for only a day when he encountered Five Mile Falls. This time he decided to push the boats along. Getting into the water, the men slowly worked their way ahead, several stepping into deep holes and nearly drowning. An even bigger hurdle was Skowhegan Falls, where steep cliffs on each side of the river made portaging impossible. The troops spent an entire day pulling and poling the bateaux through rapids a half mile apart.[3]

Meanwhile, at Fort Western, Arnold readied the main body

2. Arnold to Washington, Sept. 25, 1775, Jared Sparks, ed., *Correspondence of the Revolution: Being Letters of Eminent Men to George Washington* (Boston, 1853), I, 48; Fitzpatrick, ed., *Writings of Washington*, IV, 2-3; Graham, *Morgan*, 61-62.

3. Arnold to Washington, Sept. 25, 1775 (second letter of that date), Sparks, ed., *Correspondence of the Revolution*, I, 47; journals of Return Meigs and George Morison, in Roberts, *March to Quebec*, 175, 511-12.

of the expedition for departure, dispatching a second division under Greene on the 26th, a third under Meigs on the 27th, and a fourth under Enos on the 29th. Arnold himself canoed up-river and soon found these officers also experiencing difficulties with the falls. While with Greene's troops on October 2, he came upon Morgan, just getting the last of his baggage around Norridgewock. Arnold told Morgan that he planned to halt the last three divisions at Norridgewock to repair the badly leaking bateaux; that would give Morgan the opportunity to start his road construction before Arnold caught up with him again.[4]

But after reaching the Great Carrying Place on Saturday evening, October 7, Morgan awoke the next morning in a drizzling rain that quickly turned into a downpour. He lost a day's time because of the weather, and he and his companies spent a sleepless Sunday night around small fires trying to keep warm. Though the rain persisted on Monday, Morgan began his task, for the rear detachments were close behind him. Attired only in Indian leggins and breech clout, he worked with his men as they cleared the underbrush from the woods. Much of the time they sloshed through mud and struggled across bogs, where men sometimes sank "half-leg deep." To make matters worse, the rains and river water that had seeped into the bateaux ruined a large amount of their food.[5]

Though Arnold sent several companies forward to assist Morgan, Greene's troops passed the riflemen; and since Meigs and Enos likewise threatened to overtake him, Morgan gave up completing the road, ordering that only the heavy foliage be removed from the trail. Morgan and Febiger pushed ahead with the scouts and soon encountered a reconnaissance party sent out by Arnold. They greeted Arnold's men "kindly," and Febiger

4. Journal of Arnold, in *ibid.*, 46.
5. Journal of Henry, in *ibid.*, 327; Smith, *Arnold's March*, 117-34, 339-58.

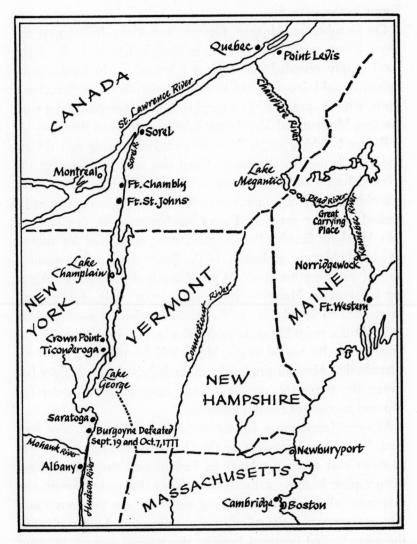

Morgan's Campaigns, 1775-1777

allowed them to drink from his canteen filled with the last bit of liquor in the army.[6]

On October 19, Morgan, Greene, and Meigs halted near the Dead River, with Enos not far behind. When a check of the food supply revealed no bread and little flour in Greene's division, Arnold detached 100 men to obtain additional flour from Enos, who supposedly had a surplus. While Arnold waited with Greene, Morgan and Meigs proceeded up the Dead River.

Before breaking camp, Morgan incurred trouble that threatened to disrupt his command. Until this time he had kept the spirited backwoodsmen in line, although there had been some grumbling at his announcement that ammunition could not be wasted in target practice. Then Chamberlin, a member of Captain Matthew Smith's Pennsylvania company, fired his rifle at an object. Morgan rushed up to the Pennsylvanian and accused him of violating his order. When Chamberlin denied discharging his weapon, Morgan seized a stick from a pile of wood and threatened to knock him to the ground unless he confessed his guilt. At this point Captain Smith, who had witnessed the altercation, swore he would strike Morgan if he placed a hand on Chamberlin. Morgan prudently conceded the issue. A fight between the two captains would only have made it harder for Morgan to control Smith's company.[7]

Morgan faced more serious difficulties when, by boat and land, his companies moved up the Dead River. The current was so swift that often the boatmen had to pull themselves along by grasping bushes on the banks. From the 19th through the 21st rain fell relentlessly, ruining much of the precious food. The greater part of the riflemen now traveled on land, with only the more skilled boatmen braving the roaring waters. William

6. Journals of Senter and Henry, in Roberts, *March to Quebec*, 205, 327.

7. Journal of Henry, in *ibid.*, 329; Graham, *Morgan*, 68.

Humphreys, first lieutenant of Morgan's Virginia company, lost his equipment when his bateau overturned, and he and his men nearly drowned before being hoisted into another craft. The route was also perilous for the troops on foot, who made long detours around swollen rivulets, sometimes losing their way.

Plodding along with his men, Morgan saw Arnold overtake them in a canoe. A council of war composed of the officers of the lead divisions met with Arnold on the 23rd. Wet and cold like his companions, Morgan listened as Arnold reviewed their critical situation—there was an alarming shortage of food, an epidemic of dysentery, no warm clothing, and a week or more of hazardous traveling remained. The diarists of the expedition suggest no talk of turning back. Certainly Arnold spoke only of going on. Since leaving Fort Western, he had moved up and down the long column, encouraging the men and sometimes working with them, lifting boats and shouldering provisions. Now, ordering the sick returned to Fort Western, he set out in advance of the army with an escort of picked men to purchase food from French Canadians in the Chaudière Valley.[8]

Morgan and Meigs drove on to the edge of the Height of Land, the watershed dividing the streams flowing north to the St. Lawrence and those running south to the Kennebec. Greene, arriving there on the 28th, gave Morgan distressing news. Three days earlier Enos's officers had voted to turn back, and while Enos himself had said he wished to go on, he had refused to countermand their decision. When Greene asked for a fair settlement of the food, Enos reluctantly gave up two and a half barrels

8. Journals of Arnold, Henry Dearborn, Meigs, Senter, and Morison, in Roberts, *March to Quebec*, 55, 136, 179, 209, 516. For Arnold's part in the expedition, see Willard Wallace, *Traitorous Hero: The Life and Fortunes of Benedict Arnold* (New York, 1954), 61-74; James T. Flexner, *The Traitor and the Spy: Benedict Arnold and John André* (New York, 1953), 62-72.

of flour. Reaching Fort Western in eleven days, Enos continued to Cambridge, where a court-martial tried and acquitted him of desertion. Luckily for him, only his own men could testify. Back in the Maine wilderness Henry Dearborn, a Massachusetts officer who later served under Morgan in the Saratoga campaign, wrote in his journal that the troops in Meigs's division prayed that Enos and his men "might die by the way, or meet with some disaster, Equal to the Cowardly[,] dastardly and unfriendly Spirit they . . . [displayed] in returning Back without orders." [9]

The most grueling ordeal yet for Morgan and the other commanders was the trek of four and a half miles across the Height of Land. If Greene and Meigs still had boats, they did not attempt to transport them to a chain of ponds that reached Lake Megantic and the Chaudière River. While the two Pennsylvania rifle captains each took a heavy craft, Morgan brought all seven of his over a snow-covered trail that traversed underbrush, ravines, and woods. The bateauxmen's exertions were painful for rifleman Joseph Henry to watch. He reported that Morgan's Virginians had the flesh "worn from their shoulders, even to the bone." By this time, declared Henry, "an antipathy had arisen against Morgan, as too strict a disciplinarian." Yet Morgan, as well as Arnold, was a hero to the youthful Pennsylvanian, who acknowledged that Morgan's forceful leadership did much to keep the expedition together. Knotty problems were "left to the energy of Morgan's mind, and he conquered." [10]

At last beyond the "Terrible Carrying Place," as one soldier described the Height of Land, the army came to Lake Megantic. Morgan loaded his bateaux and boarded the first boat. Entering the Chaudière, he found it equally as swift as the Dead. Without warning, the boats crashed into submerged rocks and sank.

9. Journal of Dearborn, in Roberts, *March to Quebec*, 137.
10. Journals of Senter, Henry, and Morison, in *ibid.*, 216, 329, 335-36, 523.

Struggling in the swirling, icy waters, Morgan finally reached shore, accompanied by all his men but one. (The lost man was the army's first death by drowning.) After the nightmare of carrying their bateaux beyond the Height of Land, Morgan's troops suffered a cruel fate—gone were their food, much of their equipment, and Dr. Isaac Senter's valuable medicine box. When Private Abner Stocking and his Connecticut company came upon the riflemen, he noted that their condition was "truly deplorable—they had not . . . a mouthful of provisions of any kind, and we were not able to relieve them, as hunger stared us in the face. . . . Some of Captain Morgan's company we were told had perished with the cold." Undoubtedly a few of the units shared what rations they had with the riflemen. Though malnutrition had weakened Morgan's sturdy frame, he trudged back and forth along the line, assuring the men that Arnold would not fail them. But he, Meigs, and Greene could not maintain any semblance of formation; some companies were strung out for miles. As their hunger increased, men ate dog meat, roasted shot pouches, and made gruel from shaving soap and lip salve. Throughout the campaign the two riflemen's wives had resolutely kept pace with the others. When Mrs. Grier waded a stream with her skirt held above her waist, Henry observed that no one made an unkind insinuation. The second woman, Mrs. Warner, left the column when her husband grew too ill to keep on. Staying with him until he died, she shouldered his rifle and hurried to rejoin the expedition.

At last, on November 2, the army met Arnold's relief force bringing oatmeal, flour, and cattle. Slaughtering the animals, many of the famished soldiers gulped the meat down raw. Pushing on, the gaunt, ragged Americans presented a strange sight to the French Canadians of the Chaudière Valley. "I thought," said Stocking, "we much resembled the animals which inhabit

New-Spain, called the Ourang-Outang." At the village of St. Marys, the army left the river and marched over frozen plains to the St. Lawrence, encamping at Point Levis by November 10.[11]

The men of the Kennebec column had little time to reflect upon their amazing 350-mile journey from Fort Western, which ranks among the most famous marches in American military history. To get to Quebec, they still needed to pass over the St. Lawrence, whose waters were dotted with British patrol boats. Arnold and his officers set to work. With the aid of friendly Indians, the Americans gathered thirty or more canoes and dugouts, constructed scaling ladders, and made iron tips for pikes.

On November 11, a scout rushed up to Morgan with word of a British force about to land at a nearby mill. Gathering a body of riflemen and Indians, Morgan hurried to a precipice overlooking the mill, only to find the threat consisted of a few sailors in a single boat. He watched as a midshipman waded ashore while the crew, desiring to locate a more suitable landing place, drew off. Convinced the boatmen had seen his men, Morgan raised his rifle and fired at the sailors, who quickly rowed beyond range. The midshipman, after trying to swim after them, soon gave up and turned back. As Morgan led his party toward the beach to make the capture, one of the Indians drew a knife and dashed ahead, intent on taking a scalp. Morgan raced forward and overtook him, persuading him to give up his victim. Morgan and Arnold hoped the prisoner would reveal the strength of Quebec's defenses but found him uncommunicative.[12]

11. Journals of Meigs, Senter, Henry, and Stocking, in *ibid.*, 181, 218, 337-38, 554-58. Perhaps as many as 60 men died during the march, while approximately 70 turned back because of illness. Enos's defection further reduced the army by about 300. Some 600 of Arnold's troops reached Point Levis. For these and other estimates, see Christopher Ward, *War of the Revolution*, ed. John R. Alden (New York, 1952), I, 450.

12. Journal of Hendricks and Chambers, *Pennsylvania Archives*, 2d Ser., XV, 48; journals of Dearborn, Senter, Henry, James Melvin, Caleb

With little knowledge of the enemy fortress, the expedition began the crossing at nine o'clock on the night of November 13. Arnold, Morgan, and Dr. Senter paddled silently in the lead canoe. When in mid-stream one of the boats broke open, all its occupants except Lieutenant Steele of the Pennsylvania riflemen scrambled into another craft; Steele held to its stern the rest of the way. Later Morgan and Arnold sighted the murky outline of a rowboat, but the men on board it did not see the Americans. Arnold landed his men at the same cove where British General James Wolfe had gone ashore sixteen years earlier to engage in his great battle with French General Montcalm. While the canoes returned to ferry additional men, Morgan sent out a reconnaissance party under Lieutenant William Heth of Virginia, who crept near the city's walls without coming upon any sentries. Heth's report convinced Morgan that the time to attack was at hand. He had no difficulty persuading Arnold to this view; both were men of action. They waited impatiently for the troops at Point Levis to be transported to the north bank. But after the second group debarked, the men built a fire in an abandoned house, presumably to warm themselves; instantly a British barge spotted the blaze and made for the cove. When Arnold shouted to the oarsmen to row toward him, they backwatered and disappeared around a bend, followed by a spray of bullets.[13]

At roughly four A.M. Arnold called a council of war and asked his officers whether an assault should be attempted; it would have to be without the assistance of the 200 men on the far bank, for the encounter with the patrol boat indicated that a further passage would be foolhardy. Arnold and most of his officers

Haskell, Morison, Stocking, and Simon Fobes, in Roberts, *March to Quebec*, 141, 223, 349-50, 441, 479, 532, 559, 586.

13. Journals of Dearborn, Meigs, Senter, Simeon Thayer, Henry, Morison, Stocking, and Fobes, in *ibid.*, 141, 182, 224-25, 264, 351-53, 532-33, 559, 586-87.

opposed immediate action: word of the patrol boat episode must have alerted Colonel Allan Maclean, acting commander of the garrison; hence the Americans had lost the element of surprise, an important factor since they were perhaps outnumbered. The opinion of the majority so upset Morgan that, oddly enough, he said very little. Having volunteered for the expedition in the hope of fighting, he and his troops had undergone incredible hardships in reaching Quebec. Now all might be lost by waiting. The enemy would strengthen their defenses; the Canadian winter was already upon them; and there was no assurance that Schuyler's army, from which Arnold had received no intelligence for weeks, would be able to reinforce them.

Evidence obtained afterward suggests that had Arnold gambled in accordance with Morgan's wishes, the city would quite possibly have fallen to the Americans. Not for six or more hours did a report of the Wolfe's Cove incident reach Maclean, whose forces were badly disorganized, particularly the French Canadian militia who showed no strong will to fight. Because of his lack of information, however, Arnold can scarcely be criticized for his stand. Morgan probably should have followed his usual habit of freely speaking his mind. After the council, discontent festered inside him.[14]

For the time being, he directed the vanguard of the army up the bluff to the edge of the Plains of Abraham. Looming ahead in the morning mist was the dim outline of a large house serving as quarters for a group of redcoats. Using this opportunity for the action he craved, he sprinted "sword in hand" at the head of his troops. They met no opposition; a few drowsy-eyed Britons meekly surrendered, while the others fled by a rear door. Then, after Arnold brought up the remaining units and while the Amer-

14. Journals of Morison and Fobes, in *ibid.*, 533, 587; Graham, *Morgan*, 85; Wallace, *Traitorous Hero*, 76-77.

icans got a few hours' sleep, a daring British squad crept out and captured one of Morgan's sentries, Virginia rifleman George Merchant. Merchant, a tall, well-built young man, was an excellent marksman and one of Morgan's favorites. Nothing had gone right for Morgan that morning.[15]

Arnold viewed Merchant's seizure as an indication that the enemy might leave their defenses and engage him in open combat. In that case, he would gladly fight. He eagerly drew up his army and hurried toward the walls of the city. But the gates did not open. Redcoats and civilians crowding the ramparts stared down on the hatless, disheveled band, exchanging taunts and insults with them. Morgan, already upset by recent events, thought the parading up and down sheer nonsense, and evidently told Arnold so that evening when he lodged a complaint with his commander: the riflemen were receiving an inadequate diet, and something had to be done about it! (Arnold had recently instituted strict rationing.) A direct account of what transpired has not been preserved, although it is clear that Morgan was in a thoroughly belligerent mood, that Arnold too became greatly exercised, and that at one point Morgan seemed ready to strike his superior. Though rejecting Morgan's demand

15. Graham, *Morgan*, 86, 465; "Morgan's Autobiography," *Historical Magazine*, 2d Ser., 9 (1871), 379. The British took a keen interest in Merchant, probably because word of the riflemen's activities at Boston had reached Quebec. Moreover, French peasants had spread a rumor that the riflemen wore hunting frocks made of sheet-iron. Justin H. Smith, *Our Struggle for the Fourteenth Colony* (New York, 1907), II, 13. Merchant was sent to England, "hunting-shirt and all . . . probably as a finished specimen of the riflemen of the colonies." Journal of Henry, in Roberts, *March to Quebec*, 354. An English periodical noted that "The Rifleman who was brought here from Quebec . . . is a Virginian, above six feet high, stout and well-proportioned. . . . He can strike a mark with the greatest certainty, at two hundred yards distance. He has a heavy provincial pronunciation, but otherwise speaks good English. The account he gives, is, that the troops in general are such kind of men as himself, tall and well-proportioned." *Remembrancer, 1776*, Pt. II, 344-45.

at the moment, Arnold reconsidered it and next day ordered an increase in the riflemen's allotments. Strict taskmaster that Morgan was, he always made every effort to provide well for his men. In the forests of Maine he had grown fond of many of them. As Private Henry wrote, when Morgan "became attached he was kind and truly affectionate." [16]

Even toward Arnold, Morgan felt a closeness, though the feeling was based more on professional respect than personal intimacy. Both the tall, sinewy Morgan and the short, stocky Arnold possessed famous tempers, were sensitive to criticism, and thirsted for glory; more significant, both were battlefield tacticians and leaders of men. Differences they had, but Arnold could count on Morgan's loyalty and co-operation. Even after Arnold's treason brought him national execration, Morgan could remember the swarthy little man as "my old friend." [17]

Just after their fracas, Arnold showed his continued respect for Morgan. Temporarily withdrawing twenty-five miles to Point aux Trembles, he ordered the Virginian to cover the retreat. When he discovered that Schuyler's army, now led by Brigadier General Richard Montgomery, was approaching, Arnold sent Morgan back to Quebec on reconnaissance.[18] Montgomery entered Point aux Trembles on December 2, bringing clothes and ammunition for Arnold's troops. Like Arnold, Montgomery had failed to hold his force together; several hundred of his New Englanders had tramped homeward after their brief enlistments expired. However, he had captured Forts St. Johns and Chambly on the Sorel River and had taken Montreal before

16. Journal of Henry, in Roberts, *March to Quebec*, 302, 354, 356; Graham, *Morgan*, 88.

17. Morgan to Jefferson, Mar. 23, 1781, Julian P. Boyd, ed., *The Papers of Thomas Jefferson* (Princeton, 1950———), V, 218-19.

18. Graham, *Morgan*, 90, 465; "Morgan's Autobiography," *Historical Magazine*, 2d Ser., 9 (1871), 379; journals of Dearborn, Meigs, and Senter, in Roberts, *March to Quebec*, 144, 184, 227.

uniting with Arnold. On December 4, he led the combined army of 975 men toward the Plains of Abraham.[19]

Morgan was reconnoitering near the city when Montgomery appeared. In launching siege operations, he stationed Morgan's companies on the north side of Quebec in the suburb of St. Roque. Again, as at Boston, the riflemen amused themselves by sniping at redcoats, who soon saw the wisdom of staying behind cover. Inside the city was Governor Guy Carleton, who had fled eastward with a small body of regulars shortly before the fall of Montreal. A steady and courageous soldier, he had reorganized Quebec's defenses and improved morale. He could muster nearly 1,800 men, including French Canadian militia and able-bodied civilians. Possessing large quantities of food and expecting reinforcements from England in the spring, he wisely decided to remain behind the walls.

Montgomery, aware of Carleton's situation, had no choice but to attack. His small cannon were ineffective against the thick bastions. Smallpox broke out, and food became increasingly short. Still worse, the enlistments of Arnold's New Englanders would expire with the end of the year. Accordingly, Montgomery planned an assault for the first stormy night. Sometime in the latter part of December, Morgan attended a meeting of the principal American officers. Montgomery and Arnold briefed their subordinates on the order of battle. Two feints were to be made against the walls of the Upper Town, one headed by Colonel James Livingston, the other by Captain Jacob Brown. The divisions of Arnold and Montgomery were to smash into the

19. Early in Sept., Schuyler became ill and returned to Fort Ticonderoga, where he worked to secure additional supplies and equipment for Montgomery. Accounts of Montgomery's Montreal campaign are in Smith, *Struggle for the Fourteenth Colony*, I, 336-491; Lynn Montross, *Rag, Tag and Bobtail: The Story of the American Revolutionary Army* (New York, 1952), 61-66; Ward, *War of the Revolution*, I, 150-62; Willard Wallace, *Appeal to Arms* (New York, 1951), 67-72.

Lower Town, Arnold from the north, Montgomery from the south; the two columns were to unite in the Sault au Matelot, a narrow, winding street near the center of the Lower Town, and drive their way into the Upper Town. The climax to the Canadian campaign was at hand.

CHAPTER IV

Defeat and Imprisonment

O N THE afternoon of December 30, snow began to fall. By evening the downfall increased, and a strong wind blew in from the northwest. Just after midnight Morgan hurried into the storm to visit his men. He inspected their rifles, spoke encouraging words, then hastened to join Arnold's officers for a brief review of the battle plan. Because of the blinding snow, the scarcely distinguishable trail, and the inexperience of the field officers, Arnold concluded that he and Morgan should lead the way—Arnold to direct a small advance party of thirty men and Captain John Lamb's forty New York artillerists with their six-pounder strapped securely to a sled; Morgan to follow with the main body of riflemen and New Englanders. At two o'clock, Arnold's corps assembled before light streaming from open doorways. While Arnold supervised, his subordinates formed the men in a single line, gave them slips of paper for their caps as identifying marks, and reminded them to hold their guns under their coats to keep powder and locks dry.

The men waited nervously, stamping their feet to lessen the cold, until four o'clock when bursting rockets signaled the beginning of the assault. Immediately the feinting parties of Brown and Livingston appeared before the walls and fired at the parapets. In the city drums beat, church bells pealed, and Carleton's men rushed to their battle stations.

Meanwhile, Montgomery, picking his way around ice cakes,

led his column over a narrow lane between the cliff of Quebec and the Saint Lawrence. After cutting a path through two undefended palisades, Montgomery and the forlorn hope, as eighteenth-century advance parties were known, charged toward a blockhouse obstructing their route. Its garrison, composed of British seamen and Canadian volunteers, fired four cannon at the oncoming Americans, killing Montgomery and six others. Lieutenant Colonel Donald Campbell, Montgomery's overly cautious second in command, ordered a retreat that quickly turned into terror-stricken flight. Had Campbell been a brave man, the outcome of the battle might have been different.

To the north, Arnold's men set out from St. Roque and passed along the bank of the Charles River. Sometimes they slipped and slid on ice disgorged by the water; sometimes they stumbled and fell while beating down mounds of snow higher than their heads. Just as Arnold and Lamb passed safely beyond the north wall of the Upper Town, sentries atop the Palace Gate sighted Morgan's column. Stopping to urge the main body on, Morgan then raced to the front of the rifle companies. Once in the Lower Town, he pursued Arnold through a maze of wharves, warehouses, and shops.

Entering a narrow street, Arnold glimpsed a barrier with two cannon at the far end. Waving Morgan to his side, Arnold tersely instructed him to move out to the left and come upon it from the rear while Lamb's six-pounder held the defenders' attention. Only then did Arnold discover that Lamb's men had abandoned their weapon in a snow drift. With a frontal attack his sole recourse, Arnold dashed forward, shouting for the others to follow. Morgan, close at his Colonel's heels, saw a flash of light as one of the enemy cannon went off and watched several of his Virginians topple into the snow. Suddenly Arnold fell sprawling as a musket ball tore into his left leg. Slowly he got up, supported by two riflemen, while Morgan and the other officers crowded around. There was no time to waste; yet Arnold could not continue. The field officers insisted that Morgan take the lead since he had seen service and they had not. Their decision was proper: throughout the campaign Morgan had borne most of the difficult assignments, never failing to perform well. Although Morgan was to lead, he was not specifically given absolute command. At any moment his superiors, individually or collectively, could overrule him.[1]

Of more immediate concern was the barrier. Morgan raced forward and placed a ladder against the wall. When he ordered a soldier to mount it, the man hesitated; so Morgan himself went up. A barrage of musketry and grapeshot greeted him as his head appeared over the top, a ball tearing through his hat and another creasing his cheek. Stunned, he fell backward into the snow, his face blackened by powder burns. The men around him halted, reluctant to face what seemed certain death. But in a moment Morgan was on his feet, climbing the ladder and leaping the barricade. His back struck a cannon—"which hurt me very much"—and he fell beneath it. In the darkness and confusion the gun momentarily offered protection from bayonet thrusts. Then the redcoats hastily retreated when riflemen poured over the wall. Lucky to be alive and experiencing considerable pain from his fall, Morgan led an assault on a nearby house where the enemy had taken cover. Rushing around to the back, he found the Britons trying to escape by a rear entrance. Though all alone, he coolly announced that they were surrounded and must surrender now or receive no quarter. His deception worked; they all gave up.[2]

1. Wallace, *Traitorous Hero*, 83-84; Ward, *War of the Revolution*, I, 190-92; Graham, *Morgan*, 96, 465; "Morgan's Autobiography," *Historical Magazine*, 2d Ser., 9 (1871), 379.

2. Graham, *Morgan*, 97-98; "Morgan's Autobiography," *Historical Magazine*, 2d Ser., 9 (1871), 379; Hill's Notes; journals of Thayer, Morison, and Stocking, in Roberts, *March to Quebec*, 275, 536-37, 564-65.

Morgan pressed on and entered the Sault au Matelot, en-countering throngs of French Canadian militia who threw down their guns and shouted, "Vive la liberté." At the end of the street was another barrier, but the defenders had fled, and its gate was open. Morgan, with an interpreter, walked through the passage and proceeded to the edge of the Upper Town and back without seeing signs of the enemy. Believing the British were reeling, he wanted to drive on. But at an impromptu coun-cil of war at the lower end of the Sault au Matelot, the other American officers overruled Morgan: they were at Montgomery's rendezvous point and feared to violate orders; countless num-bers of their men had strayed on unfamiliar streets; and their prisoners if left behind might break loose and turn the captured cannon on them.[3]

The Americans who stood arguing in the narrow street were suffering the effects of a divided command. Battlefield decisions must be made quickly by an officer with full authority to carry them out. Perhaps the fault was Arnold's in neglecting to make it clear that someone, Morgan or possibly Greene, should have that power. In any case, their rejection of Morgan's proposal may have cost the Americans the city. The garrison was badly confused. Brown and Livingston had drawn Carleton's attention from the Lower Town, and a rumor had spread throughout the Upper Town that Arnold's force was beating down all opposition.

Morgan, visibly upset, waited impatiently for Montgomery's appearance. Finally, he occupied himself by going back to the dock area to search for the men who had lost their way. After rounding up nearly 200 New Englanders belonging to Greene

3. Graham, *Morgan*, 466; "Morgan's Autobiography," *Historical Maga-zine*, 2d Ser., 9 (1871), 380; journals of Meigs, Henry, Morison, and Stocking, in Roberts, *March to Quebec*, 190, 377, 537, 565.

and Meigs, Morgan returned to the first barrier, where there was still no word of Montgomery.[4]

Carleton remained calm despite the turmoil about him. Reconnaissance parties presently informed him that the activities of Brown and Livingston were feints, that Montgomery's column was no longer in the field, and that the only threat was in the Sault au Matelot. Dispatching troops to the previously abandoned barrier in that street, he then sent other soldiers under a Captain Laws out the Palace Gate with orders to come upon Arnold's detachment from the rear.

Dawn was breaking and the storm abating when the Americans discerned new activity at the second barrier. With their position in the open street now untenable, the officers belatedly accepted Morgan's advice to advance and once again asked him to take the lead. Though readily agreeing, he must have been bitter knowing that the enemy obstacles could have been his for the taking, if only the others had given in to him earlier.

In the van with the three rifle companies, Morgan came face to face with a British squad. When the lieutenant in command called for him to surrender, Morgan shot him through the head. The redcoats fled for the barricade, pursued by the riflemen.[5] Morgan, Humphreys, Heth, and Steele scrambled up ladders propped against the wall. From upper-story windows in houses on the far side, muskets blazed, and below in the street two rows of fusiliers stood with fixed bayonets. Falling back, Morgan rallied the Americans for a second try, then a third, a fourth, and more—all of them repulsed. He seemed to be everywhere, carrying a wounded soldier to the rear, leading first one charge and then another, his stentorian commands rising above the sounds of the wind and musketry. He "stormed

4. Graham, *Morgan*, 99.
5. Journal of Stocking, in Roberts, *March to Quebec*, 565.

and raged" and was "brave to temerity," reported Henry; while George Morison declared, "Betwixt every peal the awful voice of Morgan is heard, whose gigantic stature and terrible appearance carries dismay among the foe wherever he comes." Noticing a stone dwelling with gable-end windows overlooking the British side of the barrier, Morgan sent riflemen inside to enfilade the enemy line. But Major Henry Caldwell, the British commander, saw them enter the building and ordered a ladder set against it. Fusiliers climbed up, swarmed through a window, and, after a warm contest, drove the invaders out.[6]

As the enemy, reinforced by scores of men, loosed blast after blast, the Americans suffered a frightful loss, especially in officers. Even more alarming to Morgan was the realization that most of the rifles and muskets were too wet to fire. He could scarcely complain when the troops sought cover in houses along the way. Denying himself this security, he stayed in the street with a small party of riflemen, directing the fire of those who still had dry priming. His performance was as futile as it was heroic; the enemy, aiming from portholes in the wall, were well protected. Once during a temporary lull he called for another charge, a plea his weary men refused to heed.[7]

At last grasping the hopelessness of his situation, Morgan, accompanied by Heth, returned toward the first barrier to consult with Meigs and Bigelow, who headed the rear guard. Their hasty conference resulted in a decision to withdraw behind that barrier and await Montgomery. But Heth, who carried this message back up the Sault au Matelot, found the men would not run the gantlet of the street, although they

6. Journals of Meigs, Thayer, Henry, and Morison, in *ibid.*, 190, 276, 378, 537-38.

7. Graham, *Morgan*, 101-2; journal of Henry, in Roberts, *March to Quebec*, 378.

changed their minds about nine A.M. when a British nine-pounder began hurling balls at their houses. As Morgan, Greene, Bigelow, and Meigs came up to meet them, Laws's flanking unit from the Palace Gate attacked the Americans from behind. As Carleton wrote, the patriots were hemmed in front and rear —"caught as it were in a trap." [8]

Could they break through Laws's force and escape from the town? Morgan thought there was a chance of success, and he pleaded with the field officers to let him head such an attempt, an offer they rejected. Over his protest Arnold's subordinates agreed to surrender on Carleton's assurance of good treatment. The frustrations of being blocked at every turn by his fellow officers and of failing to gain the city swelled up in Morgan. Seeing the men around him throw down their arms, he burst into tears of rage. With his back against a building, he dared the British to try and take his sword. When they threatened to shoot him, he told them to go ahead. He refused to listen when his riflemen begged him to give up. Suddenly he sighted a priest in the milling crowd. In desperation he handed the surprised man his sword, saying angrily, "Not a scoundrel of those cowards shall take it out of my hands." [9]

Morgan's anguish must have deepened after his capture, when he learned of Montgomery's death, Campbell's cowardly withdrawal, and the enemy's consternation during the initial stage of the assault. A British officer, probably Major Caldwell, wrote of Arnold's column: "Had they acted with more spirit, they might have pushed in at first and possessed themselves of the whole of Lower Town, and let their friends in at the other side, before our people had time to have recovered from a certain

8. Graham, *Morgan*, 102; Carleton's remark is in Smith, *Struggle for the Fourteenth Colony*, I, 146.
9. Graham, *Morgan*, 102-3.

degree of panic, which seized them on the first news of the post being surprised." [10]

The Americans had failed dismally, but through no fault of Morgan. Morgan, who was seldom philosophical, found little solace in his own magnificent performance. He was a prisoner hundreds of miles from home, and his rifle companies, particularly the Virginians, had received extremely heavy losses. Reputedly only twenty-five of Morgan's Frederick County men ever returned to Virginia. All told, American casualties amounted to approximately 100 killed and wounded and 400 captured as opposed to Carleton's loss of only 20 in all categories.[11] Outside the city the wounded Arnold assembled the remnant of his battered corps and assumed command of Montgomery's division. Reforming his army, he decided to spend the winter outside Quebec, having "no thought of leaving this proud town, until I first enter it in triumph." Though Arnold pleaded with Congress and Washington for reinforcements, he gave the British no cause for alarm. Never could he muster half as many troops as Carleton.[12]

While Arnold's force spent a miserable winter on the Plains of Abraham, suffering from bitter cold and short rations, the Americans within the city fared relatively well. After feeding their captives, the British imprisoned the enlisted men in a monastery, the officers in a seminary. Carleton gave them straw and blankets for bedding, and he allowed Major Meigs to enter Arnold's camp to secure what baggage they still possessed. (Meigs returned with a message in code written on the back of a playing card: "Long Nos'd" was coming with his "Black

10. Henry S. Commager and Richard B. Morris, eds., *The Spirit of 'Seventy-Six: The Story of the American Revolution As Told by Participants* (New York, 1958), I, 206.

11. Smith, *Struggle for the Fourteenth Colony*, II, 581-82.

12. Wallace, *Traitorous Hero*, 86.

Dog," which meant that aquiline-nose General Charles Lee, a dog lover, was advancing from Washington's camp to aid Arnold, a report that proved to be untrue.) [13] Soon after entering their quarters, several rooms in an upper story of the seminary, the officers received from Carleton a quantity of wine and from the Bishop of Quebec a liberal gift of tea. They could not complain of the amount of food allotted them, although there was some grumbling about their steady diet of pork, potatoes, and cabbage prepared by a grimy little French cook.

For recreation the officers were allowed occasional walks in the seminary garden, while playing cards and talking to redcoat sentries were other diversions. Morgan discovered that one of the guards had performed with him during Dunmore's War. The Americans' confinement was further enlivened by one of their own group, Lieutenant William Heth of Virginia, who recorded in his diary the lighter side of prison life. One warm spring day when several mesdemoiselles dressed in finery strolled outside his window, Heth decided to amuse his associates by attracting the attention of the young ladies. Borrowing the best clothing available, "I riggd myself out in such a Brilliant manner, that I thought I could not but attract the Eyes of *any Lady* of Penetration or Taste." His attire included a red coat, white vest, white cord breeches (which had "seen their best days"), silk hose, and cocked hat with a feather. "Thus equipt— I hung out at the windows Sunday & Monday" but made no "conquests." He ruefully explained that he was "not ... sufficiently acquainted with the French Language to keep up a Tete a Tete." [14]

Heth noted that the British officers frequently visited the Americans, especially Morgan whom they respected because of

13. B. Floyd Flickinger, ed., "The Diary of William Heth," Winchester, Virginia Historical Society, *Annual Papers*, 1 (1931), 41.
14. *Ibid.*, 46-47.

his spirited performance during the battle. Morgan became well acquainted with a Major Carleton, brother of the General, and a naval officer named McKenzie, whose brother Morgan had rescued from the Indian at Point Levis.[15]

One of Carleton's subordinates, possibly young Carleton or McKenzie, made a concerted effort to gain Morgan's good will. The two men talked on numerous subjects but always avoided topics of a political nature until, one day, the officer told Morgan that the patriots would gain nothing from their struggle with the mother country. The Briton said that he considered Morgan a brave and enterprising soldier deserving nobler employment than the American cause, and that Morgan could have a colonelcy in His Majesty's army. Indignant, Morgan replied that his services were not for sale; he was no "scoundrel."[16]

An equally upsetting experience for Morgan, one which illustrates the stormy side of his nature, concerned the conduct of a fellow prisoner, Captain William Goodrich of Massachusetts. At the time of his capture, Goodrich possessed a watch belonging to a Canadian civilian named Bromfield. In June 1776, an American enlisted man, receiving permission to leave the city for a brief time, volunteered to take the watch to its owner; but Goodrich rejected the offer, confiding to the American officers that he did not trust the soldier. Morgan then grew "pretty warm" and accused him of desiring to keep it for himself. When Goodrich remained opposed to relinquishing the watch, Morgan took him by the throat and forced him to give it up. Heth and Charles Porterfield, the diarists recording the incident, applauded Morgan's action, since they believed Goodrich had no intention of returning the watch. Both officers considered the Massachusetts officer of low moral character. Morgan may well have disliked Goodrich even before their imprison-

15. *Ibid.*, 41, 56.
16. Graham, *Morgan*, 111-12.

ment, for the latter along with Captain Oliver Hanchet of Connecticut had seriously threatened the effectiveness of the Kennebec column early the previous December by refusing to serve further under Arnold. Though Montgomery persuaded them to remain with Arnold, they became unpopular with many of the other officers. Goodrich's friends, particularly Captain Hanchet and a Lieutenant Andrews, were angry about Morgan's treatment of Goodrich. Andrews, moreover, held a personal grudge: earlier Morgan had given him "a blow or two in his Jaws" for telling a lie. Their ill feeling was triggered on July 3. While Morgan and Major Timothy Bigelow were talking in the latter's quarters, Morgan noticed Goodrich standing at the door, listening to the conversation. Morgan ordered Goodrich to be on his way, but he was slow in leaving, and Morgan shook him severely before shoving him away from the door. Overhearing the disturbance, Andrews and Goodrich's other friends seized Morgan while Andrews hit him several times. But Andrews recoiled in pain when Morgan landed a "severe kick" in his stomach. At that point Morgan's attackers withdrew to another room. After that Goodrich kept his distance from Morgan.[17]

Morgan's great physical vigor, so evident in his difficulties with Goodrich, probably made him a restless prisoner. Twice in May, he unsuccessfully petitioned Carleton for a parole. Near the end of July, however, the Governor agreed to release all his prisoners on condition they would not bear arms until exchanged for Britons in American hands. The men of the Kennebec column were the only large body of American soldiers still in Canada. When British reinforcements from England arrived at Quebec

17. Flickinger, ed., "The Diary of William Heth," Winchester, Va. Hist. Soc., *Annual Papers*, 1 (1931), 117-18; [Charles Porterfield], "Diary of a Prisoner of War at Quebec," *Va. Mag. of Hist. and Biog.*, 9 (1901), 150-52. The quotations are from Heth.

in May, the patriot besieging force had retreated toward Montreal, and by late June had retired to Fort Ticonderoga.

On August 11, Carleton's prisoners sailed from Quebec aboard transports that were scheduled to unite with a large British fleet assembling for a major assault upon New York City. Reaching Staten Island early in September after an uneventful voyage, the Americans learned that British General William Howe had defeated Washington's army near Brooklyn on Long Island and had forced the patriot commander to withdraw northward from New York City. On September 24, Howe landed the prisoners at Elizabethtown, New Jersey, and turned them over to American authorities. All the returning men were filled with emotion, reported Joseph Henry. Morgan leaped from the boat, fell upon the ground with arms outspread, and cried, "Oh my country." [18]

Though the efforts of Montgomery, Arnold, and Morgan had failed to wrest Canada from the Crown, Morgan's performance on the march through Maine and at the battle of Quebec had so impressed Arnold that he subsequently spoke highly of his subordinate in a letter to Washington. But the Commander in Chief had already heard reports of Morgan's activity and had a special position in mind for his fellow Virginian.[19]

18. Flickinger, ed., "The Diary of William Heth," Winchester, Va. Hist. Soc., *Annual Papers*, 1 (1931), 56-57, 59; "Diary of Lieutenant Francis Nichols," *Pa. Mag. of Hist. and Biog.*, 20 (1896), 506; journals of Thayer and Henry, in Roberts, *March to Quebec*, 292, 427.

19. Arnold to Washington, Nov. 6, 1776, Washington Papers, Lib. Cong.

CHAPTER V

Saratoga Campaign

O N SEPTEMBER 28, 1776, Washington wrote to John Hancock, president of the Continental Congress:

As Col: Hugh Stephenson of the Rifle Regiment ordered lately to be raised, is dead, according to the information I have received, I would beg leave to recommend to the particular notice of Congress, Captain Daniel Morgan, just returned among the Prisoners from Canada, as a fit and proper person to succeed to the vacancy occasioned by his Death. . . . His [Morgan's] Conduct as an Officer on the expedition with General Arnold last fall, his intrepid behavior in the Assault on Quebec when the brave Montgomery fell;—the inflexible attachment he professed to our Cause during his imprisonment and which he perseveres in; added to these his residence in the place Col: Stevenson [*sic*] came from and his Interest and influence in the same circle and with such men as are to compose such a Regiment; all in my Opinion entitle him to the favor of Congress, and lead me to believe, that in his promotion, the States will gain a good and valuable Officer for the sort of Troops he is particularly recommended to command.[1]

A few days later Hancock informed Washington that the rifle regiment would be "kept for Mr. Morgan." For the present

1. Washington to Hancock, Sept. 28, 1776, Fitzpatrick, ed., *Writings of Washington*, VI, 128. Since Morgan had not yet been exchanged, Washington requested that if his recommendation were accepted, the promotion not be mentioned publicly.

Morgan returned to Frederick County following an absence of fifteen months to await his exchange.[2]

Morgan found his wife and daughters in good health, though worried about his safety since Carleton had not allowed his prisoners to write letters home except just after their capture. Toward the end of the year a courier delivered Morgan's commission as colonel of the 11th Virginia, one of fifteen regiments promised by that state for Continental service. Exchanged in January 1777, Morgan set to work, assisted by his officers who included Christian Febiger as lieutenant colonel, William Heth as major, and Peter Bruin as one of the captains. Morgan was proud to gain old friends for his subordinates, and he took equal pleasure in having some enlisted men from his original rifle company join the new unit. But recruitment proved difficult; Morgan had to range over a wide area of western Virginia, and he was away from home for long periods of time. Accepting only accurate marksmen, he was perhaps too selective, an opinion held by Governor Patrick Henry, who twice urged Morgan to complete his regiment with all haste. Having but 180 men by the end of March, Morgan proceeded to Washington's camp at Morristown, New Jersey.[3]

While Morgan was in Virginia, Washington had retreated through New Jersey to the west bank of the Delaware River. Then he slipped back and scored successive triumphs at Trenton and Princeton, before taking to winter quarters in the highlands

2. Hancock to Washington, Oct. 4, 1776, Burnett, ed., *Letters of Congress*, II, 114. Probably because of Washington's request, Morgan's elevation is not recorded in the *Journals of Congress*.

3. Graham, *Morgan*, 118-21; Williamsburg *Virginia Gazette* (Purdie), Feb. 14, 1777; Worthington C. Ford, ed., *Journals and Correspondence of Samuel B. Webb* (New York, 1893), I, 85; H. R. McIlwaine, ed., *Journals...of the...Council of State of Virginia* (Richmond, 1931-1932), I, 321; McIlwaine, ed., *Official Letters of the Governors of the State of Virginia* (Richmond, 1926), I, 105.

about Morristown. His army of fewer than 4,000 men suffered from insufficient clothing, meager food supplies, and smallpox. In the spring his outlook brightened when newly raised Continental forces began arriving at Morristown. By the middle of May he had roughly 8,000 troops to oppose Howe's expected late-spring offensive.

During this month Morgan was occupied with camp duties. His orderly book shows that he exerted himself to give the 11th Regiment a martial appearance, in spite of a shortage of soap, shoes, uniforms, powder, and lead. Though preferring to wear his customary hunting shirt and leggins, Morgan was a stickler for neatness. Whatever the attire of his men—and for most of them it consisted of a motley assortment—he insisted they look as "decent and clean" as possible. The drummers and fifers were to take "particular care" in their dress and were to practice together an hour each day. There would be no finer regiment in the army; that was Morgan's ambition. But the 11th Virginia, which Washington had planned to use for scouting and guerrilla tactics once Howe took the field, had a serious deficiency in numbers.[4]

Therefore early in June, after shifting his army twenty miles southward to the heights of Middlebrook, Washington gave Morgan command of a specially created corps of light infantry, composed of nearly 500 picked Continentals outfitted in hunting shirts and leggins. The troops were from the western counties of Pennsylvania, Maryland, and Virginia, most of the Virginians drawn from Morgan's own regiment. The corps, considered an independent unit (not attached to any state line), was excused from all regular duties of the camp. Aided by his able lieutenant colonel, Richard Butler of Pennsylvania, Morgan procured rifles and requisitioned pikes.[5]

4. "Orderly Book of Major William Heth," Virginia Historical Society, *Proceedings*, 10 (1891), 332-76.

5. Fitzpatrick, ed., *Writings of Washington*, VIII, 236-37, 246.

Morgan's force soon saw action against the British. Howe had assembled the bulk of his army at Amboy, New Jersey, and on June 12 he advanced to New Brunswick, eight miles south of Middlebrook. Guessing that Howe intended to move on Philadelphia, Washington told Morgan to take a position near the junction of the New Brunswick-Delaware road and a route leading northward toward the Millstone River and the American camp. If the British took either route, Morgan was to claw at their flanks, and Washington advised him to "dress a Company or two of true Woods Men in the right Indian Style and let them make the Attack accompanied with screaming and yelling as the Indians do, it would have very good consequences." Accordingly, Morgan halted on the Millstone road before daylight on the 14th. He sent out scouts who hurriedly reported that Howe was headed in their direction. Deploying his riflemen through a wooded area, Morgan himself waited just to the rear of his center. Here, his favorite combat station, he could easily receive reports and continue in contact with the greater part of his command.

When Howe's first contingents came into view, Morgan's men opened a heavy fire that temporarily checked the enemy. As the British, strengthened by their main body, pressed forward, they heard the shrill sound of Morgan's turkey-call, an instrument he blew to assemble his men. The riflemen gathered around Morgan, who then led them to higher ground. There he bivouacked and dispatched information of his encounter to Washington's headquarters. The following day, when called in for consultation at Middlebrook, Morgan personally told Washington that Howe had encamped at Somerset Courthouse.[6]

Since Washington refused to leave his well-protected location

6. *Ibid.*, 236-37, 249; Richard Meade and Robert Harrison (separate letters) to Morgan, June 15, 1777, Theodorous B. Myers Coll., N. Y. Pub. Lib.

to risk battle, the British returned to New Brunswick. Howe next tried another device to draw his opponent out, retreating across the Raritan River toward Amboy on the night of the 21st. Cautious at first, Washington held most of his army at Middlebrook, but he dispatched Major General Nathanael Greene's division, Brigadier General Anthony Wayne's brigade, and Morgan's corps to fall upon Howe's rear guard, still at New Brunswick. After flushing a Hessian picket near the outskirts, Morgan joined Greene and Wayne inside the town, and the three American commanders drove the rear guard across the river bridge into redoubts on the east bank. Finding additional enemy troops there, Greene correctly surmised that the Americans were outnumbered. Even so, Wayne and Morgan, both intrepid fighters, urged an assault, and Greene agreed. The Americans dislodged the British and harassed them as they withdrew, sometimes advancing within thirty yards. At Piscataway the Americans gave up the chase, while the British continued to Amboy. That night when Washington wrote Congress about the happenings of the past day, he included praise for the "Conduct and bravery of Genl. Wayne and Colo. Morgan and of their Officers and Men . . . as they constantly advanced upon an Enemy far superior to them in numbers." He further stated his intention to follow Howe and observe his next move. On the morrow he came down from the heights and drew up at New Market.[7]

Having lured Washington into level country, Howe prepared to make him fight. Long before dawn on the 26th, he pointed his army toward Westfield, intent on getting between the Americans and the passes leading back to Middlebrook. But

---

7. George W. Greene, *Life of Nathanael Greene* (New York, 1871), I, 394; Timothy Pickering, Jr. to John Pickering, June 23, 1777, Timothy Pickering Papers, Mass. Hist. Soc.; Fitzpatrick, ed., *Writings of Washington*, VIII, 281-83, 295-96.

near Woodbridge a patriot reconnaissance party sighted the enemy and warned Washington in time to escape. Morgan, sent to delay the British thrust, found that Howe had wind of Washington's flight and had headed for Amboy, where he transported his entire army to New York.[8]

No one could deduce Howe's next design, and as a result Morgan's corps seldom spent two consecutive nights in the same place during the next six and a half weeks. For a time Washington thought his adversary would sail up the Hudson to assist British General John Burgoyne, then pushing down from Lake Champlain. To watch Howe, Washington sent Morgan and other regimental commanders to patrol along the Highlands of the Hudson. But Morgan could only report in his dispatches that Howe remained in New York. The British General's intentions became all the more mystifying when he put out to sea in late July. Was he bound for Philadelphia via the Delaware River? Or was he intent on slipping back to New York and thence up the Hudson while Washington was rushing to the patriot capital? Washington's uncertainty is illustrated by the frequency with which he changed Morgan's marching orders—from Philadelphia to Trenton, Germantown, Maidenhead, and, finally, Trenton again. At Trenton, Morgan was to wait until reliable intelligence of Howe came to light. Since his men were weary and foot-sore, and since the mercury had remained steadily in the nineties, Morgan must have welcomed the opportunity to halt.[9]

But the rest was short-lived: an important assignment was in store for the rifle corps. While trying to determine Howe's destination, Washington had received alarming news from upper

8. *Ibid.*, 307-8.

9. See the Morgan-Washington correspondence for July and early Aug. 1777, in the Washington Papers, Lib. Cong., and in the Myers Coll., N. Y. Pub. Lib.

New York. The American Northern army was feebly contesting the southward drive of General Burgoyne's army of 9,500 redcoats, Germans, Tories, and Indians. "Gentleman Johnny," occupying Fort Ticonderoga, had previously made the fortress untenable to the Americans by placing cannon on an elevation overlooking it. Then he overran several smaller American posts and by July 29 took Fort Miller, less than forty miles from Albany, his immediate objective. At Albany he planned to arrange with Howe for control of the Hudson River in order to cut off New England from the rest of the colonies.

Keenly aware of the danger, Washington persuaded Congress to transfer Benedict Arnold to the Northern army. He presently discovered that the legislators as well as many New Yorkers advocated his assigning Morgan's corps to the same theater. "Oh for some Virginia rifle-men!" cried an Albany gentleman. "Colonel Morgan's regiment would be of great use this way." With Howe's scheme still obscure, the American General felt reluctant to part with his "rangers." At length he agreed to give them up subject to immediate recall to the main army. On August 17, Morgan received a letter from Washington to repair to Peekskill, New York, where Major General Israel Putnam had boats ready to carry the riflemen to Albany. Washington added, "I know of no Corps so likely to check . . . [Burgoyne's] progress in proportion to their number, as the one you Command. I have great dependence on you, your Officers and Men." Since the frontier riflemen were skilled in Indian fighting methods, Washington believed they would be particularly useful against Burgoyne's savages, who, notwithstanding the British General's efforts to control them, had "intimidated" the American soldiers by their use of the torch and scalping knife. He confided to Governor George Clinton of New York that he hoped the presence of the riflemen would cause wholesale desertions among the Indians. "I should think it would be well," he said, "even before their

arrival to begin to circulate these Ideas, with proper Embellish-
ments, throughout the Country, and in the army and to take pains
to communicate them to the Enemy. It would not be amiss,
among other Things, to magnify Numbers." [10]

Major General Horatio Gates, the new head of the American
Northern army, also thought the riflemen would provide succor
against the Indians, and he gratefully thanked Washington for
dispatching Morgan's corps to the north. Though Gates hourly
expected the riflemen on August 23, contrary winds postponed
their sailing, so that they did not enter his camp near the junction
of the Mohawk and the Hudson until the 29th or 30th. On arriving, Morgan dined with Gates, his neighbor from the Valley
of Virginia.[11]

Whatever his other virtues, Gates did not look like a soldier;
he was small of stature, ruddy-faced, and bespectacled, with thin
graying hair. His enemies, who were numerous, said he looked
like a "granny," and Burgoyne allegedly referred to him as an
"old midwife." But behind him were years of military experience
in which he had displayed considerable talent as an administrator.
Born in England, the son of an upper servant of the Duke of
Leeds, Gates rose to the rank of major in the British army, only
to find additional promotion impossible because of his background and limited means. In 1772 he sold his commission and
settled in the Valley of Virginia on a farm that he called Traveller's Rest. Usually mild-mannered and convivial, he enjoyed a
racy story and a bottle of wine in the company of friends, including Charles Lee, also an ex-British regular who emigrated
to Virginia and later became an American general. At times

10. Williamsburg *Virginia Gazette* (Dixon & Hunter), Aug. 1, 1777;
Washington to Morgan, Aug. 16, 1777, and Washington to Clinton,
Aug. 16, 1777, Fitzpatrick, ed., *Writings of Washington*, IX, 71, 78.

11. Gates to Washington, Aug. 22, 1777, Sparks, ed., *Correspondence of
the Revolution*, I, 427-28; Gates to Benjamin Lincoln, Aug. 23, 31, 1777,
Gates Papers, N. Y. Hist. Soc.

Gates was petty and inconsiderate in his relations with other Continental officers, especially Washington, whom he neglected to inform of his great victory at Saratoga—news the Commander in Chief got from a second party after Gates had notified Congress. As Washington's adjutant general, Gates had rendered excellent service. Then, in June 1776 Gates was sent to assist Philip Schuyler in the Northern Department. He did not get along well with his superior, perhaps due to differences in temperament, and by December 1776 Gates felt he should be given Schuyler's job. Each man had his supporters in Congress—Gates's most influential ally was John Adams—and in March 1777 the legislators handed the position to Gates, only to reinstate Schuyler two months later. Congress then blamed Schuyler for the dismal showing against Burgoyne, perhaps with some justification, and again removed him in favor of Gates. Gates has often been called more of a politician than a soldier, an opinion which may be unfair to him. Few, if any, of Washington's generals could have surpassed his performance against Burgoyne.

But even before Gates's arrival in the north, the military situation commenced to gravitate in favor of the Americans. British Lieutenant Colonel Barry St. Leger's diversionary force of 900 redcoats, Tories, and Indians, driving through the Mohawk Valley toward Albany, was delayed by small bodies of patriot irregulars and Continentals in the vicinity of Oriskany, New York. With the approach of American reinforcements under Benedict Arnold, St. Leger's Indians fled, and the Briton pulled back to Montreal. Burgoyne encountered more trouble when he detached two German contingents toward the Connecticut River to acquire badly needed pack horses and provisions. Near Bennington, Vermont, Brigadier General John Stark and Colonel Seth Warner with their militia routed the enemy, capturing 700 and slaying 200. These two setbacks were bitter blows to Burgoyne, who now had only 6,300 effectives, having left garrisons at Ticonderoga and elsewhere. To compound his woes, patriot militia began raiding his long line of communications. During August and early September he stayed at Fort Miller, endeavoring with little success to procure supplies. Yet the playwright-soldier, still confident he could secure Albany, crossed his army to the west bank of the Hudson on September 13 and turned southward. Despite his lack of transportation, he continued to make room in his wagons for large quantities of expensive wines and his own extensive wardrobe.

Meanwhile, Gates and Arnold, assisted by Morgan and other subordinates, were reorganizing the American Northern army. The victories in the Mohawk Valley and near Bennington encouraged the militia to join Gates in large numbers, and by September 7, his army had grown to nearly 7,000. Since his camp at the mouth of the Mohawk was on level terrain, suited for regular British military formations, Gates prepared to march sixteen miles northward to Bemis Heights to await Burgoyne's attack. Before setting out, he added to Morgan's corps 300 picked musketmen, equipped with bayonets, and under Major Henry Dearborn.[12]

Morgan found that Bemis Heights was a perfect place for the use of his frontier riflemen. It was a high plateau, covered with broken elevations separated by deep ravines through which creeks turned and twisted. The region was densely wooded except for occasional farms and wagon trails stretching down to the Hudson. Here in the red and gold of early autumn forests Gates and Arnold supervised the erection of fortifications, while Morgan directed his corps in reconnoitering Burgoyne's progress and harassing his Indians and other scouts. As Washington had predicted, the riflemen proved valuable against the savages.

12. Lloyd A. Brown and Howard H. Peckham, eds., *Revolutionary War Journals of Henry Dearborn* (Chicago, 1939), 104; Gates to Morgan, Aug. 29, 1777, Gates Papers, N. Y. Hist. Soc.

Burgoyne admitted they so terrorized his Indians that "not a man of them was to be brought within the sound of a rifle shot." Morgan's men had chased all the British scouts inside their own lines by the 18th, the same day that Burgoyne encamped three miles from Bemis Heights. Although he possessed only vague information about the American location, Burgoyne resolved to bring on a showdown.[13]

Late on the morning of the 19th, American sentries scrambled down from tall trees to report to Gates that Burgoyne's army was approaching in three columns. Major General Baron von Riedesel and Brigadier General William Phillips traveled along the river road with 1,200 Germans; Burgoyne led four British regiments totaling 1,100 men across a ravine and toward the American center; and Brigadier General Simon Fraser on Burgoyne's right moved ahead with 2,200 redcoats, Tories, and Indians.

Gates decided that Morgan's corps—the "elite" of the army—should engage the enemy in a heavily wooded area north of the American camp and that Arnold, directing the left wing, should give assistance when necessary. Originally Gates had intended to await an assault upon his lines, but Arnold had proposed instead that a full-scale battle be fought in the forest, where Burgoyne could not effectively use his artillery and close-rank maneuvers. There, too, the American riflemen and other marksmen could be employed to great advantage. Gates's final plan, therefore, was a compromise between his original one and Arnold's.

Once beyond the meadow in front of the American works,

13. John Burgoyne, *State of the Expedition from Canada* (London, 1780), 122; Brown and Peckham, eds., *Revolutionary War Journals of Henry Dearborn*, 105; James P. Baxter, *The British Invasion from the North with the Journal of Lieut. William Digby* (Albany, 1887), 269-70; "Journal of Oliver Boardman," Connecticut Historical Society, *Collections*, 7 (1899), 224; E. B. O'Callahan, ed., *John Burgoyne's Orderly Book* (Albany, 1860), 113.

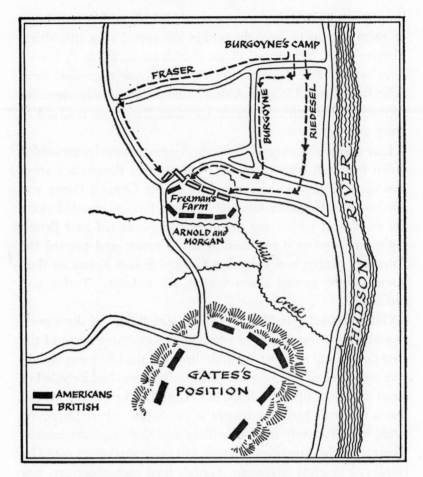

The Battle of Freeman's Farm, September 19, 1777

Morgan arranged his troops in two thin lines with orders to push through the underbrush while he took his customary station slightly to the rear of his second line. Major Jacob Morris of Maryland, in charge of the first detachment, proceeded so rapidly that he soon lost contact with Morgan. Shortly before one o'clock, just south of a farm owned by one Isaac Freeman,

Morris encountered the advance elements of Burgoyne's center. Rushing after the fleeing enemy, Morris's riflemen ran head on into Burgoyne's main force at Freeman's farm and in their eagerness to escape fanned out in all directions.[14]

Morgan heard the shooting and crashed forward to discover what had happened. Certain that Morris's haste had led to the destruction of part of his corps, he became furious. Reputedly breaking into angry tears, he exclaimed to Colonel James Wilkinson, who had ridden up, "I am ruined, by G—d! ... my men are scattered God knows where." Fortunately Morgan had his turkey-call. The sharp whistle enabled the riflemen to determine his location, and soon they gathered around him.[15]

Lucky to have lost few if any men, Morgan regrouped his corps and moved within sight of Freeman's farm, then occupied by Burgoyne's column. The farmhouse was in a clearing 350 yards long, at the north end of which the British General had placed his artillery and behind it three regiments: the 21st on the right, the 62nd in the center, and the 20th on the left. The additional regiment, the 9th, was in reserve. As Morgan stationed his men just inside the woods, Arnold dispatched two regiments of New Hampshire Continentals to the Virginian's left.

Just after one o'clock a full engagement occurred between Morgan's corps, with the support of the Continentals, and the regiments under Burgoyne's immediate command. Sheltered by the foliage, the Americans opened and sustained a brisk fire until the British retreated into a pine grove to the north. The

14. James Wilkinson, *Memoirs of My Own Times* (Philadelphia, 1816), I, 236-37; Baxter, *British Invasion from the North*, 271-72; Hoffman Nickerson, *The Turning Point of the Revolution* (New York, 1928), 306-11; Samuel Patterson, *Horatio Gates: Defender of American Liberties* (New York, 1941), 152-53.

15. Wilkinson, *Memoirs*, I, 237-38.

Continentals raced up and seized the British artillery, but the enemy gunners had rendered their weapons useless by removing the linstocks. Quickly reforming, Burgoyne's men executed a bayonet charge that hurled the Americans back across the opening. The riflemen, lacking bayonets, kept behind cover most of the time, some of them climbing trees to gain a better view of their targets. The redcoat gunners pointed their artillery at the woods; branches thundered down from shattered trees. Morgan's sharpshooters trained their weapons, and by late afternoon nearly all the gunners were dead or wounded.[16]

Arnold, feeding in additional men to the left of the New Hampshire Continentals, had thrown his entire division of seven regiments into the melee by mid-afternoon. When the American line began to extend more and more to the left, Burgoyne, fearing that his right held by the 21st Regiment might be outflanked, ordered that regiment to turn to its right. This movement caused the 62nd, in the center, to shift slightly to its right, thus exposing both its flanks. Morgan had spotted this activity and now concentrated his fire upon the 62nd. Once it almost broke. General Phillips, who had galloped across country from his post near the river, led part of the 20th to the assistance of the 62nd.

Neither side could gain a decided advantage in the bloody farmyard. Again and again Dearborn's musketmen and Arnold's regulars rolled the enemy back, only to give way themselves in the face of vicious counterattacks. Yet the scarlet-clad invaders received far greater casualties than the Americans. Veteran British officers who had observed some of the fiercest fighting of the Seven Years' War vowed they had never before witnessed such withering fire. Burgoyne lost heavily in officers, most of them brought down by riflemen. Morgan's troops were

16. R. Lamb, *Memoirs of His Own Life* (Dublin, 1809), 199; Burgoyne, *State of the Expedition*, 122; Nickerson, *Turning Point of the Revolution*, 311.

likewise "sedulous" in marking out the Tories: "This misfortune," said a redcoat sergeant, "accelerated their estrangement from our cause and army." [17]

As the afternoon wore on, Burgoyne's situation became critical. His artillery was silenced. Many of his companies were without their officers. His 62nd Regiment was almost annihilated. Fraser, for reasons unknown, had not entered the battle. Sometime after four o'clock Burgoyne slipped word to Riedesel, who waited with the Germans along the river road, to hurry and unite with the British center column. Responding with over half his men, Riedesel soon appeared on the British left, whereupon Burgoyne's forces made a final lunge, pushing the Americans from the clearing. Gates now sent out Brigadier General Ebenezer Learned's brigade, which got lost and stumbled upon Fraser's pickets. As daylight faded into dusk, the sulphurous smoke lifted, and the din of battle died away. While Morgan's corps and Arnold's Continentals tramped back to the American breastworks, Burgoyne's army threw up fortifications on the battlefield.

Gates, content with a holding action, might well have crushed the British center column had he poured in additional reinforcements earlier in the afternoon. On the other hand, he must have feared the possibility of a blow from Riedesel's Germans on his depleted lines. As it was, he could justly claim a victory: his loss was 320 to Burgoyne's nearly 600. Though Morgan's corps was the first to engage the enemy and supposedly the last to leave the field, the riflemen suffered a very small portion of the American total: 4 killed, 8 wounded, and 3 missing.[18] Accounts by British

17. Lamb, *Memoirs*, 198.
18. "A Return of the Detachment of Rifle Men Killed and taken wounded & missing the 19th Sept. Commanded by Coll. Daniel Morgan Esq., Emmet Coll., N. Y. Pub. Lib. Dearborn's losses were considerably greater: 19 dead, 22 wounded, and 3 missing. Wilkinson, *Memoirs*, I, Appendix D.

participants indicate that Morgan's corps was the most successful unit engaged that day. The riflemen were primarily responsible for reducing the 62nd Regiment to fewer than 60 effectives, and they also accounted for many of the casualties among Burgoyne's officers and gunners. One of Morgan's friends, writing in 1802, asserted that Morgan was the acting American field commander during the battle, a statement which conflicts with accounts of Arnold's presence at Freeman's farm. Whatever the truth, both officers contributed in large measure to the American success. Burgoyne could ill-afford another day like September 19 and still expect to reach Albany.[19]

That Morgan and his corps were an indispensable segment of the Northern army is clear from a letter Gates wrote to Washington, who had requested the return of the riflemen. Gates informed the Commander in Chief that the outcome of the New York campaign was balanced on a thread. "In this situation," he remarked, "your Excellency would not wish me to part with the corps the army of General Burgoyne are most afraid of." The riflemen indeed caused Burgoyne agonizing concern during late September and early October by making frequent raids upon his pickets and by enfilading his lines from treetop positions. The Americans were also active after dark. Burgoyne pointed out that not a night between September 20 and October 7 passed without skirmishing; his men always slept in their clothing, with their weapons nearby.[20]

In the American camp, Morgan's corps became a subject of

19. Hill's Notes.
20. Washington to Gates, Sept. 24, 1777, Fitzpatrick, ed., *Writings of Washington*, IX, 264-65; Gates to Washington, Oct. 5, 1777, Sparks, ed., *Correspondence of the Revolution*, I, 437; Baxter, *British Invasion from the North*, 274-75; "Journal of Oliver Boardman," Conn. Hist. Soc., *Coll.*, 7 (1899), 225-27; Brown and Peckham, eds., *Revolutionary War Journals of Henry Dearborn*, 106-7.

controversy between Gates and Arnold. Since the riflemen were serving only temporarily with the Northern army, they were not incorporated into any of Gates's divisions, although they had often been on duty with Arnold and may have been under his direction at Freeman's farm. In general orders on September 22, Gates announced that Morgan was to make all returns and reports to his headquarters and was to obtain instructions only from that source. At the time Arnold learned of these developments, he also heard that Gates had not mentioned his division's name in describing the battle of the 19th to Congress. Striding up to Gates, Arnold demanded to know why his troops had not been properly recognized and why Morgan's corps had been tampered with. One of Arnold's aides maintained that "matters were altercated in a very high strain," and Wilkinson, Gates's adjutant, said that Arnold was "in great warmth" and was "ridiculed by General Gates: high words and gross language ensued." When the men had further difficulties, Gates personally assumed the direction of Arnold's wing of the army. Though Arnold remained in camp, he received no new assignment. To what extent he had just grievances is an open question. The controversy reflected no credit on either man.[21]

Burgoyne's situation, meanwhile, grew desperate. The salt pork and flour that constituted the bulk of his provisions ran dangerously low. His men, whose uniforms had been torn during the wilderness trek, complained of the chilly October weather. They also experienced a bad case of nerves caused by the activities of the riflemen and the patriot militia. Convinced he must either retreat or fight his way to Albany, he resolved to attempt the latter. First, he would make a reconnaissance in force to place cannon on an elevation (which did not exist) overlooking the American left. Setting out on October 7, he

21. Wallace, *Traitorous Hero*, 150; Wilkinson, *Memoirs*, I, 254.

moved three-fourths of a mile south of Freeman's farm, where he spread his 1,500 men across a wheat field extending 1,000 yards. He and Riedesel looked through their spy glasses and saw nothing but trees in their front and on their flanks.

Gates took the initiative. If he devised a plan of battle, it is not known; but, according to Wilkinson, the General told him to have Morgan "begin the game." When Wilkinson performed his assignment, Morgan, "with his usual sagacity," suggested his own scheme—that he creep through the foliage on the American left to a hill near the British right flank and strike immediately after another American force burst out on Burgoyne's left flank. Impressed by Morgan's proposal, "the best ... [that] could be devised," Wilkinson presented it to Gates, who accepted it and instructed Brigadier General Enoch Poor's division to go out from the right.[22]

Poor began the assault about two o'clock, moving rapidly toward the grenadiers under Major John Acland, one of Burgoyne's drinking and card-playing companions. After a musketry barrage passed harmlessly above the Americans, Acland led a bayonet charge that crumbled under a volley from Poor's men. A British cannon was captured and turned on its disorganized owners. That was enough for the grenadiers; they sought the protection of Burgoyne's main body, leaving Acland, shot through both legs, a prisoner.

By this time Morgan was already in action. He advanced over a familiar path, for the previous day he had gone this way in reconnoitering Burgoyne's position. Reaching the hill, he gave orders: he would lead the riflemen against the flank and rear of Lord Balcarres's light infantry, stationed behind a rail fence; Dearborn would direct his Continentals against the Briton's flank and front. During Poor's onslaught the riflemen surged

22. *Ibid.*, 268.

down the hill and opened fire. As the light infantry changed
front to meet the threat, Dearborn's troops dashed forward,
halted sixty yards from the fence, and delivered a blast. Jumping the obstacle, they charged with fixed bayonets and drove the
British back in confusion. Balcarres rallied his men behind a
second fence and fought stubbornly before retiring to his own
lines.[23]

Morgan now hastened to the left of Burgoyne's center, held
mainly by Riedesel's blue-coated Brunswickers, at the same time
that Learned's brigade, recently sent up, headed in the direction
of the Germans. With Learned's men was Arnold, who had left
camp without Gates's permission. According to one report, a
messenger from Gates caught up with Arnold and ordered him
back to the American encampment; Arnold replied that he was
going to help Morgan.[24]

Morgan and Arnold, the latter assuming leadership of
Learned's units, threw their men against the Brunswickers, who
held firm and repelled their opponents. When the Americans
came on again, the outnumbered Germans withdrew toward
their fortifications. At this point General Fraser, with the light
infantry and the British 24th Regiment, attempted to form a line
slightly to the rear of Riedesel's men to cover their movement.
Mounted on a grey horse, Fraser rode back and forth shouting
encouragement to his troops. Believing Fraser's efforts were prolonging the contest, Morgan called on rifleman Timothy Murphy
to shoot the brave Scottish General. Murphy, a skilled Indian
fighter and a fine marksman, climbed a tree and trained his
double-barreled rifle upon Fraser. Allegedly his first shot sev-

23. *Ibid.*; Graham, *Morgan*, 161-62; Nickerson, *Turning Point of the
Revolution*, 360.
24. Tench Tilghman to John Cadwalader, Jan. 18, 1778, *Pa. Mag.
of Hist. and Biog.*, 32 (1908), 169.

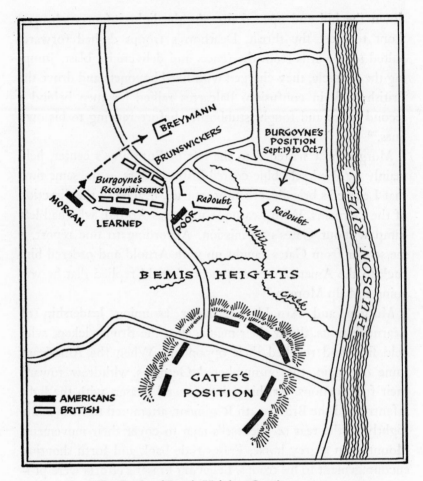

The Battle of Bemis Heights, October 7, 1777

ered the crupper of Fraser's horse, his second creased the horse's mane, and his third struck the General. In any event, Murphy mortally wounded Fraser, who was carried to the quarters of young Mrs. Riedesel. The German woman lamented that "poor General Fraser" died moaning, "Oh, fatal ambition! Poor General Burgoyne! My poor wife!" At the loss of their leader, the

74

British fell back to their breastworks. The first phase of the battle had lasted only fifty minutes.[25]

Their victory was not complete; so Arnold, assuming direction of John Paterson's and John Nixon's brigades, went at the British center, while Morgan made for Burgoyne's right redoubt held by Lieutenant Colonel Heinrich von Breymann's Germans. Though Arnold displayed great personal bravery, his drive was repulsed, but subsequently he cut to his left and led Learned's troops in driving a body of Canadians and Indians from several cabins. Then he joined Morgan, who was engaging Breymann's men, at which point the combined American force routed the Germans. Before being shot by one of his own men, Breymann killed four others in an effort to halt their flight. On the American side, Arnold received a ball in the same leg that had been hit at Quebec. Since it was growing dark, the Americans did not pursue their foe. They had inflicted approximately 600 casualties upon Burgoyne's army as against about 150 of their own. Moreover, they had exposed the flank and rear of the British defenses by seizing Breymann's redoubt. When Burgoyne retreated northward along the Hudson, Gates wisely dispatched units to surround him. With escape impossible, Burgoyne laid down his arms on October 17 at the village of Saratoga.

Admirers of Gates have often given him most of the glory for the Saratoga triumph, while giving less to Morgan and little or none to Arnold; supporters of Arnold have used the same pattern, but in reverse. None of the three should be excluded

25. Morgan told the story of Fraser's death to a British officer. [Graham], "A Recollection of the American Revolutionary War," *Va. Hist. Register*, 6 (1853), 210. Charles Neilson, whose father served in Gates's army, recorded the same story. It also appears in William L. Stone, *Burgoyne's Campaign and St. Leger's Expedition* (Albany, 1877), 324-25. Mrs. Riedesel's remarks are in her *Letters and Journals Relating to the War of the American Revolution*, trans. William L. Stone (Albany, 1867), 119-20.

from a fair share of the credit. Though slow to act offensively, Gates realized that time and terrain favored the Americans in their struggle with Burgoyne. With fall approaching and the British on rough, unfamiliar ground, he saw no need for a rash maneuver that might end in disaster. Accordingly, he dug in and allowed the British General to wear himself down in unsuccessful probes. The American officers who actually bore the brunt of the fighting in the contests of September 19 and October 7 were Morgan and Arnold. On both occasions Gates displayed his confidence in Morgan by having him begin the action. Following the second engagement, in which Morgan's plan of a double envelopment was used, Gates reputedly embraced Morgan, saying, "Morgan, you have done wonders." In his battle report to Congress, Gates declared that "too much praise cannot be given to the Corps commanded by Col. Morgan." In both encounters Arnold came to the aid of Morgan. Though the question of Arnold's presence on the field at Freeman's farm has never been answered satisfactorily, it seems probable that an officer with his combat record and fiery nature would have taken an active role in directing his own division. But Arnold's most valuable assistance to Morgan came during the action of October 7. Indeed, it is frequently said that Arnold's efforts gave the needed impetus to the attack, an opinion which may well be true. Certainly Arnold seems to have co-ordinated the American forces, which were without an over-all leader. Throughout the day Gates remained at his headquarters, a proper place for a commanding general but hardly an inspiring one.[26]

Though the value of the Kentucky rifle in the War for Independence has often been overstated, the weapon was an important factor in the two American victories on Bemis Heights, as Burgoyne and several of his officers pointed out in their memoirs.

26. Hill's Notes; Gates to Hancock, Oct. 12, 1777, Papers of the Continental Congress, No. 154, I, 272, National Archives.

Morgan was proud of his part in winning the Saratoga campaign, a triumph that encouraged France to enter the war on the side of the United States, but he shared his credit with Dearborn's men. He knew that his riflemen would have been far less effective without the support of Dearborn's troops, whose bayonets protected them from British thrusts. He no doubt expressed sincere regret at losing the services of Dearborn's contingent when, just after Burgoyne's capitulation, he and his rifle corps were called to perform elsewhere.[27]

27. William Graham, *Joseph Graham and His Papers* (Raleigh, 1904), 135.

CHAPTER VI

Service in the Middle States

WHILE Gates defeated Burgoyne in New York, Howe triumphed over Washington in Pennsylvania. Howe's mysterious sea voyage had ended at the head of Chesapeake Bay, whence he set troops in motion for Philadelphia. Though Washington raced southward and gave battle at Brandywine Creek, he lost heavily in men and failed to keep Howe from entering the patriot capital. Like a wounded animal, Washington lashed back at his opponent's advance elements at Germantown, seven miles north of Philadelphia, on the night of October 3. The fighting was fierce, the casualties numerous on both sides, and after two and a half hours the Americans left the scene, eventually encamping near the village of Whitemarsh.

Brandywine and Germantown, coupled with expiring enlistments, so weakened the American army that Washington sent Lieutenant Colonel Alexander Hamilton to secure Morgan's riflemen and other reinforcements from Gates. Hamilton was to impress upon Morgan "how essential" his services were to the army and to urge him to quicken his march. As two Virginia officers had already written Morgan, his corps had indeed been missed during the Pennsylvania campaign. Washington had created a new light unit under Brigadier General William Maxwell to replace the departed riflemen, but a number of officers believed the new corps guilty of cowardly conduct at Brandy-

78

wine, with Maxwell himself supposedly drunk. In any event, his troops did not distinguish themselves in Morgan's absence.[1]

Before hearing from Washington, Gates had ordered Morgan to return to the main army. Tramping southward over roads crowded with homeward-bound militia, the rifle corps reached Fishkill, New York, by October 31. There Morgan attended a council of war convened by General Putnam to assign regiments to garrison duty along the Hudson. On the morning of November 2, just beyond New Windsor, New York, Morgan met Hamilton and was exhilarated to learn that his corps was so valuable to the Commander in Chief; of all the officers he ever served under, Morgan respected Washington most. Morgan accelerated his pace, even though each day several of his men complained of having to throw away their worn-out shoes.[2]

When Morgan joined Washington's army at Whitemarsh, he found that his corps' performance in the north was well known. No officer took a keener interest in the riflemen than a recent arrival from France, the Marquis de Lafayette, a tall young man who wore the epaulets of an American major general. Morgan discovered that Lafayette, unlike so many foreign officers who offered the patriots their services, was not bloated with self-esteem, and that he had volunteered to perform without pay. Morgan, the crude frontiersman, and Lafayette, the polished nobleman, became fast friends. Once Lafayette, leading a party of Morgan's men on a scouting mission, came upon a large Hessian picket which he drove back over half a mile. He exclaimed to Washington that the riflemen were "above even theyr repu-

1. Washington to Hamilton, Oct. 30, 1777, Fitzpatrick, ed., *Writings of Washington*, IX, 468; Graham, *Morgan*, 177-78; John Marshall, *The Life of George Washington* (Philadelphia, 1804-1807), III, 141; Heth to Morgan, Sept. 30, 1777, Myers Coll., N. Y. Pub. Lib.

2. *The Trumbull Papers*, Massachusetts Historical Society, *Collections*, 7th Ser., 2 (1902), 180-81; Sparks, ed., *Correspondence of the Revolution*, II, 24; Fitzpatrick, ed., *Writings of Washington*, X, 95.

tation"—continually running and never halting for rest or nourishment.[3]

Washington kept the riflemen on the go after their return from the north. With Howe's army striving to consolidate its hold on Philadelphia by reducing the American forts in the Delaware River, Morgan frequently reconnoitered up and down the stream. In mid-November, he and Anthony Wayne prepared for a surprise assault on Province Island, south of Philadelphia, where British guns were bombarding Fort Mifflin on nearby Mud Island. But when the enemy forced the evacuation of the Mifflin garrison, Washington called off the attack. Immediately afterward, Morgan and Greene crossed over to the New Jersey side. Lord Cornwallis, who had swept the river of American fortifications, had assembled a large force near Haddonfield and was expected to raid the interior. When he suddenly rejoined Howe, Washington recalled Greene and, a little later, Morgan.[4]

Morgan returned with all haste because he knew that Howe and Cornwallis were approaching Whitemarsh. Determined not to miss any action, Morgan dashed into the American camp on December 7. He and his corps, assisted by Colonel Christopher Gist's Maryland militia, occupied a wooded elevation overlooking the Limekiln Road, a mile or so in front of the American center. Presently a British column under Major General Charles Grey came into view. At Morgan's command, the Americans opened and sustained a blistering fire as the British hurried toward the protection of the woods. The patriots fought heroically in

3. Louis Gottschalk, ed., *The Letters of Lafayette to Washington, 1777-1779* (New York, 1941), 7; Gottschalk, *Lafayette Joins the American Army* (Chicago, 1937), 82.

4. William Duane, ed., *Extracts from the Diary of Christopher Marshall* (Albany, 1877), 143; Douglas S. Freeman, *George Washington: A Biography* (New York, 1948-1957), IV, 551; G. W. Greene, *N. Greene,* 517, 530.

the furious contest that ensued, despite an overwhelming dis-
advantage in men. After a time the Hessian jägers (light infantry)
and Major John Simcoe's Tory Queen's Rangers gained their
opponents' flanks. Morgan, galloping back and forth in an effort
to keep a battle line, had his horse shot from under him. At
length, he and Gist retired in good order while part of the riflemen, slithering from tree to tree, covered the movement with
their deadly marksmanship.

Grey too wanted no more. While Morgan and other American unit commanders watched, the enemy officer bivouacked a
mile from Whitemarsh. Morgan, whose losses were modest compared with Grey's, estimated his casualties at about twenty-five.
Although this figure was probably higher than the number he
had suffered during the entire Saratoga Campaign, he and Gist
had checked Grey's thrust. Washington gave his "warmest
thanks" to Morgan and the men of his "intrepid corps, for their
gallant behaviour." [5]

After Howe unsuccessfully probed the American left and
withdrew to Philadelphia, Washington shifted to winter quarters
among the desolate hills of Valley Forge. Morgan, as usual, had
a special role: patrolling the area between Gulph Mills and
Radnor Meeting House on the west side of the Schuylkill River.
Mainly it involved routine tasks such as reporting the appearance
of enemy foraging parties and establishing checking stations on

5. Since the accounts vary greatly, only a general reconstruction of
Morgan's engagement is possible. *Historical Magazine,* 2d Ser., 1 (1867),
196; Henry C. Lodge, ed., *[John] Andre's Journal* (Boston, 1903), I,
128; Harry M. Lydenberg, ed., *Archibald Henderson, Lieutenant General
Royal Engineers, His Diaries and Sketches in America, 1762-1780* (New
York, 1930), 160; Benjamin F. Stevens, ed., *Facsimiles of Manuscripts in
European Archives Relating to America, 1773-1783* (London, 1889-
1895), 2,088; Joseph Reed to [Thomas] Wharton, [Jr.], Dec. 10, 1777,
Peter Force Transcripts, Miscellaneous Letters, Lib. Cong.; Fitzpatrick,
ed., *Writings of Washington,* X, 140, 142, 145-46.

various roads to prevent Loyalist farmers from supplying provisions for the British in Philadelphia. A tradition of remarkable longevity has it that Morgan won the respect of the country folk by his honesty and fair dealing; he displayed a reluctance to confiscate farm produce unless certain of its ultimate destination. Even when he seized produce, he released the Tories with a warning. Throughout the war Morgan was surprisingly moderate in dealing with Americans who retained their loyalty to the Crown. He believed that many were misguided and would respond best to peaceful persuasion.[6]

Morgan evinced less tolerance toward the Pennsylvania militia officers operating in his sector. He thought them generally narrow and petty in their determination not to take advice or instructions from Continental officers. Morgan filled his letters with complaints about the Pennsylvanians, but his discontent was not limited to them. His correspondence during this period of routine patrol duty shows a tendency to grumble, perhaps unduly. Next to the British, boredom was Morgan's worst enemy, and he tended to become fretful when performing menial military chores.[7]

Morgan's mood did not improve after his recall to Valley Forge in January 1778. Camp talk hinted of a plot to embarrass Washington or even remove him from the supreme command. Morgan was one of a host of angry officers who denounced Congress for appointing as inspector general Thomas Conway, a French veteran known to have criticized Washington's performance in the campaign of 1777. Though at least a few dis-

6. Henry Woodman, *The History of Valley Forge* (Oaks, Pa., 1921), 61.

7. See the correspondence of Morgan and Lord Stirling (William Alexander of New Jersey) for Dec. 1777, and Jan. 1778, in the Washington Papers, Lib. Cong.

satisfied persons favored the elevation of Gates, the victor of Saratoga, Gates never committed himself on the issue. But Washington's supporters felt that the Board of War, of which Gates was president in the winter of 1777-78, had deliberately made the Commander in Chief's position more difficult by urging Conway's selection as inspector general, where he would not be under Washington's direct authority. Morgan's indignation exploded when he encountered one of the alleged conspirators, board secretary Richard Peters. Peters declared that he was drawn into an unprovoked controversy with Morgan, who acted "as Champion for the General's Character." When Peters vehemently denied his part in any conspiracy, Morgan became violent, their "Dispute" proceeding "to the last Extremity." Nearly hysterical when he wrote of the affair two days later, Peters called Morgan's charge the most "villianous of all Falsehoods." His protestations were evidently sincere, just as it is also probable that no organized drive occurred to replace Washington. His critics, undoubtedly a small minority and for the most part honest in thinking him deficient as a military man, tactfully limited their discussion to their private correspondence with one another.[8]

But to the officers who recognized Washington's tremendous burdens and dedication to the American cause, the slightest reflection on their chief was tantamount to treason. Few of his subordinates revered Washington more than Morgan, who, years hence, assured George Washington Parke Custis as well as others that Washington was the sustaining force of the Revolution; without him it would have collapsed in the field. It was in this period of reputed plots that Morgan added an article to his faith:

8. Burnett, ed., *Letters of Congress*, III, 46n.; Robert Troup to Gates, Apr. 18, 1778, Gates Papers, N. Y. Hist. Soc.; Bernard Knollenberg, *Washington and the Revolution* (New York, 1940), 65-77.

"party matters" had no place in a republic—they were worse than "the devil." [9]

Leaving his army comrades to deal with intriguers, Morgan obtained a furlough to visit his family. From his home he made occasional trips to Winchester, where he was the center of attention. The Revolution had helped transform his reputation from a roistering teamster to the "celebrated" Colonel Morgan. Isaac Zane commented that his sacrifices for "thy country" deserved "sympathetic feeling in every acquaintance." To be untouched by such adulation, Morgan would have had to be less than human. He was never that. Yet a group of prominent Quakers quartered in Winchester considered him affable and unassuming in conversation. These Friends were exiled to Frederick County from Philadelphia, where they had been arrested for refusing to take an oath to the state of Pennsylvania and for urging their brethren to give no assistance to the patriots. Morgan, observed Quaker James Pemberton, felt the Pennsylvanians had been wronged since they were banished without first being granted a hearing from the state authorities.[10]

By May, Morgan was back at Valley Forge. His sharp eye detected significant changes since his departure three months before. The army was a formidable instrument now, thanks to the labors of Prussian drillmaster Baron von Steuben and Quartermaster General Nathanael Greene. Equally important, it had adequate equipment and contained an impressive number of seasoned veterans, officers and enlisted men. In Virginia, Morgan also had endeavored to advance the army's prospects by

9. George Washington Parke Custis, *Recollections and Private Memoirs of Washington*, ed. Benson J. Lossing (New York, 1860), 320-21; Charles Carter Lee Notes, Lib. Cong.; Morgan to Gates, Nov. 9, 1781, Gates Papers, N. Y. Hist. Soc.

10. Isaac Zane to Morgan, Apr. 3, 1778, Myers Coll., N. Y. Pub. Lib.; Thomas Gilpin, *Exiles in Virginia* (Philadelphia, 1848), 204-5.

recruiting additional frontiersmen for his rifle corps, an effort which bore little or no fruit.[11]

While Valley Forge continued in a whirl of activity, Morgan resumed scouting duties near Gulph Mills. He had three important visitors early in June. With letters for Washington came Joshua Loring, Jr., British commissary of prisoners, whose wife was then the subject of rebel and Tory doggerels. Blonde, fun-loving Betsy Loring was "Billy" Howe's "little Filly." Joshua seemingly did not mind; at least he did not forsake his profitable position which frequently kept him away from his wife and the dark, handsome Howe. Morgan, perhaps thinking the complacent Loring a gullible man, told him an exceedingly wild tale, which soon ended up in the journal of Howe's secretary, Ambrose Serle. Morgan said that 99 of every 100 Americans would accept peace on the King's terms and that "none (as he [Morgan] expressed it) but a few low dirty Rascals . . . in the lead of affairs" truly favored independence.[12]

A man to rival Morgan as a storyteller was portly, convivial Colonel Henry Knox, Washington's artillery chief, who administered to Morgan the oath of allegiance required by Congress of all officers in the Continental Army. The third caller, Dr. Adam Ferguson, was a noted professor of moral philosophy at the University of Edinburgh. Ferguson appeared as secretary of the so-called Carlisle Commission, which had recently landed in Philadelphia with an offer of reconciliation from George III to the Continental Congress. Morgan had no authority to grant Ferguson a pass to enter the American lines, but he agreed to give Washington a copy of the commissioners' instructions, in-

11. Fitzpatrick, ed., *Writings of Washington*, X, 401.
12. George F. Scheer and Hugh F. Rankin, *Rebels and Redcoats* (Cleveland, 1957), 208-9; Edward H. Tatum, ed., *The American Journal of Ambrose Serle* (San Marino, 1940), 305.

cluding the peace offer. The document carried the seal of a loving mother caressing her children.[13]

Even before Ferguson passed these papers to Morgan, the mission of Carlisle and his associates was doomed to fail, for the rebels knew that Sir Henry Clinton, Howe's successor as British military commander in America, was in readiness to abandon Philadelphia. Had Clinton tarried there, the commissioners could have threatened Congress with a major military offensive if it rejected the olive branch. But Clinton was about to employ 5,000 men against the French West Indian island of St. Lucia and to concentrate the bulk of his force at New York. On June 18, after the commissioners sailed from Philadelphia with the evacuating fleet, Clinton and his main army struck off across New Jersey for New York.

Morgan, whose advance parties discerned this movement, sent scouts into the Quaker City even as the last British rear units were retiring. On his command, bellmen went through the streets that night crying that the populace should stay inside until morning when patriot leaders would officially take control of the city. Long before daylight Morgan had gone, leading the rifle corps over the road toward Coryell's Ferry north of Princeton; his orders from Washington were to join the main army, then in pursuit of Clinton.[14]

After hurrying to unite with Washington by June 23 at Hopewell, Morgan found more rapid marching in store for him. Washington detached the rifle corps to assist Maxwell's brigade and General Philemon Dickinson's New Jersey militia units, which were already engaged in impeding the enemy's progress. To

13. G. D. Skull, ed., "Journal of Captain John Montressor," *Pa. Mag. of Hist. and Biog.*, 6 (1882), 290; *Huntington Papers*, Conn. Hist. Soc., *Coll.*, 20 (1923), 409.

14. Fitzpatrick, ed., *Writings of Washington*, XII, 87-88; "Extracts from the Journal of Mrs. Henry Drinker," *Pa. Mag. of Hist. and Biog.*, 13 (1889), 307-8.

bolster the rifle corps, Washington lent Morgan 25 "marksmen" and a "spirited" officer from each brigade, along with 78 men of his own Guard, bringing Morgan's total strength to 600.[15]

Here was an opportunity for the action he craved. Though moving swiftly, he had yet to come in contact with the enemy by the night of the 24th, when a courier brought him a specific assignment: to assume a position on the British right while Brigadier General Charles Scott, just ordered out with 1,500 men, operated on the enemy's left. Morgan pressed on until, slightly after four A.M., he sighted Clinton's rear guard at Crosswicks, eighteen miles south of Hopewell. As he wrote Washington a few minutes later, he could not draw near the British right before they entered Allentown, since Crosswicks Creek ran closely parallel to the Crosswicks-Allentown road. With characteristic vigor, he asserted that he would do everything in his power to "gall" them after they arrived in Allentown. He kept his word: as the British passed through the village, the rifle unit struck with such force that cannon were quickly called up to repel the Americans. Only after this sharp skirmish did Morgan give his men a refreshing three-hour rest; they had had but snatches of sleep in the past forty-eight hours.[16]

All that day and the next Clinton's troops trudged along the narrow, sandy road from Allentown to Monmouth Courthouse. Their journey from Philadelphia had been hampered by countless discomforts and distractions. Frequent rains increased the humidity of extremely hot days, and the troops were burdened with heavy uniforms and packs that often weighed eighty pounds. The American forward units sniped at them at every opportunity and demolished bridges and felled trees in their path.

15. Fitzpatrick, ed., *Writings of Washington*, XII, 106-7, 140; Carlos E. Fisher, *The Commander in Chief's Guard* (Washington, 1904), 279.

16. Fitzpatrick, ed., *Writings of Washington*, XII, 115; Morgan to Washington, June 25, 1778 (two letters of that date), Washington Papers, Lib. Cong.

Morgan continued to dog the enemy's right flank as Clinton's column bivouacked at Monmouth Courthouse on the 27th. Establishing a camp in a wooded area three miles beyond the courthouse, he sent out parties to raid and scout. One group, composed of riflemen and soldiers of Washington's Guard, surprised and captured fifteen grenadiers washing in a stream. A body of light infantry pursued the Americans, but they escaped with their prisoners. Morgan had heard shooting in the distance and had grown apprehensive for his men. Seeing them approach, he rushed to congratulate them on their conquest. He firmly believed recognition the "grand stimulus that pushes men on to great actions." Nor would a little good-natured banter prove harmful. Reputedly he laughed loudly at the sight of Washington's Guard—the "gentlemen" he always called them—whose once immaculate uniforms were now spattered with mud. As much a part of Morgan as his fiery temper was his hearty laugh.[17]

A few hours later Morgan described the capture of the grenadiers in a letter to Washington and told of his present situation. He would cling to the British right until notified to do otherwise, although they were in "so compact a body" that he could do them little damage. To be effective, Morgan was of the view that he needed reinforcements. This could not be: the previous day Washington had instructed Lafayette, then exercising nominal command of all forward units, to assemble his force at Englishtown, where it would be enlarged under General Charles Lee. Lafayette, entering Englishtown on the 27th, failed to bring Morgan along because he thought it essential to keep one American regiment, the riflemen, on Clinton's right flank.[18]

17. Morgan to Washington, June 27, 1778, Washington Papers, Lib. Cong.; Morgan to Nathanael Greene, Apr. 11, 1781, Graham, *Morgan*, 373-74; Custis, *Recollections*, 262.

18. Morgan to Washington, June 27, 1778, Washington Papers, Lib. Cong.; Gottschalk, ed., *Letters of Lafayette to Washington*, 52.

Morgan was unaware for many hours of an important conference which Washington held that afternoon with Lee, Lafayette, and the other officers of the advance force. After days of harassing maneuvers, Washington told Lee to assail the British rear next morning. At five P.M., Lee met with his subordinates but gave them no battle plan; he said that he lacked sufficient intelligence of the terrain and the enemy's location to work out a co-ordinated scheme of action.

Lee gave Morgan no hint of the approaching clash until spurred on by Washington. The Commander in Chief, fearing that Clinton might steal away in the darkness, called on Lee to dispatch 800 men to observe the enemy at Monmouth and to secure Morgan's help in delaying any British escape effort. Morgan got such a message sometime after three o'clock on the morning of the 28th. It also contained word of Lee's intention to attack after sunrise and of his desire for Morgan to assist by pushing against the British right. But Lee did not call Morgan back toward the main advance force, nor did he tell Morgan when or where he was to co-operate with Lee's troops. Morgan apparently expected further information from Lee before the battle; he failed to get it.[19]

The sound of heavy firing toward the courthouse reached him a little after ten o'clock. He sent a dragoon galloping off with a dispatch for Lee and waited impatiently for a reply. The horseman reined up at the scene of action to find the Americans in some confusion. When Lee had taken the offensive, Clinton immediately recalled a substantial body of men who had already set out that morning toward Middletown and Sandy Hook. Lee as well as his brigadiers issued commands, with the result that erratic movements occurred up and down the line. His troops were pulling back to stronger ground when Morgan's rider,

19. *The Lee Papers* (New-York Historical Society, *Collections*, Vols. 4-7 [1871-74]), III, 102, 120, 161.

looking unsuccessfully for Lee, finally sought orders from Anthony Wayne. Vaguely Wayne replied that Morgan should govern himself in accordance with the withdrawal.[20] Soon afterward Morgan's dragoon encountered Washington, who had hastily advanced with the main American army and assumed full command on the battlefield. At twelve thirty the Commander in Chief dictated a hurried note to Morgan: "I have just received your Letter by the Dragoon; as your Corps is out of supporting Distance I would have you confine yourself to observing the motions of the Enemy, unless an opportunity offers of intercepting some small Parties; and by no means to come to an Engagement with your whole Body unless you are tempted by some very evident advantage." [21]

Morgan, seeing no such opportunity, chafed at his impotence three miles beyond the courthouse; the British remained too closely bunched on the Monmouth-Sandy Hook road for him to annoy them. His anguish only increased when details of the Monmouth encounter reached him. After Washington formed a stationary battle line, Clinton discovered that he was smashing against a stone wall—Steuben's training had served the Continentals well. At dusk the struggle concluded indecisively, though Clinton's losses far exceeded Washington's. If Clinton experienced no "severe flogging," Morgan was still correct in maintaining that American arms had gained new laurels that day. He may not have exaggerated in assuring Washington that his corps could have played a major role had he been close at hand when Lee began his assault. Morgan frankly admitted his concern at not sharing in the "gloary" that the army achieved after Lee's retreat was halted.[22]

20. *Ibid.*, 23.
21. Washington to Morgan, [June 28, 1778], Fitzpatrick, ed., *Writings of Washington*, XII, 126.
22. Morgan to Washington, June 30, 1778, Washington Papers, Lib. Cong.

Recriminations soon burst forth on the American side. Charged with not attacking as directed and with retreating in disorder, Lee was adjudged guilty by a court-martial and suspended from the service. But a substantial number of the Continental officers felt he had been treated too severely. For that matter, neither Lafayette nor Wayne had performed particularly well, and there may have been some criticism of Morgan for not taking the initiative and uniting with Lee.[23]

Morgan was generally not one to exceed what he thought were his instructions, especially if Washington gave them. He is reported to have come by this attitude early in the war. Once Washington had detached him on a special mission with word to avoid tangling with the enemy, but the rifle officer had succumbed to the temptation to disperse a small group of redcoats. He blurted out his disobedience to Washington, saying his "flesh and blood" were weak. Convinced of being cashiered from the service, Morgan spent a sleepless night, but the next day he learned that Washington would forget the incident because it was "my first offense." [24]

Certainly Washington's correspondence after Monmouth contains no censure of Morgan for not establishing contact with Lee, who also saw no error in Morgan's conduct. At his trial Lee remarked that, although he had expected Morgan to act offensively, the Colonel was forced to move at his own discretion, for he was some distance ahead of the vanguard. In the last analysis, the fault was Lee's in not giving Morgan explicit information. The result was that a crack unit of the Continental Army sat out one of the major contests of the war, a fact that rankled Morgan for months to come.[25]

23. William S. Stryker, *The Battle of Monmouth*, ed. William S. Myers (Princeton, 1927), 155-56.

24. Custis, *Recollections*, 310.

25. *Lee Papers*, III, 180, 195; Thomas Posey to Morgan, June 22, 1779, Myers Coll., N. Y. Pub. Lib.

Had he tried, Morgan could have gleaned some satisfaction from his part in this New Jersey campaign. He took approximately 30 prisoners and 100 deserters. These statistics include the week following the battle, during which Morgan and Maxwell tried to prevent enemy foraging parties from ravaging the countryside along Clinton's line of retreat. On July 1, the rifle corps skirmished briskly with part of the British rear guard, then withdrew on the appearance of two redcoat reinforcing columns. Four days after that Clinton's army, having boarded transports at Sandy Hook, sailed for New York City.[26]

Morgan rejoined Washington's army, which soon crossed the Hudson at King's Ferry and encamped at White Plains, New York. For a brief period Morgan was stationed in Westchester County opposite British-held Manhattan Island. Then he returned to White Plains to take temporary charge of Brigadier General William Woodford's Virginia brigade while Woodford was on leave. Since Morgan also acquired permanent command of the brigade's 7th Regiment, he relinquished his rifle corps to a junior officer. Its manpower was now insufficient to warrant a colonel's directing it: twice that spring and summer Washington had sent companies of riflemen to help guard the Northern frontiers from Indian forays. The corps would be disbanded by the end of the year.[27]

Morgan parted reluctantly with his riflemen, described by one officer as the "pride of Washington." The "old wagoner," as he jocosely referred to himself, had been popular with his troops. Though the famous Morgan temper might explode occasionally and his powerful fists go to work on violators of camp

26. Williams G. Simmes, ed., *Army Correspondence of Colonel John Laurens in the Years 1777-8* (New York, 1867), 205; Sparks, ed., *Correspondence of the Revolution*, II, 152-53.

27. Fitzpatrick, ed., *Writings of Washington*, XI, 440; XII, 190, 251-52; XIII, 110, 439, 439n.

rules, the riflemen knew him to be a just leader. Maintaining that public whippings merely degraded a soldier and broke his spirit, he forbade such punishment in his corps. He made every attempt to fill the needs of his men and encouraged them to seek him out for personal advice and assistance. He also tried to prevent an impenetrable gulf between officers and enlisted men. An illustrative tale has it that Morgan once noticed two of his riflemen sweating and straining as they attempted to move a large rock from a road. Seeing an ensign standing nearby, Morgan said, "Why don't you lay hold and help these men?" "Sir," replied the latter, "I am an officer!" "I beg your pardon," thundered Morgan, "I did not think of that!" Jumping from his horse, he gave the soldiers a hand in rolling away the stone. A French officer, the Marquis de Chastellux, told in a similar story that when Morgan spied a number of teamsters having difficulty easing their rigs through a narrow pass, he climbed aboard one of their wagons and showed them how to handle their horses. The old wagoner was noted for his common touch.[28]

He probably saw little of the riflemen after shifting Woodford's brigade to Pompton, New Jersey, early in November. His new duties were numerous and time-consuming; doubtless he considered many of them tedious, preferring the relative freedom from detail that he had known commanding the independent rifle corps. Though Morgan was an uneducated backwoodsman with scant administrative experience, he quickly mastered his role. With businesslike efficiency, he turned in customary reports to superiors about food, equipment, and the myriad other matters concerning a brigade. Before long he came to enjoy his position; it seemed a just reward for his accomplishments with the rifle corps.

28. *The Public Papers of George Clinton* (New York, 1899-1914), V, 236; Graham, *Morgan*, 199-201; Marquis de Chastellux, *Travels in North America* (New York, 1828), 239*n.*, 240*n.*

November was an eventful, if not momentous, month. He sent out patrols to spot possible British sorties from New York; he dispatched troops as far north as Haverstraw, New York, to watch for enemy activities up the Hudson; he assigned 200 men to repair a road beween Morristown and Haverstraw. On one occasion he acquired intelligence of a projected foray by General Grey into the Highlands of the Hudson, only to obtain later information that Grey would descend on the New Jersey coast. Both reports were false. More disturbing to Morgan was a problem that had long bedeviled the Continental Army and now appeared in Woodford's brigade. Many soldiers, their term of service nearly up, were about to quit the army, despite Virginia's offer of large bounties to those who would stay. Morgan had exhausted every recourse, he dejectedly wrote Washington; he had thought he possessed a persuasive way with enlisted men, but they seemed fixed in their decision. The only way to keep a sizeable number was to grant them furloughs until spring. Washington found that other Virginia officers lent weight to this view and eventually followed Morgan's suggestion.[29]

Since Woodford was scheduled to arrive shortly, Morgan also obtained a leave of absence early in 1779; but when he returned to camp, perhaps in April, he discovered that Woodford had not arrived. Morgan continued to head the brigade until Woodford, evidently delayed by illness, took over in June. That Morgan had displayed real ability in his recent capacity, to say nothing of arousing an intense feeling of loyalty from the brigade officers, is suggested by a letter he subsequently received from Colonel John Neville of that same command. Though Neville expressed

29. Graham, *Morgan*, 217-23; Stirling to Morgan, Nov. 1, 1778, Myers Coll., N. Y. Pub. Lib.; Fitzpatrick, ed., *Writings of Washington*, XIII, 249-50, 394-95; Christian Febiger Letter Book, correspondence with Morgan and others for Nov. and Dec. 1778, Va. State Lib. (photostatic copy).

personal esteem for General Woodford, he frankly stated that the officers deemed Morgan an infinitely superior soldier. How they wished for Woodford's promotion to division commander so that "old Morgan" could again have the brigade—they would "kick the world" before them! [30]

In view of his past services with the corps of riflemen and the brigade, it is not surprising that Morgan was not fully content to resume the leadership of a single regiment. Then, scarcely a week or more after Woodford set foot in camp, a new corps of American light infantry was formed. Much larger than Morgan's old light unit, it consisted of sixteen companies chosen from Washington's army, each one previously acting as light infantry with its own division. The men were veterans of two years' Continental duty, young, healthy, and strong, and proficient with the bayonet.[31]

No post could have been more in line with Morgan's desires and experience. He became obsessed with the idea of leading the new force; no officer, he vowed, had equaled his performance with light troops. Accurate as his evaluation was, at least two factors militated against him. First, the new body was of adequate strength for a brigadier general. Second, Brigadier General Anthony Wayne had lately been replaced by Major General Arthur St. Clair as commander of the Pennsylvania line. The impulsive Wayne, implying that he might retire from the service if forced to perform in a secondary role, was, like Morgan, angling for the light infantry assignment.

Morgan became indignant when he heard rumors that the corps would go to Wayne, and he determined to face about and head for home if that happened. Nothing would hold him back but the possibility that his staying might save America from

30. Neville to Morgan, Nov. 9, 1779, Myers Coll., N. Y. Pub. Lib.
31. John W. Wright, "The Corps of Light Infantry in the Continental Army," *American Historical Review*, 31 (1926), 455.

destruction. He would not divulge his intention, he confided to a friend in Winchester, for fear of arousing further discontent in his fellow officers, who were already greatly exercised over low pay and inflationary prices.[32]

While it might appear as gross hypocrisy to threaten resignation and express concern for army morale in the same breath, it was all too clear to Morgan that his part in the war had not been looked upon as significant. That he would retain his loyalty to the cause he demonstrated in not revealing his likelihood of retiring. So well did he keep his secret that on June 30, 1779, the field officers of the right wing of Washington's army elected him chairman of a permanent committee to set maximum prices on food stuffs to be purchased.[33]

That same day Morgan learned of Wayne's elevation to the coveted post and informed Washington of his decision to give up the service. At Morgan's request, the Commander in Chief gave his disappointed subordinate a pass to Philadelphia along with a letter to the President of Congress: "Sir: Col Morgan of the Virginia troops, who waits on Congress with his resignation will have the honor of delivering you this. I cannot in justice avoid mentioning him as a very valuable officer who has rendered a series of important services and distinguished himself upon several occasions." [34]

Morgan was in Philadelphia on July 18, when he wrote a letter of resignation to the politicians. Writing did not come easily to Morgan, and this long letter must have been a difficult undertaking. But the characters are fairly well proportioned, and the message is coherent. He reviewed his successful military career in detail, then added:

32. Morgan to Dolphin Drew, June 16, 1779, Gates Papers, N. Y. Hist. Soc.

33. *William Heath Papers,* IV, 305-7.

34. Washington to the President of Congress, June 30, 1779, Fitzpatrick, ed., *Writings of Washington,* XV, 342.

From these considerations I could not but flatter myself, that if at any time a respectable corps of light troops should be formd I should be honored with the command of it. . . . I am however disappointed, such a corps has been form'd and the command of it given to another—As it is generally known that I commanded the light troops of our army and that the command is now taken from me, it will naturally be judged that this chang of officers has taken place either on account of some misconduct in me, or on account of my want of capacity—I cannot therefore but feel deeply effected with this Injury done my reputation. . . . I can with sincerity declare that I engaged in the service of my country with a full determination to continue in it as long as my services were wanting [wanted]—I must conclude from what has happend, that my country has no more occasion for me, I therefore beg leave to retire.[35]

Although Morgan admitted that Wayne outranked him, he pointed out that his military experience exceeded the Pennsylvanian's. Wayne was "still enjoying the sweets of domestic life" while he had fought in two Indian wars. Morgan was not without supporters. He wrote William Woodford that many people in the capital felt the light corps should have been his. He also said Congress studied his letter on July 19, and though the lawmakers did not approve of his resignation, they felt he had been "Neglected, but not intentionally." They treated him with "great respect" and persuaded him to accept an "honorable furlough" until "something offers." [36]

If Morgan correctly stated that Congress believed him slighted, why did that body not make amends by raising him to brigadier general? (An increase in rank was all the legislators could have done for him.) In July 1780 Washington gave the answer: "Custom (for I do not recollect any Resolve of Congress author-

35. Morgan to the President of Congress, July 18, 1779, Papers of the Continental Congress, No. 78, XV, 473, National Archives.
36. Morgan to Woodford, July 22, 1779, Chicago Hist. Soc.

izing it) has established a kind of right to the promotion of Brigadiers in State lines (where there are Regiments enough to require a Brigr. to command [)]." In July 1779 Virginia had four brigadier generals, more than the state deserved on the basis of its troops in service. Had there been an opening in the Virginia line for a brigadier, Congress would undoubtedly have given it to Morgan, who stood first in seniority among the state's colonels.[37]

Congress may have sympathized with Morgan, but Washington thought the former rifle officer had no reason to be discontented. The next year he wrote that Morgan was "a brave Officer, and a well meaning man, but his withdrawing from Service at the time he did last year, could not be justified on any ground; there was not, to my knowledge, the smallest cause for dissatisfaction; and the Season and circumstances were totally opposed to the measure, even if cause had existed, till matters assumed a different aspect than they were at the time of his proffered resignation." [38] That Morgan left the army at a critical period is unlikely. Washington's main army, quartered in an arc of camps stretching across the Hudson, had attempted no major operation in the twelve months following Monmouth. Though Sir Henry Clinton had recently disturbed the relative calm along the Hudson by seizing American forts at Stony Point and Verplancks Point, he soon sailed back to New York.

Whatever the military situation, Morgan was only one of many officers to leave the army because of dissatisfaction over rank and injured pride; an equal number, including Nathanael Greene, John Sullivan, Benedict Arnold, and Henry Knox, seriously contemplated doing so. Washington repeatedly described the spirit of discontent among his subordinates as "truly

37. Fitzpatrick, ed., *Writings of Washington*, XIX, 225; "List of the officers . . . of the Virginia line," U. S. Rev. Coll., Lib. Cong.
38. Fitzpatrick, ed., *Writings of Washington*, XIX, 226.

alarming," especially in the Virginia line where it raged "like an epidemical disease." John Adams expressed a similar view in saying he was "wearied to death with the wrangles between military officers, high and low. They quarrel like cats and dogs. They worry one another like mastiffs, scrambling for rank and pay like apes for nuts." But Adams failed to understand the military mind's sensitivity concerning recognition and honor. American officers of that day fought for their country, but they fought for glory too. And while few were more ambitious or thin-skinned than Morgan, scarcely a handful could match his combat record.[39]

39. *Ibid.*, XI, 180; C. F. Adams, ed., *Familiar Letters of John Adams and His Wife*, 276. Most historians commenting on Morgan's retirement have sustained the rifleman's contention that his past accomplishments had been inadequately recognized. They include Montross, *Rag, Tag and Bobtail*, 328, 403; Sidney G. Fischer, *The True History of the American Revolution* (Philadelphia, 1902), 269, 412; John Fiske, *The American Revolution* (Boston, 1891), II, 249-50; John R. Alden, *The South in the Revolution* (Baton Rouge, 1957), 252; Ward, *War of the Revolution*, II, 735.

CHAPTER VII

Morgan Joins the Southern Army

MORGAN spurred southward over frontier trails. Congress might call his departure a furlough, but he had been treated shamefully and would not return, though he would still wish Congress and the army well. Proud and indignant but not wrathful, he returned to an agrarian life.[1]

How Abigail Morgan had managed the farm in his absence is not apparent, but Morgan maintained that she underwent numerous difficulties. He had been able to send her little money; his meager salary, often in arrears, had gone for much of his food, clothing, and lodging, all of which enlisted men obtained from the public. Despite her best efforts, Morgan found that his farm demanded attention, and he devoted the fall and winter of 1779 to improving it; his land, dwellings, horses, cattle, and slaves all required supervision.[2]

Busy though he was, he kept up with the war as best he could. In letters to Woodford, he pleaded for his old friend to write of every important happening. How was the brigade, he asked, and how were Muhlenberg, Smallwood, and Stirling? From Woodford and other army associates he learned of developments in the North, where neither Washington nor Clinton undertook a major offensive during the remainder of 1779. Far

1. Morgan to Woodford, July 22, 1779, Chicago Hist. Soc.
2. Richard K. Meade to Morgan, June 30, 1779, and Neville to Morgan, Nov. 9, 1779, Myers Coll., N. Y. Pub. Lib.

more alarming to Morgan was the British invasion of the South, an area without previous major conflict since an unsuccessful redcoat thrust at Charleston, South Carolina, in 1776. Then, in 1778, the London government had decided to launch a vigorous Southern campaign. The King's ministers mistakenly thought great Tory strength lay slumbering in the South, waiting to be aroused by the unfurling of a royal standard. Moreover, this thinly settled region of innumerable rivers, creeks, and swamps was far-removed from the main American army which opposed Clinton in the New York area. The first step in the new plan saw British forces from New York and Florida subdue Georgia in the winter of 1778-79. Nearly a year later Clinton sailed southward and in February 1780 landed thirty miles below Charleston, where American Major General Benjamin Lincoln worked frantically to shore up the city's defenses. Beware "Charles Town," cried Morgan to an army comrade, when he got wind of Clinton's approach.[3]

In Morgan's opinion, Lincoln, a jovial, obese officer from Massachusetts, lacked the ability to head the Southern Department during this time of crisis. He wrote Colonel William Grayson of the Board of War that Gates was ideally suited for the post; just as Gates had stopped Burgoyne's invasion, so now he was the man to halt Clinton. Gates was spending the spring of 1780 at his farm, Traveller's Rest, in Berkeley County, Virginia. Morgan seems to have made several trips to Gates's retreat. On the high front porch during warm spring days the two Saratoga veterans reviewed the war over a pipe and a glass of rum. If he had believed Gates hostile to Washington in the winter of 1777-

3. Febiger to Morgan, Sept. 3, 1779, Febiger Letter Book, Va. State Lib.; Morgan to Woodford, Oct. 3, 1779, Ferdinand J. Dreer Coll., Generals of the Revolution, Hist. Soc. of Pa.; Neville to Morgan, Nov. 9, 1779, Myers Coll., N. Y. Pub. Lib.; Morgan to Otho Holland Williams, Mar. 10, 1780, Elizabeth Merritt, ed., *Calendar of the General Otho Holland Williams Papers* (Baltimore, 1940), 19.

78, Morgan harbored no ill will toward him now; they were on the best of terms.[4]

For several weeks Morgan did not see Gates. He was suffering from an ailment—he called it sciatica—which he first contracted on the arduous march to Quebec and which caused him discomfort while heading Woodford's brigade in 1779. It was in this condition that he heard grave news from South Carolina: Charleston had fallen on May 12. Though Lincoln had more ability than Morgan would admit, he was forced to surrender his army of 5,500 men, the greatest American defeat of the war in numbers captured. Lincoln, who had followed the wishes of the South Carolina civilian leaders in defending Charleston and was subsequently surrounded by Clinton's army, drew stern criticism from Washington and other patriots. For political reasons, however, Lincoln could hardly have abandoned the South's largest city without a fight. As for Clinton, he soon returned to New York, leaving Lord Cornwallis to head the mopping up operations in the lower South.

Roughly six weeks after Lincoln's capitulation, Morgan opened a letter from Gates which brought momentous consequences for him. Gates wrote that Congress had appointed him commander of the Southern Department and that the lawmakers contemplated calling Morgan to active service with the Southern army. Involved with last-minute details before taking up his new station, Gates could not visit Morgan but hoped his neighbor would come to Traveller's Rest for the "particulars." In his immediate reply, Morgan expressed great enthusiasm for Gates's appointment. "Would to god youd a had it six months ago," he exclaimed; "our affairs would have wore a more pleasing aspect at this day than they do." He had no doubt that Gates would "stir up" the Southern people and give them "fresh life."

4. The letter to Grayson is described in Morgan to Gates, June 24, 1780, Gates Papers, N. Y. Hist. Soc.

Although Morgan was more than willing to travel to Gates's home, he felt physically unable to ride that far. Instead he suggested they meet at the gap in the Blue Ridge where Gates would pass on his journey south. "I am very desirious to see you," he added, "and must and will see you." [5] Gates answered that he would look for his friend at Berry's Tavern, Ashby's Gap, on the morning of the 28th. Enclosed was a resolution of Congress calling on Morgan to join the Southern army. [6]

Morgan fairly leaped at this opportunity once he talked with Gates at Berry's Tavern. Whereas the previous year Morgan had felt neglected as a regimental commander with Washington's army, Gates was prepared to recognize Morgan's particular ability with light troops. He asked his former subordinate to head a special light unit similar to Morgan's old rifle corps. Not only was the position to Morgan's liking; he knew that Gates needed his assistance. The American General had few troops to oppose the British, who, already in possession of South Carolina and Georgia, were preparing to slash their way northward. In return for his services, Morgan stipulated only that Gates try to persuade Congress to promote him to brigadier general so that he would not have to perform under Virginia militia officers recently elevated above him. Gates, thinking this a reasonable request, agreed, but could he succeed? His relations with Congress fluctuated between good and bad, and Morgan had retired against the legislators' wishes. But Morgan, eager to fight again, and under an officer who trusted him, was content to hope for the best.

From Berry's Tavern, Gates proceeded to Fredericksburg,

5. Gates to Morgan, June 21, 1781 [1780], Graham, *Morgan*, 233-34; Morgan to Gates, June 24, 1780, Gates Papers, N. Y. Hist. Soc.
6. Gates to Morgan, June 26, 1780, Myers Coll., N. Y. Pub. Lib.; Ford, ed., *Journals of Congress*, XVII, 519.

where he wrote Samuel Huntington, president of Congress, an urgent plea that Morgan be appointed a brigadier general:

... Colonel Morgan requests me to represent to Your Excellency, that the State of Virginia have appointed some Junior Officers to himself Brigadiers General who will take Command of Him, should he take the Field in his present Rank.—This is not only a galling Circumstance to so old and deserving an Officer, but must impede, and possibly entirely defeat my Intention, in placing Colonel Morgan at the Head of a Select Corps from whose Services I expect the most brilliant Success. Therefore I humbly entreat your Excellency, will move Congress to order a Commission to issue immediately, appointing Colonel Morgan a Brigadier General.—I am confident the Rank, the Services and the Experience of Colo Morgan is such as will prevent any officer, from thinking Himself agrieved by His Promotion—I shall impatiently expect the arrival of this Commission as I wish the Service in which I design to employ Colonel Morgan may meet with the least possible Delay.[7]

Morgan, meanwhile, impatiently waited to gain enough strength to ride the distance to Gates's camp in North Carolina. He busied himself by circulating an order from Gates to all Continentals in western Virginia to assemble on July 15 at Fredericksburg; from there they would leave for North Carolina. He also arraigned several Southern army deserters before the Frederick County Court. At his recommendation, the justices sentenced them to two months' military service beyond their period of enlistment. Perhaps these activities caused Morgan to have a relapse: sharp pains once more shot through his back and thighs, confining him to bed. He rested, he massaged his aching muscles, he took cold baths—nothing seemed to help. His physical anguish was more than equaled by the disappointment of not being able to take the field. Probably never before or after did he so hunger

7. Gates to Samuel Huntington, July 4, 1780, *Magazine of American History*, 5 (1880), 282.

for action. But he was possessed of sturdy frame and even stouter heart, and he "mended amazingly"; this he wrote Gates on August 15, over six weeks after their meeting at Berry's Tavern. Though he had "suffered much," in body and in spirit, he was overjoyed at the prospect of departing within a fortnight; the pains were almost completely gone. He confidently assured Gates that he would "make up" for "lost time." [8]

How Gates could have used Morgan that very next day, August 16! He was so decisively defeated near Camden, South Carolina, that the Southern army was all but destroyed. On joining his new command in North Carolina on July 25, Gates had discovered it amounted to only 1,400 Delaware and Maryland Continentals and 120 dragoons. Its numbers, inadequate provisions, and meager equipment should have led him to demonstrate the caution that had marked his conduct in the Saratoga campaign. He needed time to build and equip a genuine army; few officers could rival his talents in organization and administration—even his critics admitted that.

He failed to employ his talents. Instead he advanced through desolate Loyalist country to attack the British garrison at Camden. On August 15, after being reinforced by 2,000 untrained North Carolina and Virginia militia, he unexpectedly came upon a British force under Lord Cornwallis, who had heard of Gates's approach and had hurried from Charleston with fresh units to reinforce the Camden outpost. Though Gates might well have avoided battle, he resolved to make a stand, and the following morning the two armies clashed. His militia, comprising the left side of the American line, soon fled, at which point Cornwallis concentrated on the American right held by the Continentals. For a time the American regulars stubbornly maintained their ground, only at length to break and scatter. Gates, lathering his

8. Gates's General Order, June 29, 1780, and Morgan to Gates, Aug. 15, 1780, Gates Papers, N. Y. Hist. Soc.; Order Books, XVII, 355.

horse ahead of his battered force, made Hillsboro, North Carolina, three days later, 160 miles from the scene of action, a remarkable ride for a man of fifty-one. Hamilton, a friend of Washington and inimical to Gates, asked if there were ever such an instance of a general running away from his own army. "And was there ever so precipitous a flight?" But Gates, denying he had fled, said his purpose was to reach a suitable location for reorganizing his army.[9]

Camden was a crushing blow to the Americans. Cornwallis, counting 324 British casualties, estimated Gates's losses as 1,900, killed, wounded, and captured. Gates was largely responsible for his own misfortune. He had never been recognized as a tactician. Entrusting half of his main line to raw militia was perhaps the biggest mistake of his military career.[10]

Word of the Camden disaster came to Morgan while he was still at home, and though not completely recovered, he resolved to leave immediately for North Carolina. In so doing he would risk more than his health; he would deplete his financial resources as well. Gates, who had promised that the service would meet his traveling costs, had sent no money, and Morgan had almost no ready cash. But he set out, leading an extra mare to sell for expense money. He rode slowly, stopping often to rest and stretch his muscles. Unpleasant as the journey must have been, it was lightened somewhat by several companions, young Virginians who wished to enlist in Morgan's new light corps; one,

9. John C. Hamilton, ed., *The Works of Alexander Hamilton* (New York, 1851), II, 124.

10. For accounts of Camden, see Otho H. Williams, "A Narrative of the Campaign of 1780," in William Johnson, *Sketches of the Life and Correspondence of Nathanael Greene* (Charleston, S. C., 1822), I, Appendix B, 486-99; Scheer and Rankin, *Rebels and Redcoats*, 404-11; Christopher Ward, *The Delaware Continentals* (Wilmington, 1941), 335-50; Ward, *War of the Revolution*, II, 717-30.

Major Peter Bruin, was beginning his third tour of duty with Morgan.[11]

Entering Hillsboro, North Carolina, in late September, Morgan alighted before the pillared brick courthouse that served as Gates's headquarters and the temporary meeting place of the state legislature. Gates greeted Morgan warmly and told the North Carolina civilian leaders that Morgan's appearance was a great lift to the patriot cause in the South. After he saw the Southern army encampment a mile outside of town, Morgan may have wondered what he or anyone else could do. Barely 700 Maryland and Delaware Continentals were there. (The Camden militia were hopelessly dispersed, many having returned to their homes.) These regulars, along with 500 additional men, mostly new arrivals from Virginia, slept in wigwams made of fence rails and cornstalks. Colonel Otho Holland Williams of Maryland, whose acquaintance with Morgan dated from the Boston siege, described the soldiers as destitute of clothing, almost without pay, and with never more than half rations. They had also lost their artillery, wagons, and most of their muskets at Camden.[12]

There were other bitter fruits from Camden. The British victory confirmed Cornwallis in his resolution to occupy North Carolina, a move Clinton had sanctioned provided his venturesome subordinate could retain control of South Carolina. The forty-two-year-old Cornwallis, a veteran of the Seven Years' War, and far more energetic than Howe or Clinton, felt it essential to gain North Carolina in order to preserve his hold on the lower South. With Gates in no condition to retaliate, this was a dubious assumption. Moreover, by spreading his army over

11. Morgan to Gates, Nov. 9, 1780, Gates Papers, N. Y. Hist. Soc.; Boyd, ed., *Jefferson Papers*, V, 53; deposition of Peter Bruin, Revolutionary War Pension Files, National Archives.

12. Williams's narrative, in Johnson, *Greene*, I, Appendix B, 506-7.

three states, he would leave his lines of communication and remote garrisons subject to bands of rebel partisans under such
leaders as Thomas Sumter and Francis Marion—men who burst
from ambush to kill and destroy and then disappear into the
forests and swamps. Cornwallis failed to consider these possibilities as he advanced from Camden to Charlotte, the first step in
his invasion of the Tar Heel State.

Alarmed by this threat, the North Carolina Board of War
urged Gates to send westward all the Continentals having shoes
to assist the state militia, which was to be headed by Brigadier
General William Smallwood, a Maryland regular then at Hillsboro. The board also requested that Colonel Morgan, "the
famous Partisan," accompany Smallwood. As the board wrote
Morgan, his well-known "Character as a Soldier" would infuse
new morale into the militia.[13]

Gates agreed to detach Morgan and instructed Smallwood to
impede Cornwallis's progress through guerrilla operations. This
strategy, which Gates himself should have employed earlier
instead of pressing down on Camden, was already being put to
good use by the North Carolina irregulars in the Charlotte
vicinity under Brigadier General William L. Davidson and
Colonel William R. Davie. They hindered Cornwallis's every
move to forage in the country, deploying their men in wooded
areas and ravines near the village. Militia used this way were
often effective, far less so when arranged in close rank formation
against British regulars with bayonets, as was true at Camden.

Gates knew from his experience in the Saratoga campaign
that Morgan was unexcelled in directing the kind of harassing
activities the North Carolinians were engaged in; it was mani-
festly for this reason he agreed to let Morgan go with Smallwood.

13. Walter Clark, ed., *The State Records of North Carolina* (Winston
and Goldsboro, 1895-1907), XIV, 397, 400.

The only difficulty involved in his decision was Morgan's opposition to taking orders from militia officers, and certainly in performing with the irregulars several of the state officers would equal his rank or surpass it. Morgan was already on edge because he had received no word from Congress about his promotion; he correctly considered himself a superior soldier to the North Carolinians. That Morgan's explosive nature might collide with the imperious attitude of certain Southern militia leaders who saw their own locales as private preserves was alarmingly clear to Gates. He urged Smallwood to beware of trouble, and he wrote the President of Congress that the only sure solution was to elevate Morgan to brigadier general. The North Carolina Board of War echoed Gates's concern in advising its delegates in Congress to work for Morgan's promotion. To Gates, Smallwood, and the state Board of War, the problem demanded immediate attention. They could only trust that the politicians in far-off Philadelphia would so view the matter.[14]

In the meantime, Gates helped eliminate the chances of friction between Morgan and the local officers by keeping an old promise: he gave Morgan an independent light corps. Though the new unit consisted mainly of picked men, its size—three companies of Continental infantry, sixty Virginia riflemen, and seventy cavalrymen—must have disappointed Morgan. He was more fortunate in his principal subordinates. Lieutenant Colonels John Eager Howard and William Washington, commanding the infantry and cavalry respectively, were capable officers who had battlefield experience with Washington's army. Howard was a Marylander who later served his state as governor, delegate to the Continental Congress, and member of the United States

14. Gates to Smallwood, Oct. 3, 1780, and Gates to Samuel Huntington, Oct. 5, 1780, Papers of the Continental Congress, No. 154, II, 210-11, 267-68, National Archives; Clark, ed., *State Records of North Carolina*, XIV, 405.

Senate. Washington was a portly, good-natured Virginian and a relative of the Commander in Chief. Morgan was also lucky in getting a suit of clothing for each of his men from the North Carolina Board of War. Since clothing was extremely scarce for the bulk of the Southern army, Gates resolved to remain with most of his troops at Hillsboro until he could raise and outfit a formidable striking force.[15]

Delayed nearly forty-eight hours by rains, Morgan's corps at last began marching westward on October 7; Smallwood came on a few days afterward. With his corps small, his assignment vague, and his body further weakened by a recent bout with malaria, Morgan could hardly have ventured forth with great optimism. Yet he showed his customary vigor by inquiring of the roads to the west, of the ability of the militiamen, and of the number of men who owned rifles. Though interested in adding experienced fighters to his corps, Morgan's immediate attention was directed to his shortage of food; he found nothing to purchase except meat and flour. To an officer concerned with the welfare of his men, this was a sad state of affairs. It also thwarted his plan to have an elaborate dinner for Washington, Howard, and the company leaders. "An officer looks very blank when he hain't it in his power to ask his officers to eat with him at times," he moaned to Gates. For a man without formal military education, Morgan had developed a keen sense of the amenities of army life.[16]

15. Williams's narrative, in Johnson, *Greene*, I, Appendix B, 508; William Seymour, *A Journal of the Southern Expedition, 1780-1783*, Delaware Historical Society, Papers, 15 (1896), 8; *The Journal and Order Book of Capt. Robert Kirkwood*, Del. Hist. Soc., Papers, LVI (Wilmington, 1910), 11; "Journal of Lieutenant Thomas Anderson," *Historical Magazine*, 2d Ser., 1 (1867), 208.

16. Clark, ed., *State Records of North Carolina*, XIV, 407; W. Graham, *J. Graham*, 135; Morgan to Gates, Oct. 20, 1780, Myers Coll., N. Y. Pub. Lib.

Reaching the east bank of the Yadkin River on the 13th, he encountered Brigadier General Jethro Sumner with a contingent of militia, waiting for Smallwood. That afternoon Sumner and Morgan learned that Cornwallis had abandoned Charlotte. His scheme for the subjugation of North Carolina was destroyed on October 7, at King's Mountain in upper South Carolina. A large body of frontier patriots from North Carolina, Virginia, and east Tennessee caught up with 1,100 Loyalists under British Major Patrick Ferguson, who, like Morgan, excelled in rifle tactics. The hardy backwoodsmen, aroused by Ferguson's plundering and burning of rebel homes, went to work with a vengeance, and before the struggle ended many of the Loyalists had been killed or wounded while trying desperately to surrender; others were hanged after the battle. Ferguson's command was demolished.[17]

This setback was especially jarring to Cornwallis because Ferguson's men formed one of the two British light units in the Southern states; the other was Banastre Tarleton's Tory Legion. The General knew the inestimable value of such units in the rough and forested Carolina terrain, where they gathered intelligence, protected flanks of marching columns, and hunted down rebels picking at British posts and supply lines. Now fearful that Ferguson's conquerors might strike at Camden or Ninety-Six in the west, Cornwallis pulled back from Charlotte in the direction of the threatened region.

Two days after learning of Cornwallis's retreat, Morgan crossed the Yadkin and headed toward Charlotte. In response to an offer from Sumner to lend him 100 men should he desire to annoy Cornwallis, Morgan declined, for as he told Sumner, he had no idea what Smallwood wanted him to do; so he would

17. Clark, ed., *State Records of North Carolina*, XIV, 693; Lyman C. Draper, *King's Mountain and Its Heroes* (Cincinnati, 1881), *passim*.

march on slowly until orders arrived. In closing, he asked that Sumner tell Smallwood of his march toward Charlotte.[18]

Most of the other American commanders between the Yadkin and Charlotte also expected instructions from Smallwood, a fact that may explain why Sumner, Morgan, Davie, and Davidson avoided a co-ordinated move against the retiring enemy, whose extended wagon trains would have been an inviting target. When Smallwood finally came up with the militia and Morgan's men about October 20, he assembled his force at New Providence, twelve miles south of Charlotte. A more aggressive general might have endeavored to obstruct Cornwallis, since heavy rains had churned the enemy's escape route into a quagmire.

By November 1, Cornwallis had established winter quarters for his army at Winnsboro, South Carolina, between Camden and Ninety-Six. Neither Smallwood nor Cornwallis undertook large scale operations that month. On the 3rd, Smallwood sent Morgan's corps on an uneventful mission into the Waxhaws country, below the South Carolina line, to protect a group of foragers under Davie. Meanwhile, Gates, thinking there would be more food available in the vicinity of New Providence, started westward with his troops. But, uniting with Smallwood on the 22nd, he discovered that the surrounding country was almost bare of provisions. Three days later he held a council of war attended by Smallwood, Morgan, and Davidson. Owing to the lack of food and the probability that Cornwallis would soon gain reinforcements and attempt another push into North Carolina, the council voted to withdraw the army to Charlotte. Gates, leaving on the 27th, ordered Smallwood to follow the

18. Sumner to Morgan, Oct. 17, 1780, Jethro Sumner Papers, William L. Clements Lib., Univ. of Mich.; Morgan to Sumner, Oct. 17, 1780, Lloyd Smith Coll., Morristown National Hist. Park, Lib.

next day and told Morgan to stay on guard at New Providence.[19]

A few hours after Gates's departure, Smallwood heard of a quantity of corn and forage still in the Waxhaws. Morgan was eager to bestir himself after a monotonous month at New Providence and begged Smallwood's permission to collect it. Though Smallwood opposed the scheme, Morgan ardently persisted. "What shall I do with Morgan?" Smallwood wrote despairingly to Gates. "He is in a fever to go below." The same day Morgan wrote Gates that the supplies in the Waxhaws would temporarily feed the horses, which had not "a morsel of forage." To make the excursion Morgan needed several of Smallwood's wagons and the assurance that the General would remain at New Providence to aid his corps if it encountered a superior British force. The following day Gates gave in to Morgan, perhaps to humor his restless subordinate.[20]

Morgan's Waxhaws expedition, while failing to locate any corn and forage, did result in a minor military success. Journeying back to New Providence, Morgan passed the plantation of Tory Colonel Rowland Rugeley. Finding that Rugeley and 100 of his Loyalist supporters were nearby in a barn converted into a fort, Morgan dispatched Washington's cavalry to dislodge them. The fort was surrounded by an abatis; so Washington resorted to a ruse. He secured a log, shaped it into the semblance of a cannon, and propped it up. Placing the "cannon" in sight of the garrison, he called upon Rugeley to surrender. After the Tory officer and his men marched out with their hands above their heads, Morgan slyly remarked that the British were not likely

19. Smallwood to Morgan, Nov. 3, 1780, Myers Coll., N. Y. Pub. Lib.; Seymour, *Journal of the Southern Expedition*, 9; Clark, ed., *State Records of North Carolina*, XIV, 160-61.

20. Smallwood to Gates, Nov. 27, 1780, *ibid.*, 760; Morgan to Gates, Nov. 27, 1780, Gates Papers, N. Y. Hist. Soc.; Gates to Morgan, Nov. 28, 1780, Myers Coll., N. Y. Pub. Lib.

to judge Rugeley's performance as that of a "great military character." He was correct. "Rugeley," said Cornwallis, "will not be made a brigadier." [21]

Morgan would have readily traded this small victory for an opportunity to destroy the British counterpart to his own light corps, Banastre Tarleton's Tory Legion, composed of both infantry and cavalry. An advocate of smashing, head-on attacks, Tarleton had led his men in numerous raids through South Carolina. The brutality he several times displayed had brought him the epithet of "Bloody Tarleton"; and his useless slaughter of Colonel Abraham Buford's Continentals in the Waxhaws as they attempted to surrender caused Americans to define his brand of mercy as "Tarleton's Quarter" (an expression shouted by the patriots at King's Mountain as they butchered the Loyalists). Short and thickset, vigorous and resourceful, the twenty-six-year-old Tarleton was intensely proud of his Legion, and its success had gained him the favor of Cornwallis. In November 1780 the British General had told his subordinate, "I wish you would get three Legions, and divide yourself in three parts: We can do no good without you." Cornwallis had indeed kept Tarleton and his Legion active in beating back guerrillas and in keeping communications open between British stations in South Carolina. Morgan knew that his corps must be made equal or superior to Tarleton's Legion, and as a beginning he persuaded Colonel Isaac Shelby, a King's Mountain fighter, to recruit 500 North Carolina riflemen for his command. Elated by this prospect, Morgan dashed off a letter to Gates requesting formal permission for this undertaking.[22]

21. Graham, *Morgan*, 249; Banastre Tarleton, *A History of the Campaigns of 1780 and 1781, in the Southern Province of North America* (London, 1787), 205.

22. Robert D. Bass, *The Green Dragoon: The Lives of Banastre Tarleton and Mary Robinson* (New York, 1957), 117; Morgan to Gates, Nov. 23, 1780, Gates Papers, N. Y. Hist. Soc.

Gates was unable to comply. The Camden fiasco led Congress to recall him from the Southern Department. Rumor of the recall had reached Morgan in early November, and even before that he had heard reports that certain Southern army officers had formed a cabal to weaken Gates's prestige with the army and urge Congress to replace him. Morgan maintained he did not know who these officers were, but his friend Otho Williams later singled out Smallwood as their leader. Whatever Morgan thought of the Camden defeat, he was steadfastly loyal to Gates so long as the little man continued in charge, and he heatedly assured Gates that no one dared attempt to draw him into a plot. Morgan's rough handling of Richard Peters, the alleged enemy of Washington, two years before was common knowledge in the Continental Army. Evidently no conspirator in the South wanted the same treatment.[23]

New laurels had not come Morgan's way during his service in the South under Gates. With the Southern army inactive in late November, awaiting its new commander, Morgan's career seemed to have reached a standstill. Supremely confident of himself to perform well if given the opportunity, he doubtless attributed his inaction to the adversity that afflicted the Southern Department. In addition to the staggering reversals at Charleston and Camden, the states had inadequate administrative machinery to raise enough food and war materials for the army. It was not entirely the fault of the civil officials, who complained with some justification that many of their resources had been drained in supplying the troops that fought at Charleston and Camden. Morale too had fallen precipitately; military enlistments were few, for men stayed home to protect their property and families from Tory marauders. These difficulties explain Gates's avoid-

23. Williams's narrative, in Johnson, *Greene*, I, Appendix B, 508; Bruin to Morgan, Nov. [?], 1780, Myers Coll., N. Y. Pub. Lib.; Morgan to Gates, Nov. 9, 1780, Gates Papers, N. Y. Hist. Soc.

ance of combat since Camden and the failure of Morgan's efforts to build a large, well-equipped light corps.

As for the North Carolina riflemen Morgan hoped to add, Gates would have to let his replacement decide on that. No one knew who the new commander would be. One story had it that Congress had appointed Smallwood. Major Peter Bruin, called back to Virginia by Governor Jefferson, confided to Morgan that Richmond gossip indicated Lincoln as the man; he supposedly had been exchanged since Charleston's fall. Uncertain as to when Gates would depart, Morgan had written him a consoling note on November 9. "I am informed you are to be recalled," he said, "for which I am sorry and glad both, for I don't think it will be in the power of any Genl. officer who commands in this country to add to his reputation." After the Yorktown victory, Morgan told Gates that he was "a great officer, a patriot, & an honest man." Though Morgan was overly flattering to his Valley neighbor, his statement bears some truth. The diminutive Horatio had performed ably as adjutant general and as commander of the Northern army. Had he not served in the South, he would have ranked among the leading figures of the Revolution.[24]

Despite his disappointments that autumn of 1780, Morgan could point to some pleasant developments. He had no real problem with the North Carolina brigadiers, and he got along exceptionally well with General Davidson, an enterprising backwoodsman and former Continental whom he had known at Valley Forge. Morgan's health appeared to be completely restored by mid-November; he felt as strong and energetic as ever. And, finally, the news arrived that Congress had elevated him to brigadier general.[25]

24. Bruin to Morgan, Nov. [?], 1780, Myers Coll., N. Y. Pub. Lib.; Morgan to Gates, Nov. 9, 1780, May 20, 1782, Gates Papers, N. Y. Hist. Soc.
25. Gates to Morgan, Oct. 27, 1780, Graham, *Morgan*, 243.

It was well for Morgan, considering his sensitive nature, that he was ignorant of the lengthy discussion in Congress preceding his promotion. The congressmen first took up the question on July 14, 1780, when they heard a report from the Board of War stating why Gates desired Morgan's advancement. Though Virginia did not have enough troops in Continental service to warrant another general officer, the board pointed out that this obstacle would be removed when the state met its quota of men for 1780. In any case, the board believed Morgan had "great pretensions to promotion from personal merit." He had "early embarked in the present war, and uniformly distinguished himself as an active, brave, and useful officer." [26]

Congressional approval came slowly. On the motion of Joseph Jones, delegate from Virginia, the legislators decided to study the matter further before bringing it to a vote. Jones asked Washington for his opinion, reminding him that Morgan had "left the army in disgust under your immediate command." Washington replied that the delicate situation between Gates and himself made him reluctant to comment on a subject concerning Gates. So he would merely "state facts." There could be no opposition to Morgan's elevation through the Virginia line if that state supplied the troops it had promised; but, recalling Virginia's deficiencies in the past, he thought it unlikely that Virginia would do so. Washington was always rigidly proper where Virginia officers were involved in questions of rank, since he feared charges of favoritism to men from his own state. With officers from other states he was somewhat more flexible.[27]

His remarks obviously did not help Morgan, whose retirement the previous year had no doubt placed him in a bad light with

26. Ford, ed., *Journals of Congress*, XVII, 612-13.
27. Burnett, ed., *Letters of Congress*, V, 270-71; Fitzpatrick, ed., *Writings of Washington*, XIX, 224-26; Howard Swiggett, *The Great Man* (New York, 1953), 13.

many of the legislators. But after Congress received letters in support of Morgan from Governor Thomas Jefferson of Virginia and Governor John Rutledge of South Carolina, Gates's campaign for Morgan brought results; the lawmakers raised the rifleman to brigadier general on October 13. In their resolve they did not mention Morgan's past accomplishments but merely declared his promotion would remove "several embarrassments" in the Southern Department.[28]

Congress, in grudgingly adhering to the pleadings of the Southern leaders, could call Morgan's promotion irregular in that it violated the tradition of moving up through state lines. But was this procedure really desirable? Under it able officers were passed over if their lines were filled, while inferior men from other states were advanced if vacancies existed. Though Congress on the whole did its work well, surviving one crisis after another during the war, it was never free of state and regional jealousies, which explains its peculiar attachment to placing state quotas above merit. But some of the legislators may have realized the unfairness of their approach, as well as its possible harm to the war effort, when in 1781 Morgan as a brigadier general gained one of the most one-sided patriot victories of the war.

28. Graham, *Morgan*, 243; Burnett, ed., *Letters of Congress*, V, 424.

CHAPTER VIII

An Independent Command

G ATES's long-awaited successor was Nathanael Greene. He arrived in Charlotte on December 2, 1780, and only then did Morgan and the other officers determine his identity. Unlike Gates, Greene had little military experience before the Revolution; he had served a few months in the Rhode Island militia. A self-educated man, with a penchant for books about war, he was read out of the Society of Friends for advocating forceful measures to resist Britain's policy toward America. After Lexington and Concord the short, chunky Greene marched to Cambridge as brigadier general in charge of all Rhode Island troops. With Washington's command during the next five years, he gained a sound reputation for his activities at Trenton and Princeton and for his performance as quartermaster general of the army. When Congress asked Washington to select Gates's replacement, he chose Greene, his most valuable subordinate, whose talents lay chiefly in administration and strategy. Then thirty-eight years old, Greene was mild-mannered and made friends easily.[1]

Having tried with scant success to obtain supplies for the Southern army at Philadelphia, Annapolis, and Richmond, Greene continued southward to Gates's camp, taking over there

1. Greene, whose career long escaped careful examination, is the subject of a recent study. Theodore Thayer, *Nathanael Greene: Strategist of the American Revolution* (New York, 1960).

on December 3. Never on cordial terms, the two generals treated each other politely, making the change in leadership without incident. Colonel Otho Williams remarked that the officers present had "an elegant lesson of propriety exhibited on a most delicate and interesting occasion." Greene had no illusions that he could better Gates's performance in the months after Camden and was far less critical of Gates's part in that action than many American officers. Moreover, he evaded Congress's order to hold a court of inquiry into his predecessor's conduct.[2]

While Gates returned to Traveller's Rest, forever without an independent command, Greene found his situation similar to Gates's before Camden. His army was "rather a shadow than a substance, having only an imaginary existence." Its paper strength of 2,450 men compared dismally with the number actually present at Charlotte, 1,632, of whom fewer than 800 were adequately clothed and equipped. With the surrounding country picked clean of provisions, Greene sent his engineer, Thaddeus Kosciuszko, to locate a more promising campsite on the Pee Dee River. Then he called a council of war to consider a hit-and-run assault on Winnsboro, where Cornwallis was preparing for another thrust at North Carolina; Greene hoped to cripple his opponent and delay the invasion until he could bolster the Southern army. Morgan and Smallwood, mindful of the Camden disaster, opposed the idea. Since some military men in the North thought Greene inclined to hasty decisions and overconfidence, Morgan may have been surprised and pleased to find that the ex-Quaker deferred to his opinion and Smallwood's. Though a man of action, Morgan could be cautious, and caution in this instance was the wiser policy; another crushing defeat on the

2. Williams's narrative, in Johnson, *Greene*, I, Appendix B, 510; Williams to Greene, Dec. 6, 1780, Papers of the Continental Congress, No. 155, I, 489; Greene to Washington, Dec. 7, 1780, Greene Letter Book, Oct.-Dec. 1780, Lib. Cong.

order of Charleston and Camden might have been fatal to the patriot cause in the South.[3]

Fundamentally, both Greene and Morgan were exponents of mobility in warfare. As early as November 2, a month to the day before he first rode down the red mud streets of Charlotte, Greene had resolved to avoid open battle and to concentrate on partisan-type operations, slashing at Cornwallis's flanks, breaking up his communications, and intercepting his wagon trains. In keeping with this idea, Greene took over half his force to Cheraw, the spot selected by Kosciuszko on the Pee Dee. At this new site he would raise, train, and outfit an army; he could also aid the guerrilla Marion, threaten Camden, and watch British troop movements from Charleston. With the rest of his command, Greene fulfilled a project long in mind: the creation of a "flying army to consist of Infantry and horse." He singled out Morgan as the obvious officer to lead such a unit.[4]

For Morgan it was the realization of his desire for a larger light corps. Composed of the troops Gates had given him previously and two companies of Maryland Continentals, it also included 250 veteran Virginia militia. With this unit Morgan was to move southwest from Charlotte into the country just below the border of the Carolinas.

Greene, the student of military history, knew this arrangement violated the classic maxim of warfare that to divide an army before a superior enemy would invite the enemy to go after each part in detail. On the other hand, his shift to the Pee Dee might discourage the backcountry people whose assistance he needed in the field: he expected no large Continental reinforcement for

3. Francis V. Greene, *General Greene* (New York, 1897), 174; Greene to Sumter, Dec. 12, 1780, Draper Papers, 7VV135, State Hist. Soc. of Wis.

4. Greene to Samuel Huntington, Nov. 2, 1780, Papers of the Continental Congress, No. 155, I, 459-60, National Archives.

some time, and he feared the Tories might be tempted to take up arms after his withdrawal. Morgan's detachment would animate the patriots, help keep down the Loyalists, and harass Cornwallis's rear and left flank should the British General turn on Greene.[5]

Morgan received his marching orders on December 16. He was to cross to the west side of the Catawba River, call out the militia under Thomas Sumter and William Davidson, and then take post between the Broad and Pacolet rivers. As the two wings of the American army would be separated by 140 miles, Greene wisely avoided giving Morgan minute instructions but merely advised him to act offensively or defensively, letting "prudence and discretion" be his guides. Above all, Greene urged Morgan to guard against a surprise blow, believing it very possible that Cornwallis would divide his army and drive Morgan from his left flank before beginning his push into North Carolina.[6]

On December 21, the day after Greene's departure for the Pee Dee, Morgan headed westward, forded the Catawba, tramped over hills and through swamps, crossed the Broad, and on Christmas Day established a camp on the north bank of the Pacolet River at Grindal's Shoals. Toward evening Morgan greeted sixty new volunteers, South Carolina militia under tall, raw-boned Colonel Andrew Pickens, a man of known competence. In contrast to Morgan, Pickens, a Presbyterian elder, bore a grave countenance and spoke little. It is said that he put his words "between his fingers, and examined them before he uttered them."

5. Sparks, ed.,*Correspondence of the Revolution*, III, 189-91; Greene to Steuben, Dec. 28, 1780, Greene Letter Book, Oct.-Dec. 1780, Lib. Cong.

6. Graham, *Morgan*, 260-61. Possibly Davidson influenced Greene to send a Continental detachment into western South Carolina. In Nov. 1780, Davidson had advanced a detailed plan for Morgan almost identical to the one Greene formed in Dec. Chalmers G. Davidson, *Piedmont Partisan: The Life and Times of General William Lee Davidson* (Davidson, N. C., 1951), 98-99.

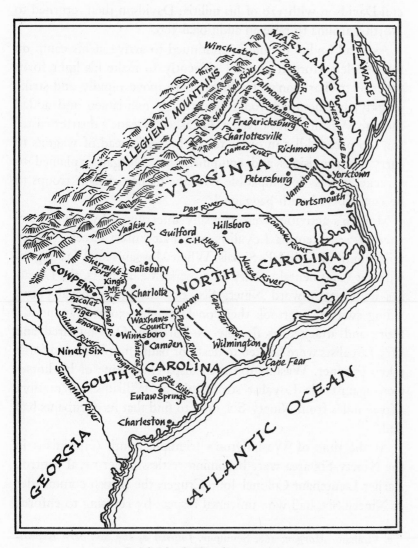

Service in the South, 1780-1781

The next week Morgan's force was further augmented by General Davidson with 120 of his militia; Davidson then returned to North Carolina to raise an additional 500.[7]

As small bodies of militia continued to arrive at his camp on the Pacolet, Morgan worked diligently to make his light force superior to Tarleton's. To enable it to move rapidly and strike quickly, he mounted 100 rifle-carrying militiamen and added them to Washington's cavalry. He asked Greene's quartermaster for 100 packsaddles in order to use horses instead of wagons to carry his provisions and equipment. As Morgan explained to Greene, it was "incompatible with the nature of light troops to be encumbered with baggage." [8]

Morgan's activities were partially interrupted by the appearance of 250 Georgia Loyalists near Fair Forest Creek, twenty miles south of Grindal's Shoals. When Morgan sent Washington with the Continental cavalry to disperse the invaders, the Loyalists withdrew toward Ninety-Six. But the plump cavalryman, riding swiftly, overtook them on December 30 at Hammond's Store and attacked as fiercely as Tarleton. One hundred and fifty Loyalists were hacked to death or badly mutilated and forty taken prisoner. Washington then dispatched some of his horsemen against the Loyalist stronghold at Williams's Plantation, fifteen miles from Ninety-Six, only to find that its occupants had fled.[9]

At the time of Washington's triumph, South Carolinians in the Ninety-Six area were becoming restless under royal control. Earlier Lieutenant Colonel John Cruger, the British commander at Ninety-Six, had won universal respect by refusing to enforce

---

7. Graham, *Morgan*, 268; Seymour, *Journal of the Southern Expedition*, 11-12; Thayer, *Greene*, 305; Davidson, *Piedmont Partisan*, 104-5.

8. Morgan to Greene, Dec. 31, 1780, Graham, *Morgan*, 268-69.

9. *Ibid.*, 267-68; John W. Barnwell, ed., "Letters of John Rutledge," *South Carolina Historical and Genealogical Magazine*, 18 (1917), 65.

one of Cornwallis's harshest proclamations, that all who had previously fought against the King must actively support British forces in order to warrant paroles. But a wave of angry resentment swept through western South Carolina when Loyalist parties began to pillage and burn the property of their rebel neighbors, causing many who had put down their arms, including Andrew Pickens and his followers, to once more take the field. Advancing to assist these patriots, a band of Georgians under Elijah Clarke and William Few was repulsed by British and Loyalist troops at the battle of Long Canes on December 11, 1780. Soon afterward the Georgians broke up into small groups and scattered throughout the back country.[10]

The Georgians were veterans of numerous skirmishes, and Morgan was eager to have them join his light corps. There were few things that enlisted men would not do for Morgan, and when he addressed a stirring appeal to the Georgians, they responded warmly. He played upon their pride and bravery, at the same time admonishing them for becoming separated and consequently serving no useful purpose. This message shows how Morgan instilled fighting spirit into his troops, and how he dealt with partisans, who were accustomed to operating independently of Continental forces:

Gentlemen, Having heard of your sufferings, your attachment to the cause of freedom, and your gallantry and address in action, I had formed to myself the pleasing idea of receiving in you, a great and valuable acquisition to my force. Judge then of my disappointment, when I find you scattered about in parties subjected to no orders, nor joining in any general plan to promote the public service. The recollections of your past achievements, and the prospect of future laurels should prevent your acting in

10. Edward McCrady, *The History of South Carolina in the Revolution, 1780-1783* (New York, 1902), 18-23; William O. Foster, "James Jackson in the American Revolution," *Georgia Historical Quarterly,* 31 (1947), 257.

such a manner for a moment. You have gained a character and why should you risk the loss of it for the most trifling gratifications. You must know, that in your present situation, you can neither provide for your safety nor assist me in annoying the enemy. Let me then entreat you by the regard you have for your fame, and by your love to your country, to repair to my camp, and subject yourselves to order and discipline. I will ask you to encounter no dangers or difficulties, but what I shall participate in. Should it be thought advisable to form detachments, you may rely on being employed on that business, if it is more agreeable to your wishes: but it is absolutely necessary, that your situation and movements should be known to me, so that I may be enabled to direct them in such a manner, that they may tend to the advantage of the whole.[11]

After vigorously rounding up able militia, Morgan was ready for action—there had been too much inactivity in past months for his warm blood. His plan was to stab through the back country at Savannah in north Georgia. He did not expect to hold the ground permanently—he would need to draw back to act in conjunction with Greene should the occasion arise—but he felt that even a limited triumph would encourage scores of South Carolinians and Georgians to shoulder their muskets; nothing attracted irregulars like an occasional victory. And Cornwallis's already shaky hold on Ninety-Six would become more precarious if the area teemed with partisans.

Though at liberty to act on his own, Morgan asked Greene if he objected to the Georgia raid, pointing out that in any event he would have to give up his station on the Pacolet. The influx of new recruits made it difficult to find sufficient food and forage in that vicinity. A retreat into North Carolina was one solution, but such a maneuver in Morgan's opinion would

11. T. U. P. Charlton, *The Life of Major General James Jackson* (Augusta, 1809), 24-25; Febiger to Greene, Feb. 18, 1781, Febiger Letter Book, Va. State Lib.

put a damper on the growing spirit of resistance in the back-woods.[12]

While Morgan waited impatiently for Greene's reply, his food shortage grew more acute because of trouble with Thomas Sumter. Greene had instructed Morgan to call on Sumter's followers for help in getting provisions. But when Morgan detached a Captain Chitty to seek out Colonel William Hill of Sumter's command, Chitty reported back that Hill refused to take directions from Morgan or any Continental officer; Hill had maintained these were Sumter's orders. This development infuriated Morgan, and though he knew that Sumter was temperamental, he also knew that both Greene and Governor John Rutledge of South Carolina had urged the little "Gamecock" to co-operate. In a tactful letter to Sumter, Greene had praised the guerrilla leader but tried to show him that small raids, however important, never won wars: "You may strike a hundred strokes and reap little benefit from them, unless you have a good army to take advantage of your success."

If Morgan's first reaction to Chitty's message was to give Sumter a sample of his temper, he soon thought better of it. He was in Sumter's country and needed all the support he could muster. He turned the problem over to Greene.

Greene cautiously sounded Sumter out and concluded that the South Carolinian resented Morgan's failure to inform him fully of the objectives of the light corps in the Broad-Pacolet region. Sumter also believed Morgan possessed orders to assume direct command of his partisans. Actually, as Governor Rutledge had assured Sumter, Greene was anxious for him to fight under Morgan. Sumter was then at his home supposedly recuperating from a wound he received the previous November in opposing Tarleton's Legion. Greene felt he was sulking, unduly

12. Morgan to Greene, Jan. 4, 1781, Graham, *Morgan*, 274-75.

prolonging his convalescence. At any rate, he rendered very little assistance of any kind to Morgan.[13]

For the moment Morgan's attention was diverted from his supply problem. From Greene came news of British regiments under Major General Alexander Leslie landing at Charleston and marching to join Cornwallis at Winnsboro. Fearful that this reinforcement would encourage Cornwallis to hammer at Morgan's corps, Greene repeated his prior warning to watch for a surprise attack, and, recalling the scattering of Gates's army after Camden, advised Morgan to designate a rendezvous in case of defeat. Greene was beginning to worry about his west wing under Morgan, which was so far from his own force at Cheraw. The Southern commander's letters to Morgan took on a patronizing tone: use good men for sentries; employ scouts; keep spies near the enemy ("short persons" would not arouse suspicion); expect little from militia in battle; write regularly.[14]

Apparently Morgan failed to resent Greene's remarks—Gates too had been free with superfluous advice. But Greene's decision that his corps should remain where it was did upset him. As Greene viewed the situation, Cornwallis would soon push against his own division of the Southern army, in which case Morgan could not annoy the enemy's flank if the light corps retired from its present location. Morgan, however, had his own British threat to worry about. On January 14, American reconnaissance parties reported that an enemy force under Tarleton was sweeping northward across the Enoree and Tiger rivers toward Morgan's encampment. Similarly Morgan learned that Cornwallis's main

13. Rutledge to Sumter, Dec. 20, 1780, and Andrew Pickens to Henry Lee, Nov. 25, 1811, Draper Papers, 7VV146, 1VV108, State Hist. Soc. of Wis.; Greene to Sumter, Jan. 8, 1781, Sumter Papers, Lib. Cong.; Morgan to Greene, Jan. 15, 1781, Graham, *Morgan*, 285; Sumter to Greene, Jan. 29, 1781, *S. C. Hist. and Geneal. Mag.*, 16 (1915), 97-99; Anne K. Gregorie, *Thomas Sumter* (Columbia, S. C., 1931), 128-33.

14. Greene to Morgan, Jan. 3, 4, 1781, Myers Coll., N. Y. Pub. Lib.

army was advancing up the east bank of the Broad River "like Bloodhounds" after prey. Leaving scouts at the fords on the Pacolet, he pulled back ten miles toward the Broad and established a temporary camp at Burr Mills on Thicketty Creek. But many of his militia were widely dispersed between the Broad and the Pacolet; the shortage of food made it impossible to keep them in a compact body.[15]

His anxiety increasing, Morgan wrote Greene on the evening of the 15th, telling of Tarleton's approach and reminding him that provisions were scarce. Even with an adequate supply, he added dejectedly, it would be almost "beyond the art of man" to keep the militia from straggling. Nothing he could accomplish would equal the risk he faced by remaining in upper South Carolina. Requesting Greene to recall the light corps, Morgan suggested the possibility of leaving Pickens's and Davidson's militia to hold down the Loyalists, since Tarleton would not likely go after such a small force. As Morgan was concluding his letter, he obtained a report that Tarleton's troops were regulars, and he added a final sentence: "We have just learned that Tarleton's force is from eleven to twelve hundred British." Even then a dragoon was racing across country with a dispatch from Greene to Morgan. In it Greene had written, "Col. Tarleton is said to be on his way to pay you a visit. I doubt not but he will have a decent reception and a proper dismission."[16]

Tarleton's maneuver against Morgan had begun two weeks before when Cornwallis rushed his lieutenant to the defense of Ninety-Six. The British General had feared that Washington's victory over the Georgia Loyalists indicated Morgan was about

15. Greene to Morgan, Jan. 8, 1781, and Morgan to Greene, Jan. 19, 1781, Graham, *Morgan*, 273, 309; Morgan to William Snickers, Jan. 26, 1781, Gates Papers, N. Y. Hist. Soc.

16. Greene to Morgan, Jan. 13, 1781, and Morgan to Greene, Jan. 15, 1781, Graham, *Morgan*, 275, 285-86.

to besiege the garrison. Though Tarleton discovered that Morgan was nowhere near Ninety-Six, he saw that Cornwallis could not afford to begin another invasion of North Carolina with Morgan in position to hit the British flank and rear or to sweep down on Ninety-Six. Accordingly, he proposed to force Morgan into battle or, failing in that, to drive him over the Broad River, where Cornwallis, coming up the east bank, could corner him.

Cornwallis agreed and gave his subordinate 200 men of the 7th Regiment, 50 of the 17th Light Dragoons, and a few artillerymen with two light pieces. Since Tarleton already had his Legion of 550 and 200 of the 71st Regiment, his total command now numbered nearly 1,100 rank and file. He started forward on January 6; Cornwallis left two days later. Heavy rains, swelling creeks and rivers, delayed both British forces so that Tarleton did not get beyond the Enoree and Tiger rivers until the 14th. Cornwallis, meanwhile, slowed his pace to allow Leslie, then struggling through the swamps along the Pee Dee River, to catch up with him. Tarleton hurried on toward the Pacolet, unaware that Cornwallis was waiting for Leslie. When he neared it on the 15th, he learned that Morgan had abandoned Grindal's Shoals but had left men to watch the fords on the river. That night Tarleton resorted to a stratagem. After traveling upriver for three hours, causing Morgan's patrols to follow him on the opposite bank, he silently wheeled about and traversed the stream at unguarded Easterwood Shoals.[17]

Early the next morning pickets rushed into Morgan's camp with word that Tarleton had crossed the Pacolet and was heading for the American position. Morgan shouted for the wagons to be loaded. The men, preparing breakfast around small fires, scrambled to their feet, and soon the little army was ready to move. Morgan set out in the direction of the Broad River, his

17. Bass, *Green Dragoon*, 142-51; Tarleton, *Campaigns of 1780 and 1781*, 210-13, 218-20.

troops eating their half-cooked food as they went. He pushed them as rapidly as possible, bawling commands to the teamsters and the men on foot, while Washington's cavalry rode on the flanks and scouted in front and rear. But the roads were rough, several swamps lay ahead, and by sunset the Americans were still five miles from the Broad. Earlier in the day Morgan had hoped to cross the river and occupy the rough country near Thicketty Mountain before dusk. There he wanted to make a stand against Tarleton. Now a passage would be difficult because darkness was fast falling, and the river was swollen from recent rains. Tarleton might surprise the Americans and cut their rear to pieces.[18]

Morgan resolved to spend the night on the west side of the Broad at a place known as the Cowpens, where Carolina farmers grazed their cattle before sending them east to market. The Cowpens was a long, gently sloping ridge covered with open woods of red oak, hickory, and pine. Beyond the crest of the ridge was a swale extending northward for eighty yards. Then came a smaller ridge behind which the ground gradually leveled into a plain, stretching toward the Broad River. Morgan knew he would have to fight there if Tarleton caught up with him that night or early the following morning. The open woods would give Tarleton room to maneuver his cavalry, and there were no swamps or thickets to protect the American flanks. It was "certainly as proper a place for action as Lieutenant colonel Tarleton could desire," wrote Tarleton in his memoirs. "America does not produce many more suitable to the nature of the troops under his command." [19]

18. *Ibid.*, 213-14; Morgan to Snickers, Jan. 26, 1781, Gates Papers, N. Y. Hist. Soc.; memoir of Thomas Young, in Joseph Johnson, *Traditions and Reminiscences Chiefly of the American Revolution in the South* (Charleston, 1851), 449.

19. Tarleton, *Campaigns of 1780 and 1781*, 221.

Because Morgan received criticism for his choice of ground, he offered a defense of his location in later years, failing to mention that he had originally intended to oppose Tarleton on the east side of the Broad River:

> I would not have had a swamp in the view of my militia on any consideration; they would have made for it, and nothing could have detained them from it. And as to covering my wings, I knew my adversary, and was perfectly sure I should have nothing but downright fighting. As to retreat, it was the very thing I wished to cut off all hope of. I would have thanked Tarleton had he surrounded me with his cavalry. It would have been better than placing my own men in the rear to shoot down those who broke from the ranks. When men are forced to fight, they will sell their lives dearly. . . . Had I crossed the river, one half of the militia would immediately have abandoned me.[20]

Whatever the truth of his statement, Morgan was anxious for a stroke at Tarleton, and while he wanted the battle near Thicketty Mountain, he was not afraid to engage his antagonist at the Cowpens. Morgan was a fighter by nature, utterly fearless of physical danger. William Washington, a brave officer himself, said he had never seen a man more collected in time of peril than Morgan. The big ex-teamster had great confidence in himself as a battlefield commander—even when his force included militia. A former militiaman, he had led such troops many times before in this war as well as earlier. Moreover, the Southern frontier militia equated his activities with light infantry with the hit-and-run operations they preferred. They also considered the old wagoner one of them; he too was a backwoodsman and had the speech and manners of the ranks. In the preceding fall two large bodies of Southern militia had asked permission to serve under him; one, the band that had destroyed

20. Johnson, *Greene*, I, 376.

Ferguson's force at King's Mountain.[21] A contingent of these same King's Mountain patriots was with Morgan at the Cowpens; they were Davidson's North Carolinians under the immediate direction of Major Charles McDowell. Morgan also had other veteran militia: the Georgia partisans, the Virginians (who were former Continentals), and Pickens's South Carolinians.

Morgan realized that these men were capable guerrilla fighters; they were excellent shots with the musket and rifle. With the exception of the Virginians, however, they could not be counted on if forced to perform in open battle against the military formations of Tarleton's regulars; so Morgan devised a plan that would make the most of their ability with firearms without compelling them to stand for long in combat.

He placed his scheme on paper for his officers to see: his main line—composed of the Continentals and the seasoned Virginia and Georgia militia under Howard—at the crest of the southern and higher elevation; his second line—formed of the bulk of the militia commanded by Pickens—150 yards down the slope; his third line—made up of a small body of skirmishers with rifles—150 yards in front of Pickens. Behind these three lines, in the swale between the elevations, he intended to station Washington's cavalry, to be used wherever necessary.

Morgan's disposition of his troops was far from orthodox in that he posted his most unreliable units far in advance of the main line of defense. But Morgan thought he knew his militia, and he told his officers how he proposed to use this formation in the event Tarleton attacked. When the British drew near, the skirmishers in the front line were to open a scattered fire and then fall back into Pickens's line. After being joined by the skirmishers, Pickens's men were to hold their fire until the enemy ad-

21. Brent to Sparks, Aug. 22, 1827, Sparks Papers, Harvard College Lib.; Clark, ed., *State Records of North Carolina*, XIV, 663-64; Boyd, ed., *Jefferson Papers*, IV, 40.

vanced within fifty yards of them. Then they were to take careful aim and shoot twice, attempting to pick off Tarleton's officers. Having completed this assignment, they were to retire in good order around the left side of Howard's main line to a position where they were to be re-formed and held in reserve.[22]

Since the success of this plan of battle depended upon the militia, Morgan himself told them of their assignments. He moved from campfire to campfire, explaining his plan, and talking and joking with the men about the prospects of defeating Tarleton. The old wagoner could crack his whip over "Ben," but he needed help. If they held up their heads and fired twice, he exclaimed, they could seek the protection of Howard's bayonets. And if Tarleton's dragoons came after them, "Billy" Washington's cavalry would cover their escape. Victory would bring them glory, he continued, and when they returned home, the old folks would cheer them and the girls would kiss them. Morgan's appeal was effective; the men crowded around, assuring him that he could count on their support. "It was upon this occasion," said Major Thomas Young, who had watched Morgan mingle with the men, that "I was more perfectly convinced of General Morgan's qualifications to command militia, than I had ever before been." Far into the night, as additional militia units arrived at the Cowpens, Morgan repeated his rounds of the campfires. "I don't believe he slept a wink that night," wrote Young.[23]

22. Memoir of Samuel Hammond, in Johnson, *Traditions and Reminiscences of the Revolution*, 526-30; Johnson, *Greene*, I, 378-79; Morgan to Greene, Jan. 19, 1781, Graham, *Morgan*, 309-10.

23. Young's memoir, in Johnson, *Traditions and Reminiscences of the Revolution*, 449; "Memoir of Thomas Young, A Revolutionary Patriot of South Carolina," *The Orion*, 3 (1843), 88.

CHAPTER IX

Cowpens and Its Consequences

W HILE the Americans prepared for the possibility of battle at the Cowpens, Tarleton's force halted for a few hours' sleep at Morgan's former camp on Thicketty Creek. During the night British pickets captured a patriot militia officer who informed Tarleton that Morgan was heading toward the Broad River; later intelligence confirmed the man's story. Fearing that Morgan would escape if allowed to cross the river unmolested, Tarleton ordered his wagons loaded and at three A.M. set out after his opponent. He experienced Morgan's earlier difficulties with the roads which ran through cuts and ravines. Behind the infantry his wagons mired in the ruts, causing whole companies to halt and push them forward. At length, instructing his teamsters to follow at a slower pace, he moved ahead with his cavalry and infantry.

An hour before daylight a reconnaissance party reported that Morgan was encamped at the Cowpens, five miles away. Calling in his guides, Tarleton inquired of the ground Morgan occupied and of the country in his rear. In his memoirs, he said: "These people described both with great perspicuity: They said that the woods were open and free from swamps; that . . . part of Broad River . . . was about six miles distant from the enemy's left flank, and that the river, by making a curve to the westward, ran parallel to their rear." [1]

1. Tarleton, *Campaigns of 1780 and 1781*, 215; Bass, *Green Dragoon*, 153, 155.

Soon afterward the American scouts warned Morgan that Tarleton was only five miles away and advancing rapidly. Morgan shouted to his troops, "Boys, get up, Benny's coming." After a hurried breakfast the officers arranged their units according to plan, and Morgan went to each line and spoke to the men. To the skirmishers in front of Pickens, he said, "Let me see which are most entitled to the credit of brave men, the boys of Carolina or those of Georgia." Moving to Pickens's militia, he delivered a fiery speech, pounding his fist into his palm as he spoke. He expected to see their usual zeal and courage, and he reminded them not to withdraw until they had fired twice at close range. His words to Howard's line were equally impassioned: "My friends in arms, my dear boys, I request you to remember Saratoga, Monmouth, Paoli, Brandywine, and this day you must play your parts for your honor & liberty's cause." Battlefield oratory was not uncommon in the eighteenth century, but it was seldom more effectively employed. Morgan struck a spark in his men. The often unpredictable militia were, as one American officer wrote, "all in good spirits and very willing to fight." [2]

Astride his horse, behind Howard's Continentals, Morgan caught sight of green-jacketed dragoons moving among the dense foliage at the far end of the slope; they were followed by infantrymen in scarlet and white. It was now about seven A.M. As the British gathered at the edge of the open wood, Tarleton sent a detachment of dragoons to disperse Morgan's skirmishers. When the horsemen approached the Americans, they received

2. Graham, *Morgan*, 297, 309; Morgan to Snickers, Jan. 26, 1781, Gates Papers, N. Y. Hist. Soc.; memoirs of Joseph McJunkin and Christopher Brandon, Draper Papers, 23VV189-90, 23VV235, State Hist. Soc. of Wis.; Henry Lee, *Memoirs of the War in the Southern Department*, ed. R. E. Lee, 2d ed. (London, 1869), 227; Henry Lee, Jr., *The Campaign of 1781 in the Carolinas* (Philadelphia, 1824), 96n.; Seymour, *Journal of the Southern Expedition*, 13.

a volley that emptied fifteen saddles, and the survivors galloped to their rear. At this point Tarleton began forming his battle line, without having clearly ascertained Morgan's dispositions. Although his men were fatigued, he found them eager to attack, confident they could destroy Morgan's detachment. Ordering his rank and file to discard all gear and equipment except their guns and ammunition, he formed his light infantry on the right, the Legion infantry in the center, and the 7th Regiment on the left. In the center he also posted his artillerymen with their two small guns. At the same time he placed fifty dragoons on each flank. One hundred and eighty yards to the rear of this line, to act as a reserve, he stationed the bulk of his cavalry and the 71st Regiment.[3]

As drums rolled and fifes shrilled, the British "Raised a prodigious yell, and came Running at us as if they Intended to eat us up," said Morgan. "They give us the British halloo, boys," he shouted, "give them the Indian whoop." The American skirmishers fired a few scattered shots before drifting back into Pickens's line. At Pickens's command, the militia loosed a deadly blast that momentarily staggered Tarleton's force. When the enemy came on again, their bayonets raised for a charge, the militia filed off toward the left end of Howard's line, as Morgan had instructed them. The retreat, orderly at first, became disorganized when Tarleton sent the dragoons on his right flank to disperse the militia. At the moment, the troops composing Pickens's far right had only reached the center of the field. Private James Collins feared his "hide" would soon be "in the loft," but Morgan, seeing the enemy horsemen dash forward, ordered Washington's cavalry to drive them away. As Tarleton's men rode among the Americans, Washington's horsemen struck with such force that the British soon fled. Though Washington pur-

3. Tarleton, *Campaigns of 1780 and 1781*, 216; Roderick Mackenzie, *Strictures on Lt. Col. Tarleton's History* (London, 1787), 97, 107.

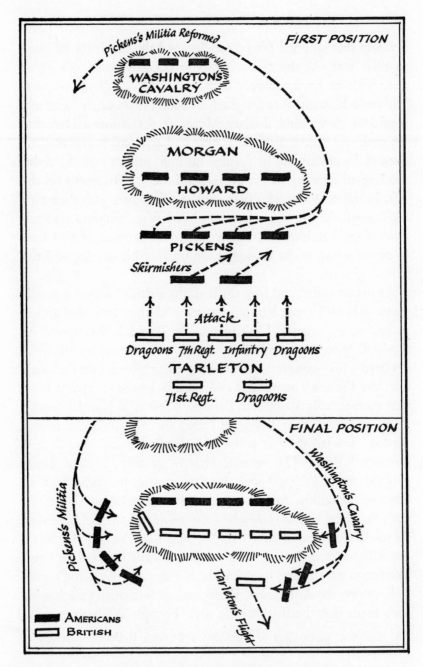

The Battle of the Cowpens, January 17, 1781

sued them, Collins reported they were as hard to catch as a "drove of wild Choctaw steers." [4]

Meanwhile, Morgan had galloped to the end of Howard's line to rally the militia. While brandishing his sword and shouting encouragement to the last units to leave the field, he saw that many of the irregulars were heading for their horses near the second elevation. Riding after them, he shouted, "Form, form, my brave fellows.... Old Morgan was never beaten." Assisted by Pickens, Morgan managed to halt most of the militia, and the two officers began to assemble them just behind Howard's men. [5]

Tarleton, taking the withdrawal of the militia for flight, regrouped his Legion and sent it up the slope. Howard's veterans gave the enemy a "well-directed and incessant fire," wrote Morgan in his battle report to Greene; while Tarleton declared, "The fire on both sides was well supported and produced much slaughter." Finding that Howard's line stood firm, the British commander called up his reserve regiment, the 71st, and deployed it on his extreme left. Since the 71st now extended beyond the American right, Howard ordered the Virginia and Georgia companies on his far right to turn to their left, wheel about, and engage the flanking regiment. These instructions resulted in some confusion, and the militia began retreating toward the second elevation. The rest of the line, believing Howard had called for a general disengagement, followed the Virginians and Georgians to the rear, all the American units retiring in good order. Morgan dashed up to Howard, who explained the situation.

4. Morgan to Snickers, Jan. 26, 1781, Gates Papers, N. Y. Hist. Soc.; Young's memoir, in Johnson, *Traditions and Reminiscences of the Revolution*, 450; [James P. Collins], *Autobiography of a Revolutionary Soldier*, ed. John M. Roberts (Clinton, La., 1859), 57.

5. "D. Wallace's History of Union...," Draper Papers, 13VV188-89, State Hist. Soc. of Wis.; [Collins], *Autobiography of a Revolutionary Soldier*, 57.

Both officers considered the retrograde movement advantageous, for it extricated Howard's right from the flanking threat.[6]

Sensing still another advantage, Morgan rode ahead of Howard's men and chose a location for them to turn around and fire a blast at the pursuing British. Tarleton's men had observed the Americans falling back and thought victory at hand. In their eagerness to overtake their foe, they broke ranks and surged forward in disorder. Washington, returning from his pursuit of the dragoons, sent word to Morgan and Howard that he would charge the British if Howard gave them a volley. Howard's troops had just reached the position selected by Morgan; Morgan ordered them to halt and face about. When Howard shouted the command to fire, the Americans blazed away at the onrushing British, only ten or fifteen yards distant. Taken completely by surprise, the line of red and green staggered, at which point Howard yelled for a bayonet charge. Then, as Washington's cavalry crashed down upon Tarleton's right, Morgan and Pickens threw the re-formed militia at his left.[7]

The result was a double envelopment, perfectly timed. The British were thrown into a "panic," admitted Tarleton. Morgan watched many of the Legion infantry and the light infantry drop their muskets and cartridge boxes and take to their "heels for security—helter-skelter." When the Continentals pushed forward, the cry "Tarleton's Quarter" is said to have sounded, but there was no useless slaughter, for Morgan and Howard shouted that quarter was to be given. In the center the British surrendered, while those who had fled to the rear were headed off by Washington's cavalry. Simultaneously, a detachment of Con-

6. Morgan to Greene, Jan. 19, 1781, Graham, *Morgan*, 468; Tarleton, *Campaigns of 1780 and 1781*, 216.

7. William Moultrie, *Memoirs of the American Revolution* (New York, 1802), I, 117; Hugh McCall, *The History of Georgia* (Savannah, 1811-1816), II, 357-58; Johnson, *Greene*, I, 380-81; Graham, *Morgan*, 468-69.

tinentals, led by Lieutenant Thomas Anderson of Delaware, captured the enemy artillery. On the American right the 71st Regiment, composed of Scottish Highlanders, continued to fight. Finally, with Pickens's militia hammering at one flank and Howard's troops at the other, its commander, Major Archibald McArthur, yielded his sword.[8]

At this point Tarleton's only hope of averting disaster was to bring up his reserve dragoons. Galloping toward them, he had his horse shot from under him. Mounting another, he soon reached the dragoons but found they were frightened and confused by the flight of his foot soldiers. "All attempts to restore order, recollection, or courage, proved fruitless," he said. "Above two hundred dragoons forsook their leader, and left the field of battle." Yet fourteen officers and forty horsemen heeded his call, and he rashly decided to make a stand against Washington's cavalry. For a moment Washington and Tarleton engaged each other in combat. Morgan described the encounter: "Tarleton & two of his Officers Charged Coll. Washington; Tarleton fired both his pistols at Washington & wounded his Horse[,] ... before two of Washington's men came up & cut the two Officers very much—Tarleton cleared himself by the swiftness of his Horse." Realizing the battle was lost, Tarleton called to his dragoons to follow and raced from the field. While Washington, chasing after the enemy, took the wrong road, Tarleton came upon part of his baggage that had been left in the care of a party of Tories. Seeing that they were looting his wagons, he drove them away, set fire to the wagons, and hurried to join Cornwallis, who was encamped at Turkey Creek, twenty-five miles away.[9]

8. Tarleton, *Campaigns of 1780 and 1781*, 217; Morgan to Snickers, Jan. 26, 1781, Gates Papers, N. Y. Hist. Soc.; see also the sources cited in the preceding footnote.

9. Tarleton, *Campaigns of 1780 and 1781*, 218; Morgan to Snickers, Jan. 26, 1781, Gates Papers, N. Y. Hist. Soc.; Graham, *Morgan*, 469; Bass, *Green Dragoon*, 159-60.

At the Cowpens, Morgan was so elated that he picked up his nine-year-old drummer boy and kissed him on both cheeks. His joy had in no way diminished a few days later when he informed his friend William Snickers of the outcome. "When you left me," he wrote, "you remember that I was desirious to have a stroke at Tarleton—my wishes are gratified & [I] have given him a devil of a whipping, a more compleat victory never was obtained." He had "entirely Broke up Tarleton's Legion," which was the "flower" of Cornwallis's army. As Morgan told Snickers, his victory was "a great thing Indeed." With fewer than 1,000 troops opposing Tarleton's 1,100, the husky frontiersman had gained one of the most decisive American triumphs of the war. British losses in men amounted to 110 killed and 702 captured as against Morgan's 12 killed and 60 wounded. The Americans also took 2 field pieces, 2 regimental flags, 35 wagons, 100 horses, and 800 muskets, plus 70 Negroes who had been officers' servants.[10]

Word of the success of January 17 quickly spread to all parts of the country. Morgan's aide, Major Edward Giles, dispatched northward with the news, admitted that he was so excited over the good tidings he forgot to inform Governor Jefferson. Abigail Adams elatedly wrote Mercy Warren that Morgan was now "the rising Hero in the South." A North Carolinian in Philadelphia declared that the military men there considered the battle one of the "most well conducted actions of the war." Greene, too, praised Morgan's arrangements, assuring Sumter that no contest during the Revolution had been "more glorious or more timely." The Virginia House of Delegates resolved to present him a saber and a horse with accompanying "furniture." Perhaps most gratifying of all to Morgan was the response of the

10. "From the Diary of a deceased officer of the Revolution," Draper Papers, 29CC100, State Hist. Soc. of Wis.; Morgan to Snickers, Jan. 26, 1781, Gates Papers, N. Y. Hist. Soc.; Graham, *Morgan*, 469.

Continental Congress. The lawmakers thanked him and his command for their "complete and important victory" and voted him a gold medal. (William Washington and Howard were to receive silver medals and swords and Pickens a sword.) [11]

Cornwallis, meanwhile, was severely jarred by the loss of the Tory Legion, which had been a bulwark of strength to him during the siege of Charleston, at Camden, and in operations against the South Carolina partisans. He wrote Clinton that it was "impossible to foresee all the consequences that this unexpected and extraordinary event may produce"; and to Lord Rawdon he confided that the "late affair" had almost broken his heart. Tarleton placed part of the blame for his catastrophe on Cornwallis, arguing that his superior should not have waited for Leslie to join the main army, that instead Cornwallis should have been in a position to pin Morgan against the Broad River when the Legion attacked. Tarleton, however, failed to mention that he had earlier expressed the opinion that his corps alone was capable of destroying Morgan's force. Moreover, he had erred in making his customary head-on assault, for in recklessly throwing his men forward he had received heavy casualties at the beginning of the battle. Still, he had a real chance for victory at the time Howard's men became confused and started to withdraw. But in his eagerness to strike a telling blow, he had lost control of his troops when they broke ranks and dashed after the Americans. The stage was set for Howard's line to face about and fire and for Washington and Pickens to attack the enemy flanks.[12]

Though Tarleton's mistakes helped pave the way for his

11. Boyd, ed., *Jefferson Papers*, IV, 441*n*.; *Warren-Adams Letters*, II, 166; Griffith J. McRee, *Life and Correspondence of James Iredell* (New York, 1857), I, 486; Greene to Sumter, Jan. 30, 1781, Draper Papers, 7VV190, State Hist. Soc. of Wis.; Ford, ed., *Journals of Congress*, XIX, 246-47; *Journals of the House of Delegates*, [1781], 19.

12. Bass, *Green Dragoon*, 160; Tarleton, *Campaigns of 1780 and 1781*, 219-20.

reversal, they hardly lessened Morgan's contribution to the final outcome. Morgan's courage and confidence, as well as his compelling personality, enabled him to gain the utmost service from militia unaccustomed to open-field fighting. Realizing their limitations, he had adopted a plan of battle specifically designed for them. It was also decidedly to Morgan's credit that he recognized Tarleton's errors and was able to achieve the double envelopment of the British flanks. Morgan's successful use of militia at the Cowpens influenced Nathanael Greene to try similar tactics in deploying regulars and militia together in open battle. Both at Guilford Courthouse and Eutaw Springs the Southern army commander stationed large numbers of militia in front of his main line of defense, and while his success with irregulars on these occasions was less than Morgan's at the Cowpens, these contests were extremely costly to the British.[13]

But however impressive his performance, the question for Morgan that cold, raw morning at the Cowpens was this: could he preserve his victory by escaping from Cornwallis? Morgan assumed the British General would attempt to destroy his light corps and free the Cowpens prisoners. Encumbered with Tarleton's men and equipment, Morgan knew that additional offensive operations were out of the question. Nor could he join Greene, for Cornwallis's position was such that the British could intercept any movement eastward. Consequently, Morgan decided to retreat toward the fords of the Catawba River in North Carolina, where he expected militia reinforcements under General Davidson and where he hoped to hear from Greene.

Morgan ordered part of Pickens's militia to remain behind under a flag of truce to care for the wounded and bury the dead.

13. A useful discussion of the militia's importance in this theater of the war is by Robert C. Pugh, "The Revolutionary Militia in the Southern Campaign, 1780-1781," *William and Mary Quarterly*, 3d Ser., 14 (1957), 154-75.

While Dr. Richard Pindell, a physician serving with the light corps, directed their work, other troops collected the enemy's abandoned muskets and tents. Some clothing also fell into Morgan's hands, though hardly of sufficient quantity to clothe all his ragged men.[14]

Early in the afternoon of January 17 Morgan left the Cowpens and bivouacked that night on the north side of the Broad River at Cherokee Ford. Up and away before dawn, he marched rapidly, sighting Gilbert Town, North Carolina, by dusk. Fearing that Cornwallis might be close behind, he sent a detachment with the prisoners northward toward Island Ford on a branch of the Catawba, instructing his men to avoid the enemy if possible and to meet his own force at Sherrald's Ford on the main stream. He then pushed due east over roads that were frozen ruts at night, yet deep with mud by noonday. On the 23rd, having gotten over the Catawba, he made camp at Sherrald's Ford. He had traveled a hundred miles and traversed two rivers in slightly more than five days, no mean pace for a corps short of food and shoes. It was in such circumstances that Morgan was at his best. If this hasty retreat was hardly as grueling as the march to Quebec, it was difficult enough. As in the Maine wilderness, Morgan seemed indefatigable, helping his men here and there, and cheering them on with praise for their industry and spirit. He did this despite a recurrence of his sciatica, mild at first but now considerably worse, probably because of his strenuous activity.[15]

Since he had no authoritative word of Cornwallis, Morgan decided to rest and reorganize his small command on the Catawba.

14. N. B. W., ed., "Captain Samuel Shaw's Revolutionary War Letters to Captain Winthrop Sargent," *Pa. Mag. of Hist. and Biog.*, 70 (1946), 321; Pickens to Henry Lee, Aug. 28, 1811, Draper Papers, 1VV1075-76, State Hist. Soc. of Wis.

15. *Journal and Order Book of Capt. Kirkwood*, 13; Seymour, *Journal of the Southern Expedition*, 15; "Journal of Lieutenant Thomas Anderson," *Historical Magazine*, 2d Ser., 1 (1867), 209; Graham, *Morgan*, 328.

If possible, he hoped to continue there until he received instructions from Greene. Presently Morgan got a dispatch from Dr. Pindell enclosing letters from Tarleton and Robert Jackson, a redcoat surgeon's mate who had been captured at the Cowpens. Though Tarleton requested permission to send medical aid to his wounded, Jackson believed the British could not be adequately cared for as prisoners and asked that they be paroled. Perhaps Morgan was influenced by his high opinion of Jackson, who had performed his duties without regard to his own personal safety during the battle—after the surgeon's mate had surrendered, Morgan treated him with respect and allowed him to tend the wounded. In any case, Morgan accepted the proposal and had Jackson released without parole. Courage and bravery Morgan recognized in any man, friend or foe.[16]

While waiting at Sherrald's Ford, Morgan thought of sending Pickens south on a raiding expedition that would temporarily divert Cornwallis from his own corps. Morgan considered ordering Pickens to intercept a shipment of cloth bound from Charleston to the British garrison at Ninety-Six, as well as destroy British draft horses in the Congaree region. South Carolina's Governor Rutledge, offering Morgan his "warmest and most cordial thanks" for the Cowpens victory, also favored a diversion in his state and suggested that Morgan strike at Ninety-Six. Such a venture, Rutledge slyly pointed out, would probably give Morgan's troops an opportunity to carry the Governor's own slaves away from that post. Morgan evinced no enthusiasm for Rutledge's scheme. Then reliable news of Cornwallis caused him to abandon the idea of dividing his force.[17]

16. *Ibid.*, 328-29; "A Militant Surgeon of the Revolution. Some Letters of Richard Pindell, M. D.," *Maryland Historical Magazine*, 18 (1923), 316-18; Bass, *Green Dragoon*, 163-64.

17. Greene to Morgan, Jan. 13, 1781, and Morgan to Greene, Jan. 23, 1781, Graham, *Morgan*, 329-32; Rutledge to Morgan, Dec. 22, 1780, Jan. 14, 25, 1781, Myers Coll., N. Y. Pub. Lib.

Cornwallis had heard rumors of Tarleton's disaster the night after the battle. They were confirmed early the next morning when the remnants of the Legion galloped into camp, just as Leslie's reinforcements appeared. According to an American prisoner who reputedly witnessed Tarleton's report to Cornwallis, the British General leaned forward on his sword as he listened to his subordinate. Angered by what he heard, he pressed so hard that the sword snapped in two, and he swore loudly that he would recapture Morgan's prisoners no matter what the cost.[18]

At any rate, Cornwallis, with his entire army, headed for the Cowpens on the 19th, only to discover a day later the real direction of Morgan's flight. Had Tarleton's fast and far-ranging Legion been intact, Cornwallis would hardly have needed twenty-four hours to determine his error. Slowed by his heavy supply train, he failed to reach Ramsour's Mill until the 25th, two days after Morgan's arrival at Sherrald's Ford. With no mobile unit to corner Morgan and hold him at bay, Cornwallis's sole recourse was to strip his army of all non-essentials and employ it as a light force. He demolished his baggage, provisions, and rum, and set his men an example by burning his personal possessions before their eyes. He spared only salt, ammunition, medical supplies, and four ambulances. Then, having risked the future efficiency of his army, he resumed his chase.[19]

Morgan, meanwhile, waited nervously for some message from Greene. He believed the two divisions of the American Southern army should come together and perhaps offer Cornwallis battle in order to prevent the British General from conquering North

18. McJunkin's memoir, Draper Papers, 23VV193, State Hist. Soc. of Wis.

19. A. R. Newsome, ed., "A British Orderly Book, 1780-1781," *North Carolina Historical Review*, 9 (1932), 284-96.

Carolina and uniting with a redcoat raiding party in Virginia under Major General William Phillips.

Morgan wrote three letters to Greene on the 25th concerning reports that Cornwallis had reached Ramsour's Mill. In the second one, he declared, "I am convinced Cornwallis will push on till he is stopped by a force able to check him." Using one of his familiar phrases, he vigorously asserted that he would "do every thing in my power" to obstruct the enemy's advance. By the time he sent his third dispatch, written at two P.M., he had word that the British were already moving from Ramsour's in the direction of the Catawba. But after sending his prisoners and baggage to Salisbury on the road to the Yadkin River, he learned that Cornwallis was still at Ramsour's, burning his supplies. Soon Morgan was reinforced by 800 militia under General Davidson who had taken advantage of the bargaining spirit of his Scotch-Irish neighbors by offering them credit for three months' duty provided they remained with him for six weeks.[20]

Southern militia, though valuable when properly used, were unreliable for extended periods of service with Continentals, especially long distances from their own communities. Davidson's force appeared just as Morgan's veteran Virginia militia, whose enlistments had expired, departed for their homes. The South Carolina irregulars further depleted Morgan's command by returning to their state, some to look after their families, others to engage in partisan warfare under their own leaders. Morgan, however, could depend upon Davidson's men through the existing emergency. He stationed them at various fords along the river with orders to block the crossings with felled trees. Davidson himself watched the principal ford, Beattie's, left open as an escape route for citizens fleeing ahead of the oncoming British, while Howard's Continentals guarded at Sherrald's.

20. Morgan to Greene, Jan. 25, 1781 (three letters of that date), Graham, *Morgan*, 335-36; Davidson, *Piedmont Partisan*, 110-11.

Though Morgan was confined to bed by his sciatica, his sense of duty would not permit him to relax. From the tent that served as his headquarters, he gave instructions for erecting the river defenses, sent his prisoners northward into Virginia to keep them out of Cornwallis's reach, and issued a call for all militia companies in the area to rally to him. He informed Greene on the 28th that "nothing in my power shall be left undone to secure this part of the country, and annoy the enemy as much as possible." As rumors reached Morgan on the 29th that the British were about to resume their advance, he left his bed, despite a high fever and the protests of his aides. Mounting his horse with difficulty, he rode to inspect his defenses. He could see Cornwallis's forward detachments on the opposite bank of the Catawba, but heavy rains had swollen the river so that a crossing without boats was impossible.[21]

One hundred and twenty-five miles away, at his camp on the Pee Dee River, Greene had waited anxiously for a report on Tarleton's thrust at Morgan. On January 23, one of Morgan's officers arrived with news of the Cowpens triumph. Greene was elated, but he knew he must act quickly to extricate Morgan from a precarious situation. He canceled his first plan to draw Cornwallis's attention by striking at Ninety-Six, when he realized the term of service of Brigadier General Edward Stevens's Virginia militia was about to end. Then he decided that to assist Morgan as well as obstruct Cornwallis he must combine the two wings of his army somewhere in North Carolina. Accompanied only by an aide, a guide, and a sergeant's guard of cavalry, Greene set out through Tory-infested country to join the force on the Catawba. Before leaving he had instructed his quartermaster to assemble boats on the Dan River, along the border between North Carolina and Virginia, for use in the event

21. Morgan to Greene, Jan. 28, 29, 1781, Graham, *Morgan*, 336-37.

of a retreat. Brigadier General Isaac Huger of South Carolina, left in command on the Pee Dee, was to lead the main army toward Salisbury.[22]

Greene, tired and mud-spattered, dashed into Morgan's camp on the 31st. The two commanders of the American Southern army, accompanied by Davidson and William Washington, traveled a short way from the camp, seated themselves on a log, and held a council of war. The Catawba was falling rapidly, and within a few hours Cornwallis would undoubtedly try a crossing; the militia were not present in as large numbers as had been hoped; Davidson's men were mostly inexperienced; and Morgan's regulars were fewer than 300. Though details of this meeting have not survived, the officers obviously felt that the east bank of the river could not be held against a British onslaught. The council concluded that Davidson, with a reputation for quick escapes, should conduct a delaying action to give Morgan and his Continentals time to head for Salisbury and the Yadkin, where they would meet the main army.[23]

Sometime after midnight, before putting his column in motion, Morgan returned to his tent and by candlelight wrote an apprehensive letter to Governor Jefferson:

The British army are on the ... [far] side of the River and I with my Little Detachment on the other. I think they will attempt to cross this morning. Never the less, we have filled up all the fords and thrown every obstruction immaginable in their way, they are in force and I have about two hundred and thirty Reguler infantry, and about sixty horse, Genl. Davidson near five hundred [800] Malitia. The inhabitents seem to make a stir, what they will do is unceartain, but I fear not much. Genl. Green arrived yesterday, he has ordered his little army to join us, they are not more than seventeen or eighteen hundred. This number

22. Williams to Morgan, Jan. 25, 1781, *ibid.*, 323.
23. W. Graham, *J. Graham*, 289.

and my detachment when join'd will be much inferior to the enemy, who must be Near three thousand, well supplyd and provided for, and our men almost Naked.

Great god what is the reason we cant Have more men in the field—so many men in the country Nearby idle for want of employment. How distressing it must be to an anxious mind to see the country over Run and destroyed for want of assistance which I am realy afraid will be the case if proper exertion are not made. . . . I have been so harassed and exposed this winter that I am entirely emmaciated. An old pain in my breast and Hip aceazed me so that [I] shant be of much use in the field this winter—if [e]ver I am, but as I have been broke down in the services of my country [I] shall bear the infirmitys of old age with more satisfaction.[24]

Long before daylight Morgan's troops were on the road to Salisbury. With only brief periods of rest they marched thirty miles, "every step being up to our Knees in Mud—it raining On us all the Way," declared Lieutenant Thomas Anderson. Morgan withdrew none too soon, for at one o'clock in the morning Cornwallis had assembled his men for an attack. Sending one division under Lieutenant Colonel James Webster to make a feint at Beattie's Ford, he personally led the other in smashing across the Catawba at Cowan's, a private ford six miles from Beattie's. Davidson was killed, and his men were dispersed. Some of them, gathering a few miles away at Tarrant's Tavern, were routed by Tarleton, who that day had instructed his newly formed corps to "remember the Cowpens." After barely escaping capture, Greene, who had stayed behind to supervise Davidson's retreat, hurried after Morgan.[25]

On February 3, Greene and Morgan passed through Salisbury,

24. Morgan to Jefferson, Feb. 1, 1781, Boyd, ed., *Jefferson Papers,* IV, 495-96.

25. "Journal of Lieutenant Thomas Anderson," *Historical Magazine,* 2d Ser., 1 (1867), 209; Tarleton, *Campaigns of 1780 and 1781,* 226.

finding that Huger was nowhere in that vicinity, and came to Trading Ford on the Yadkin, seven miles beyond the town. Though Greene had foreseen that boats were stored there for such an emergency, rain and wind had churned the river into foam-crested waves, and a crossing would be extremely hazardous. It was a desperate choice: traversing the river or standing and fighting. The American commanders were expecting General Stevens's homeward-bound Virginia militia. Even with the Virginians, whom Stevens himself called cowardly—"Their greatest Study is to Rub through their Tower [tour] of Duty with whole Bones"—Greene and Morgan would have been decidedly outnumbered. Gambling on getting over the turbulent waters, they found that luck was with them; apparently not a man or boat was lost.[26] That same day Cornwallis's advance units reached the river and exchanged shots with the last of the American rear guard as it set out across the river.

The day's exertions were evidently too much for Morgan. That night a physician, Dr. William Read, visited Morgan in his tent. The commander was lying on leaves and covered with a blanket, "rhuematic from head to feet." Read was concerned to see Morgan at the water's edge later in the evening, inquiring about one of his reconnaissance parties.[27]

The next morning Morgan, with most of his men, started for Guilford Courthouse, leaving Cornwallis waiting impatiently for the Yadkin to fall. While Greene organized the rear guard, Morgan pushed his troops the forty-seven miles to Guilford in forty-eight hours; they marched on short rations during a continuous rain. Besides his sciatica, Morgan now suffered from hemorrhoids. His "piles" made him so uncomfortable that he could not sit on his horse. "This is the first time that I ever ex-

26. Boyd, ed., *Jefferson Papers*, IV, 561-62.
27. R. W. Gibbs, ed., *Documentary History of the American Revolution* (Charleston, S. C., and New York, 1853-1857), I, 277-78.

perienced this disorder," he lamented to Greene, "and from the idea I had of it, [I] sincerely prayed that I might never know what it was." Though disabled, he did his utmost to assist Greene. He assigned men to repair the carriage of a field piece, and he sent out baggage wagons to collect forage, corn, wheat, and other provisions.[28]

Greene, all the while, was watching Cornwallis. On learning his antagonist was rushing north to cut off his escape into Virginia, Greene directed Huger, still on his march from the Pee Dee, to join Morgan at Guilford, which Huger made on February 9. With the American Southern army once more united under Greene, Morgan prepared to return home to recover his health. As he told Greene, "nothing will help me but rest"; continuing in this strenuous campaign would totally disable him from further army duty. His last official service under Greene was to attend a council of war that discussed the feasibility of Greene's 2,000 troops making a stand against Cornwallis's 2,500. By unanimous vote the council resolved that the retreat should be continued over the Dan River into Virginia. As a matter of courtesy, Greene asked Morgan to direct a recently organized light force that was to act as his rear guard, an offer Morgan regretfully declined; the position then went to Otho Williams. Morgan's assistance was also requested by patriot leaders in the Charlotte area, who unsuccessfully petitioned Greene to have Morgan take charge of their militia.[29] On February 10, as Greene began his race to the Dan, he announced in general orders that

28. *Journal and Order Book of Captain Kirkwood,* 13; Seymour, *Journal of the Southern Expedition,* 16; Morgan to Greene, Feb. 6, 1781, Graham, *Morgan,* 354-55; Morgan to Greene, Feb. 7, 1781, photostat in the possession of Dr. Joseph Fields, Joliet, Ill.

29. Morgan to Greene, Jan. 24, 1781, Graham, *Morgan,* 354; proceedings of Greene's council of war, Feb. 9 or 10, 1781, Papers of the Continental Congress, No. 155, I, 569, National Archives; Lee, *Memoirs of the War in the Southern Department,* 237; Johnson, *Greene,* I, 412-13.

Morgan would have a leave of absence until able to fight again.[30]

Morgan also left Guilford Courthouse that day, traveling by a direct route toward Fredericksburg, Virginia. Accompanying him were "Nat" and "Toby," two Negro slaves captured at the Cowpens, both of whom were to serve him for the rest of his life. Behind him were over four months' service with the Southern army in the Carolinas, a period mainly of gloom for the American cause in that theater of the war. With the exception of King's Mountain, the one outstanding patriot victory was achieved by Morgan at the Cowpens. Though compelled to leave the army, Morgan knew he had insured his victory: his prisoners were beyond Cornwallis's grasp, and his light detachment was reunited with Huger's division.[31]

Moreover, Morgan's Cowpens triumph and his successful retreat wrought momentous consequences. Two British officers, Charles Stedman and Roderick Mackenzie, asserted that the destruction of Tarleton's Legion was an important factor in accounting for Cornwallis's failure to gain a complete victory at the subsequent battle of Guilford Courthouse and for his eventual downfall in Virginia. In any case, it was Tarleton's defeat that had spurred Cornwallis into a reckless pursuit of Morgan in which he destroyed most of his equipment and abandoned South Carolina, a province Clinton had urged him to hold at all cost. Instead Cornwallis undertook his second North Carolina invasion, which ended in disaster at Yorktown. William Gordon, the future historian of the Revolution, wrote prophetically: "Morgan's success will be more important in its distant consequences, than it was on the day of victory." [32]

30. Graham, *Morgan*, 358.
31. Suit Papers, Packet 14.
32. Charles Stedman, *The History of the Origins, Progress, and Termination of the American War* (London, 1794), 324-25; Mackenzie, *Strictures on Tarleton's History*, 88-89; Eric Robson, an English historian,

Morgan's performance helped to make Greene's division of the Southern army brilliant strategy. Greene's reputation would have plummeted with those of Lincoln and Gates—his Southern predecessors—had the enemy demolished Morgan's corps and then routed his own command. That he submitted himself to these dire possibilities is explained by more than his desire to split his army and undertake guerrilla warfare; the answer also lies in the fact that Greene, a canny judge of men, recognized Morgan as the one subordinate he trusted to operate independently at a great distance from his own encampment and very near that of the enemy. Morgan had fulfilled Greene's confidence to the utmost. As the Rhode Islander remarked after Morgan left the Southern army, "Great generals are scarce—there are few Morgans to be found." [33]

---

believed the Legion's destruction virtually equal to the loss of a complete army. *The American Revolution* (New York, 1955), 100; see also Robson, "British Light Infantry in the Mid-Eighteenth Century: the Effect of American Conditions," *Army Quarterly*, 62 (1950), 209-22; Mass. Hist. Soc., *Proceedings*, 2d Ser., 62 (1930), 452.

33. Graham, *Morgan*, 395.

CHAPTER X

Defending the Old Dominion

MORGAN was greatly dejected at having to retire at this point in the Southern campaign. He believed that Greene needed him more than ever before, for Cornwallis would probably overtake the Southern army and compel it to fight. Once Morgan even toyed with the idea of turning back and rejoining the American forces. But, as he explained to Greene, that was impossible, for his pains were now accompanied by a high fever.

His journey over the rough roads of back-country Virginia proved so slow and painful that he twice stopped for a few days' rest. From the home of Brigadier General Robert Lawson, Morgan informed Greene that he was doing his best to persuade the militia in southern Virginia to take the field. He predicted they would turn out in strength. Later, after halting at one Carter Harrison's, Morgan's anxiety for Greene increased. He bluntly wrote his superior how he could win a pitched battle against Cornwallis. Since the Southern army would contain many militia, their performance would be decisive. It was highly "advisable" to put all the veteran militia in line with the regulars and station sharpshooters on the flanks and well in front of the Continentals. Between these forces Greene should place the bulk of the militia, with picked men behind them to shoot down the first man who tried to flee. "If anything will succeed, a disposition of this kind will." Basically, this was the battle plan Morgan used at the Cowpens.[1]

1. Morgan to Greene, Feb. 17, 20, 1781, Graham, *Morgan*, 370.

Reaching Frederick County by late February, Morgan spent March and April at home. Though cold baths relieved his physical ailment, his mental attitude continued apprehensive. He longed for news of Greene, but weeks passed without any word. In a long and impassioned letter Morgan unburdened himself to Jefferson. Nothing outside heaven would give him more pleasure than to aid Greene at this "critical juncture," he exclaimed. All he could do now was request Jefferson's permission to recruit a troop of cavalry in Frederick County.

Morgan was also troubled by the state of his finances. Having received no salary since going to the Southern army in September 1780, he pleaded with Jefferson to find out whether some of his back pay was available. He had previously asked the state's auditors to advance him part of his money, but they had denied him on the grounds of not having the date of his brigadier general's commission. Morgan, never one to bother with petty details, told Jefferson that the ways of bureaucrats were beyond him. If the money were forwarded on account, why would the date matter? Not only was he almost in "poverty" because of taxes and army expenses; he also felt concern over reports that the state would no longer provide any clothing for officers. In Morgan's opinion, now was hardly the time to halt this practice, for he and others had drawn no issues in some months, whereas many had. Could the politicians in Richmond not find a coat and a pair of stockings for a veteran so "bare of cloaths" he was ashamed to appear in public? [2]

To make his point, the old wagoner had doubtless exaggerated. But while his business transactions of the following year indicate he was not as financially strained as he averred, he had undeniably felt a serious pinch because of his salary being in arrears, to say nothing of wartime inflation and the dearth of hard money

2. Morgan to Jefferson, Mar. 23, 1781, Boyd, ed., *Jefferson Papers*, V, 218-19.

in Virginia. To some extent his physical ailment and absence from the service may have stoked his unhappiness. Often temperamental, he seldom hid his feelings when he considered himself wronged.

Besides appealing to Jefferson, Morgan tried still other measures to improve his personal fortunes. He sent the Board of War a certificate for a sum of money due him in return for providing the Southern Department with a quantity of his own corn at a time when no one else in his community would give the government credit. He also requested final payment for the horse he had sold the previous September while on his way to join the Southern army. Duncan Rose, of Petersburg, who had purchased the animal, confided to Jefferson that Morgan's family was hard-pressed for the money.[3]

Early in April, Morgan finally received a letter from Greene reviewing in detail his activities following the flight from Guilford Courthouse. With Cornwallis close behind, Greene had barely escaped across the Dan River. Cornwallis, sorely needing the supplies he had destroyed in his chase after Morgan, did not pursue him. In Virginia, Greene obtained more Continentals and, as Morgan had predicted, a heavy militia reinforcement. He returned to North Carolina and clashed with Cornwallis at Guilford Courthouse in a battle that Greene described to Morgan as "bloody and severe." Greene's arrangements show he accepted Morgan's advice, his main line consisting of Continentals with two lines of militia in their front. But in his dispositions Greene made one serious error: his forces were too far apart to enable the militia to make an orderly retreat if pressed. (From front to rear, 300 and 400 yards respectively separated

3. Morgan to [William Grayson], Mar. 22, 1781, Papers of the Continental Congress, No. 78, XVI, 147-48, National Archives; Ford, ed., *Journals of Congress*, XIX, 393; Rose to Jefferson, Mar. 3, 1781, Boyd, ed., *Jefferson Papers*, V, 53.

Greene's three lines as compared with the 150-yard intervals between Morgan's three lines at the Cowpens.) After the North Carolina militia—Greene's advance force—fired two rounds, they fled the field. The Virginia irregulars, holding the second line, thinned the redcoats with a withering fire but were soon pushed aside. The heaviest fighting took place at the line held by the Continentals. Cornwallis was unable to drive the Americans from their position, but he held against their counterattacks, and eventually Greene gave up the field. The British victory came at the expense of 93 killed, 413 wounded, and 26 missing. Greene informed Morgan that his own losses, 78 killed and 183 wounded, were "much less" than the enemy's.[4]

Greene's letter brought an enthusiastic reply from Morgan, who found "great satisfaction" in these statistics. He exclaimed that he was proud to have served with the Southern army and with Greene.[5] Though Southern army prospects seemed brighter, Morgan was chagrined and angry to find mounting opposition to high taxes, impressments, and drafts from the militia in western Virginia. He might complain about taxes himself, fume over his back pay, and ask for a suit of clothes, but actually obstructing the Revolution was another matter. Opposing superior armies was less depressing to him than disaffection at home. If ever the laws were "trampled on with Impunity," only then would he "despair." Morgan assured Jefferson that such was not likely to happen in Frederick County: he had personally warned certain discordant elements that he would tolerate no rebellious conduct, and the people knew him to be a man of his word.[6]

4. Greene to Morgan, Mar. 20, 1781, Graham, *Morgan*, 372-73. For accounts of the Guilford Courthouse battle, see Wallace, *Appeal to Arms*, 236-39; Ward, *War of the Revolution*, II, 777-94; Montross, *Rag, Tag and Bobtail*, 412-16.

5. Morgan to Greene, Apr. 11, 1781, Graham, *Morgan*, 373-74.

6. Morgan to Jefferson, Mar. 23, 1781, Boyd, ed., *Jefferson Papers*, V, 218-19.

In neighboring Hampshire County discontent erupted in violence. A state official, attempting to impress beef and draft men, was driven out by an angry mob. To celebrate their triumph, the malcontents got hilariously drunk, then damned Congress, toasted George III, and talked of joining Cornwallis. When local authorities tried to arrest them, they were supported by other dissatisfied persons, many of them carrying guns.

It is probable that few of these Hampshire men were British sympathizers. Still, they refused to surrender their arms, and their aims were unclear to county officials. That such flagrant conduct, if allowed to pass without notice, would elicit similar responses to impressments and drafts was abundantly clear to Valley patriot leaders. When a militia army drawn from several counties marched against the Hampshire insurgents, Morgan was in command. Word of his approach brought the uprising to a sudden end. Most of the disgruntled men, including their principal leader John Claypool, gave themselves up, and the remainder fled.[7]

Leaving his command under his friend Christian Febiger, now a resident of western Virginia, Morgan hurried home in preparation to rejoining Greene's Southern army. His good health during the campaign in Hampshire County had convinced him of his fitness for more strenuous duty. While at his farm, Morgan learned that all the Hampshire rebels who had voluntarily surrendered would be freed except John Claypool and several other instigators. Claypool, a Scotsman, was a prominent farmer and before the outbreak was generally recognized as an honest and upstanding man. After turning himself over to the authorities, he begged Morgan to help him obtain a pardon, acknowledging his recent error and promising to obey the laws of Virginia. Morgan wrote the Governor that "Humanity as well as policy" required him to speak in favor of Claypool: he was the father of

7. Eckenrode, *Revolution in Virginia*, 246-49.

fourteen children; he could be depended on to prevent another revolt because the people respected him and would follow his example; he would encourage the last of the rebels to emerge from hiding and submit themselves to the authorities. Though Claypool's request was rejected by the Virginia Executive Council, he eventually was released.[8]

Morgan was still at home when he received a letter from Lafayette that completely changed his plans. With "the freedom of an old and affectionate friend," the Marquis pleaded for Morgan's assistance. He was at Richmond with 3,000 regulars and militia. Menacing the town were 7,200 redcoats under Cornwallis, who, several weeks after Guilford Courthouse, had marched into Virginia, taking charge of all British forces there. Desperately needing reinforcements, Lafayette wanted Morgan to raise a contingent of riflemen and personally assume command. "I ever [have] had a great esteem for riflemen," he assured his friend, and nothing would give him more pleasure than to have Morgan at his side. On June 2, the Virginia House of Delegates also called on Morgan to enlist a body of civilians and militia to perform under Lafayette.[9]

With Cornwallis abandoning the Carolinas, Morgan saw the

8. Febiger Letter Book, correspondence for May 1781, Va. State Lib. Morgan's letter cited herein was his second appeal for Claypool. According to Claypool, the first letter was lost, and the Scotsman persuaded Morgan to write another. Presumably the second message repeated the arguments in the earlier one. Claypool to Morgan, May 31, 1781, Myers Coll., N. Y. Pub. Lib.; Graham, *Morgan*, 381; Morgan to Benjamin Harrison, Feb. 10, 1782, William W. Palmer, ed., *Calendar of Virginia State Papers and other Manuscripts* (Richmond, 1875-1893), III, 57-58; David Jameson to Morgan, Feb. 27, 1781, Gaillard Hunt, ed., *Fragments of Revolutionary History* (Brooklyn, 1892), 23-24; Greene to Lafayette, June 17, 1781, Greene Papers, Lib. Cong.

9. Lafayette to Morgan, May 27, 1781, Graham, *Morgan*, 375-76; Jefferson to Morgan with enclosures, June 2, 1781, Boyd, ed., *Jefferson Papers*, VI, 70, 71n., 72n.; *Journals of the House of Delegates*, [1781], 1-10.

struggle in the South centering in the Old Dominion. Here in his own state his presence was needed most and his opportunity for glory greatest. Writing on June 7 to a friend, Morgan announced triumphantly, "I have now taken the field." With the same zeal he displayed in battle, he threw himself into the work of raising his force.[10]

First, he sought advice and aid from several back-country leaders: General Gates, three county lieutenants, and his friend of long standing, the Reverend Charles Mynn Thruston. They met with Morgan at Winchester on June 14 and recommended to the legislature that magazines for provisions and military equipment, to be used by Lafayette, be established at Winchester and nearby towns. To provide for Morgan's immediate needs, they suggested that the assembly undertake a series of actions: empower the authorities to make and collect all kinds of army gear; obtain horses for cavalry purposes; authorize Morgan to employ skilled workmen; allow Morgan's commissaries and quartermasters authority to obtain food and clothing; and pass a forceful measure for raising troops, since the critical condition of spring crops and the approaching harvest season would discourage the inhabitants from volunteering in large numbers. Most of these proposals were already under consideration in the legislature, and several were presently enacted into law.[11]

Morgan plunged ahead as best as he could. He secured cavalry horses, mostly by impressment. He boasted to Thomas Nelson, who had succeeded Jefferson as governor, that the three troops of dragoons he had raised would ride the fastest mounts in western Virginia. He took time from his own work to assist Major William Nelson's state cavalrymen, who had halted at Winchester to have their animals shod and acquire equipment.

10. Morgan to Taverner Beale, June 7, 1781, *Pa. Mag. of Hist. and Biog.*, 21 (1897), 488.

11. Boyd, ed., *Jefferson Papers*, VI, 71*n.*, 72*n.*

Since there were no public funds available in Winchester, the local artisans refused to take care of Nelson's troop until Morgan promised to make good the bill should the state's auditors fail to honor it. Morgan's most difficult task was to obtain volunteers for his infantry. As his advisors at Winchester had predicted, the crop situation and the nearness of harvest time reduced enlistments.

The delays he encountered provoked the speakers of the two houses of the assembly to urge him to speed his preparations. Lafayette, retreating northward in the face of the British advance, was thirteen miles from Charlottesville, and though 700 south Valley riflemen had joined the Frenchman, the legislators believed still other frontier militia would come forth when Morgan appeared in the field—"they wish to be commanded by you." Speaking of these same irregulars, Colonel John Smith remarked to Horatio Gates that they earnestly desired Morgan as their leader.[12]

Morgan assured Governor Nelson on June 26 that he had wasted no time. He had spent the weeks recruiting good men and equipping them adequately. In North Carolina, he had seen regiments of ill-clad militia, some almost completely without weapons, arrive at the Southern army encampments. These men had been virtually useless, and Greene had pointedly warned Jefferson never again to offer him such miserable soldiers. Morgan was sure the militia he was raising would be much better off than most he had encountered in the war.

Morgan admitted to Nelson that his biggest disappointment was not being able to raise 2,000 men. The Governor could not "conceive how reluctantly the people leave their homes at this

12. Morgan to Nelson, June 26, 1781, Charles Roberts Autograph Coll., Haverford College Lib.; Palmer, ed., *Virginia State Papers*, II, 162-63; Graham, *Morgan*, 383-84; Smith to Gates, June 18, 1781, Gates Papers, N. Y. Hist. Soc.

time of year." Morgan felt the urgency of time more than he cared to tell the Governor. He feared the youthful Lafayette lacked the training and combat experience to oppose the veteran Cornwallis in battle. Finally, late in June, with as many able riflemen and dragoons as he could muster, Morgan struck off at a rapid pace to overtake the Marquis and steady him in the event of action.[13]

Meanwhile, Lafayette, realizing he was in no position for a full engagement, had nimbly avoided Cornwallis's grasp. At Ely's Ford on the Rapidan River, he was reinforced by Anthony Wayne and 1,000 Pennsylvania Continentals. Cornwallis, after detaching Tarleton and John Graves Simcoe on raiding expeditions, retired through Richmond in the direction of Jamestown. Up to this point Morgan could have found little to criticize in Lafayette's performance. But now the Marquis misjudged the enemy's withdrawal, taking it as a sign of Cornwallis's reluctance to engage his increased American army, whereas the Briton was actually slipping down the coast to be in closer contact with Clinton in New York. Having added fresh militia under Baron von Steuben, Lafayette followed Cornwallis closely, and on July 6, he threw Wayne with the advance units at what he thought was only the British rear guard preparing to cross to the south side of the James.

It was a rash step that could have been fatal to Lafayette's entire army. Cornwallis, anticipating this stroke, had sent only his baggage over the river and had concealed the bulk of his force in a strip of woods behind his rear guard. In the opening stages of the contest Wayne met with success before finding that Cornwallis's overwhelming numbers were fanning out to encircle him. His eventual escape resulted from his own sterling performance, the approaching darkness, and Cornwallis's wish to con-

13. Morgan to Nelson, June 26, 1781, Roberts Coll., Haverford College Lib.; Smith to Gates, June 18, 1781, Gates Papers, N. Y. Hist. Soc.

tinue toward Portsmouth, which he reached without further interruption.[14]

Ironically, Morgan rode into Lafayette's camp the day after the battle. Morgan must have thought the near catastrophe with Cornwallis bore out his view of Lafayette's military immaturity, but he greeted the Marquis warmly. Morgan was genuinely fond of the young man, whom he had not seen since the fall of 1778, when Lafayette was about to return to France on a visit. Just before sailing, the Marquis had written Morgan not to forget his friend "on the other side of the great water." [15]

Taking post at Malvern Hill, about equal distance between Richmond and Williamsburg, the Americans entered a period of inactivity, marked only by the efforts of Lafayette and his subordinates to strengthen their forces. Morgan wrote several letters to the Governor about additional accouterments for his cavalry.[16] He also brought a personal matter to Nelson's attention. He had discovered that the state's auditors had refused to accept the bill of the Winchester artisans who had equipped Major Nelson's cavalry. According to Morgan, the auditors had said that he had allowed the workmen to charge the state an exorbitant sum; he would have to pay the money himself. Morgan, who remembered that the auditors had withheld his back pay, was in a fury when he unfolded the story to the Governor. He wondered what these officials who fought from behind desks in Richmond knew about the realities of war. Major Nelson's cavalry had come to Winchester for aid when Tarleton and Simcoe were devastating the Virginia countryside. They had needed help quickly, and he had seen that they got it. There was no time to haggle about prices—

---

14. Lafayette's campaign is treated fully in Louis Gottschalk, *Lafayette and the Close of the American Revolution* (Chicago, 1942), 189-306.

15. Lafayette to Morgan, Nov. 28, 1778, Graham, *Morgan*, 224.

16. Morgan to Nelson, July 12, 1781, Myers Coll., N. Y. Pub. Lib.; Palmer, ed., *Virginia State Papers*, II, 215, 242.

"Trifles" never won wars. The Governor considered Morgan a man of sound sense who, in his brusque way, had a knack for getting to the heart of a problem. At Nelson's instigation, the state government promised to settle the account in question.[17]

At Malvern Hill, Continental cavalry and light troops increased Morgan's unit. But Morgan's sciatica had returned to plague him so badly that it was only a question of time before he would once again have to return home. He did not hesitate, however, to accept an important assignment that promised action. Tarleton was on a raiding expedition in Bedford and Amelia counties, and Lafayette hoped Morgan and Wayne could head off the dashing cavalryman and bring him to battle. Morgan hurried to Goode's Bridge on the south side of the James River, only to find Tarleton opposed to engaging him in further combat. Tarleton, his new Legion decidedly inferior to his original one destroyed at the Cowpens, swept in a wide arc around Morgan and Wayne on his ride back to Portsmouth.[18]

Though Morgan had notified both Nelson and Nathanael Greene as early as July 24 of his being "broke down," he did not give Lafayette a candid account of his condition before returning to Malvern Hill about July 31. As long as he had a chance for a blow at Tarleton, Morgan would have struggled against illness.[19]

After receiving a furlough and returning home, Morgan probably gave little thought to Lafayette's activities or, for that matter, to anything but his health. Several months later he wrote to an old army friend in terms that indicate he had been fighting for his life. Though still in the "land of the living," as he lightly

17. *Ibid.*, 473; Morgan to Nelson, Nov. 25, 1781, Harvard College Lib.
18. Lafayette to Wayne, July 15, 1781, Wayne Papers, N. Y. Pub. Lib.; Gottschalk, ed., *Lafayette's Letters to Washington*, 208.
19. Palmer, ed., *Virginia State Papers*, II, 473; Morgan to Greene, July 24, 1781, Greene Papers, Clements Lib., Univ. of Mich.; Lafayette to Wayne, July 29, 1781, Wayne Papers, Hist. Soc. of Pa.; Graham, *Morgan*, 393-94.

phrased his survival, he had dropped to the "very lowest stage of life." He had relapsed five times and each time had a "glimmering glimpse" of eternity. Twice he had "literally peeped into the other world." Unafraid of death, he nevertheless hated to "quit the stage" because of illness; a warrior like himself could die "more gloriously" in combat. But his sturdy constitution had "baffled" death—"that grand enemy to mankind." [20]

During his illness Morgan had received gratifying letters from Lafayette and Greene. "You are the general and the friend I want," wrote Lafayette, "and both from inclination and esteem, I lose a great deal when you go from me, and will think it a great pleasure and a great reinforcement to see you again." But do not depart "so soon as to expose your health," he cautioned. Greene's letter was equally complimentary. After Cornwallis had marched to Virginia to create a new theater of operations, Greene had turned toward the conquest of the enemy posts in South Carolina and Georgia. Though repulsed by Lord Rawdon near Camden and at Ninety-Six, the Americans had gained several sparkling triumphs in the South, including the capture of British garrisons at Forts Motte, Granby, Orangeburg, Georgetown, and Augusta. Yet Greene said that the patriot successes would have been greater had Morgan been in the field with him. Unaware that Morgan had left the service, Greene advised him to "Nurse your old bones and stick by the marquis, until the modern Hannibal [Cornwallis] unfolds his great designs. While you and Wayne are with him, I think he will be well supported, and I shall feel perfectly easy." [21]

Even as Greene's letter was traveling northward by courier, Lafayette's campaign in Virginia took on a new complexion.

20. Morgan to Butler, Jan. 17, 1782, Draper Papers, 27CC69, State Hist. Soc. of Wis.

21. Lafayette to Morgan, Aug. 15, 1781, and Greene to Morgan, Aug. 26, 1781, Graham, *Morgan*, 395-98.

General Washington, with most of his army and French forces from Rhode Island under Comte de Rochambeau, was speeding toward Virginia in hopes of hemming Cornwallis in by land, while French Admiral de Grasse blockaded him by sea. Though lacking authoritative knowledge of Washington's plan, Morgan was convinced the war in Virginia was approaching a climax. Frustrated by the thought of missing an exciting campaign in which he could demonstrate his military prowess, he poured out his feelings to the Commander in Chief in a letter of September 20:

I know you can have but little leisure for private letters—but the feelings of my heart will not permit me to be silent... I wish you success, and how much I wish that the state of my health would permit me to afford my small services on this great occasion. Such has been my peculiar fate, that during the whole course of the present war, I have never, on any important event, had the honor of serving particularly under your excellency. It is a misfortune I have ever sincerely lamented. There is nothing on earth [that] would have given me more real pleasure than to have made this campaign under your excellency's eye, to have shared the danger, and let me add, the glory too.[22]

Apparently Washington was genuinely moved by this letter, which, he wrote in reply, "breathes the Spirit and Ardor of a Veteran Soldier, who, tho impaired in the Service of his Country, yet retains the Sentiments of a Soldier in the firmest Degree." "Be assured," he added, "that I most sincerely lament your present Situation, and esteem it a peculiar Loss to the United States, that you are at this Time unable to render your Services in the Field."[23]

Morgan's presence in eastern Virginia, however, would have

22. Morgan to Washington, Sept. 20, 1781, *ibid.*, 399.
23. Washington to Morgan, Oct. 5, 1781, Fitzpatrick, ed., *Writings of Washington*, XXIII, 174.

counted little. Cornwallis was effectively cornered at Yorktown; and on October 19, 1781, he surrendered his army of 7,000 men, while his bands appropriately played "The World Turn'd Upside Down." Farther south, Greene had largely confined the enemy to Charleston and Savannah, where they remained until hostilities ended.

Morgan derived "unspeakable satisfaction" from Cornwallis's capitulation. When a large contingent of the British prisoners was brought to Winchester for confinement, he at first assisted in making arrangements for them and then took charge of the operation. Huts and barracks erected near Winchester for red-coats imprisoned there earlier in the war proved insufficient for the Yorktown prisoners; so Morgan hired some of them to local farmers. More serious was his lack of provisions for the captives. With little surplus food in Frederick and nearby counties, he found people reluctant to exchange their meager supply for promissory notes. Morgan wrote Washington, Nelson, and other officials of the difficulties confronting him.[24]

As Morgan went about his duties, Captain Joseph Graham, senior officer among the prisoners, watched him with curious interest. Sometimes stern and impassive, sometimes loud and boisterous, often given to jokes and rustic witticisms, the mus-cular General who avoided formality and used nicknames was almost a natural phenomenon in himself; or so it seemed to Graham. When Graham secured permission from an American officer to quarter some of his men in a Winchester church, Mor-gan overruled his subordinate. In his memoirs, Graham declared he remonstrated in a tone designed to "melt the heart of the

24. The following letters are all dated Nov. 25, 1781: Morgan to Washington, Graham, *Morgan*, 400; Morgan to Nelson, Harvard College Lib.; Morgan to Nelson (second letter of that date), Dreer Coll., Hist. Soc. of Pa.; Morgan to Joseph Holmes, Simon Gratz Autograph Coll., *ibid.*

rugged Republican [Morgan]." Though Morgan acknowledged that the British had grievances, he wrote Graham that housing was not one of them. Since there were not enough barracks, the British would have to build their own. A little work would not hurt them, and if Englishmen did not know how to labor, now was a good time to learn. Certainly his Frederick County neighbors, who had not sent for the prisoners, should not be responsible for quartering them. Morgan claimed that Washington approved his policy for dealing with the prisoners. With pride—and some exaggeration—he added that the Commander in Chief had never found fault with his conduct. The letter might appear "rough," Morgan admitted, but it was best that he and Graham understand each other. He hoped Graham would not be offended.[25]

Apparently Graham found Morgan too intriguing to be piqued. In order to know his captor better, he invited Morgan to dinner, and he recalled afterward that the men passed a pleasant evening together. With undisguised enthusiasm Morgan related his part in the Saratoga campaign. "Oh, we whopped" Burgoyne's regiments "tarnation well," he exclaimed, rubbing his hands; "though to be sure they gave us tough work." But in the battle of October 7, 1777, his riflemen had "settled the business." Morgan told Graham of the shooting of General Fraser by his rifleman Timothy Murphy. "Me and my boys" had a bad time until "I saw that they were led by an officer on a grey horse—a devilish brave fellow." Then "says I to one of my best shots [Murphy], says I, you get up into that there tree, and single out him on the . . . horse. Dang it, 'twas no sooner said than done. On came the British again, with the grey horseman leading; but his career was short enough this time. I jist tuck my eyes off

25. Morgan to Joseph Graham, Nov. 28, 1781, *Virginia Historical Register*, 6 (1853), 209-10.

him for a moment, and when I turned them to the place where he had been—pooh, he was gone!"

Graham, though finding Morgan fascinating company, thought the frontiersman spoke with more "volubility" than "good taste" of his own accomplishments. In striking contrast to this observation, the Marquis de Chastellux once noted that Morgan talked with modesty of his own part in the victory at the Cowpens. The Frenchman likewise recalled the "simplicity of his deportment, and the nobleness of his behaviour." [26] Morgan was accustomed to the company of a wide variety of military men and he undoubtedly could adjust his behavior to suit a particular listener.

Toward the end of the year, 1781, Morgan relinquished command of the prisoners to Colonel James Wood of Winchester. Within a few months the British were transferred to various points in the north.[27]

If Morgan had not bowed out of the service in a blaze of glory, it was through no fault of his own. Thwarted twice by illness in 1781, he had missed the greater part of Greene's masterful campaign in the Carolinas and all of the eventful Yorktown drama. His contributions during this period, if not spectacular, were none the less important. He had supplied Greene with the tactics for Guilford Courthouse and had reinforced Lafayette with light troops from the Valley. After six and a half years in the service of his country, years in which his health had been greatly impaired, Morgan, now about forty-six years old, returned to peacetime pursuits.

26. [Joseph Graham], "A Recollection of the American Revolutionary War," *ibid.*, 209-11; Chastellux, *Travels in North America*, 240*n*.
27. Fitzpatrick, ed., *Writings of Washington*, XXIII, 382-83.

CHAPTER XI

Peacetime Pursuits

THE DECADE or so that followed saw Morgan involved in a host of activities, business, civic, and personal. This period also marked a change in his standing among his fellow citizens. Because of his impressive record as a soldier, he was now looked upon as one of the most distinguished men of the Valley.

It is hardly surprising, with his increased prestige, that Morgan endeavored to control the fiery temper which had involved him in so many fracases as a younger man. A steadying influence on Morgan at this time was the Reverend Charles Mynn Thruston, who, after trading his clerical garb for a Continental commission in the war, had returned to Frederick County. Once Thruston gently rebuked Morgan for soundly thrashing a man who accused him of an unethical financial transaction. Why did Morgan contest with his inferiors, asked the minister? The world was full of little people leveling popguns at their betters. They were only shrubs at the feet of stately oaks. Morgan should remember that his position was "much altered." Life demanded "greater complacency, affability, and condescension" from Morgan the military hero than it did from Morgan the backwoods pugilist.[1]

Morgan did feel his new importance, despite occasional violent outbursts. On his farm eleven miles from Winchester, he constructed a large two-story house, which he called "Saratoga."

1. Thruston to Morgan, Aug. 24, Nov. 23, 1783, Myers Coll., N. Y. Pub. Lib.

After borrowing a considerable sum of money from Thruston, Morgan began the work in 1780 or 1781, and completed it in 1782. Atop a rocky elevation, Saratoga today is almost obscured by trees as one approaches it on the old, narrow road that Morgan himself must have built. Valley tradition holds that much of the work on Saratoga was done by Hessian prisoners of war quartered near Winchester, these Germans reputedly carrying the stones in handcarts from the banks of Opequon Creek several miles away.

Certain considerations lend credence to this allegation. The stones used in Morgan's house are not found in that immediate area but are available near Opequon Creek. Assuredly a good deal of labor—by the Hessians or other men—went into acquiring the building materials needed for Saratoga. Moreover, if Morgan personally profited from public service, odious as it may seem today, it was not unusual for the eighteenth century. Benedict Arnold's mixing of private business and army affairs is well known, but his activities were not an isolated instance in the American army, a case in point being such a distinguished figure as Nathanael Greene, who as quartermaster general sold supplies to the army from his own mercantile establishment.[2] Whatever the truth about Saratoga, the General was extremely proud of his "mansion," one of the finest in the Valley.

There is further testimony of Morgan's desire for an affluent existence. He bought a carriage and filled his house with furniture appropriate for a man of his position—including seven feather beds, three carpets, seven mirrors, two tea tables, twelve mahogany chairs, a sideboard, and a desk.[3]

2. Suit Papers, Packet 10; T. K. Cartmell, *Shenandoah Valley Pioneers and Their Descendants* (Winchester, 1909), 270-71.

3. Superior Court Deed Book 4; Deed Book 20, 22; Personal Property Tax Book, 1782, Va. State Lib.

Even with a higher living standard, life was not completely satisfying to the General who thrived on activity and fame; idleness brought boredom and perhaps a sense of frustration. Memories of his illustrious past weighed heavily upon him. He asked the state authorities for the horse and "furniture" promised him in return for his éclat at the Cowpens. After his repeated prodding, they awarded him a mount having "almost every bad quality." This would not do for a retired hero of the Revolution. Morgan secured another horse from his planter friend, William Snickers, and eventually persuaded the politicians to pay for it.[4]

The General was equally tenacious in seeking the Cowpens medal promised by Congress. When he inquired about the medal in 1782, Secretary at War Benjamin Lincoln replied that all available money was needed to feed the army. But the old soldier was persistent. He was growing "very rusty," and his laurels were fading away; the medal would revive his flagging spirits. Morgan wrote Lincoln again and also referred the question to his friend Congressman John Francis Mercer of Maryland, expressing his hope that the engraving would be commensurate with his great victory at the Cowpens.[5]

Mercer replied that Congress had finally provided for the Revolutionary medals due Washington, Morgan, and other officers. His letter reveals Morgan's role in a current controversy between the army officers and Congress. Angered by the lawmakers' slowness to offer them extra pay and other favors for their hardships during the war, many officers bitterly attacked

4. Morgan to Greene, July 28, 1782, Graham, *Morgan*, 404-5; Palmer, ed., *Virginia State Papers*, II, 231, 549, III, 504, 552; Thomas Nelson to Morgan, July 20, Oct. 16, 1781, Myers Coll., N. Y. Pub. Lib.; Morgan to Benjamin Harrison with enclosures, Aug. 23, 1782, Roberts Coll., Haverford College Lib.

5. Lincoln to Morgan, Sept. 17, 1782, Mar. 11, 1783, Myers Coll., N. Y. Pub. Lib.; Morgan to Mercer, Feb. 6, 1783, Graham, *Morgan*, 405-6.

Congress. Their hostility reached a climax early in 1783 with the circulation of two anonymous papers, the Newburgh Addresses, suggesting that the army should resist disbandment until it received satisfactory compensation. Realizing that this threat bordered on mutiny, Washington moved with skill and diplomacy, persuading the officers to leave matters in his hands by recognizing the justice of their complaints and promising to urge Congress to heed them. According to Mercer, Morgan made efforts in behalf of moderation with the Virginia line comparable to Washington's with the main army. Fortunately, the views of Washington, Morgan, and other moderates prevailed. As Mercer pointed out to Morgan, these were perilous days for the young republic which suffered from economic dislocation and state and local prejudices. Now was the time for the supporters of "union and harmony" to stand together and resolve their differences quietly. Morgan had done his share of complaining about his horse, medal, and back pay. Yet in a crisis he refused to allow his own grievances to diminish his concern for state and country. Congress, responding to the officers' claims, gave them a bonus of full pay for five years and offered enlisted men four months' extra salary.[6]

Morgan's response to a call from the Virginia legislature in April 1783 is also indicative of his loyalty. In that month the 1st Regiment of Continental Dragoons, composed mostly of Virginians, mutinied at their camp on the Congaree River in South Carolina and set out for Virginia. Maintaining they suffered for want of adequate food and clothing, the men headed for Richmond to place their grievances before state officials. On assurances that their problems would be investigated, the dragoons promised to encamp at Winchester. Morgan, leaving a thriving grist mill business, agreed to meet them in the southern part of the

6. Mercer to Morgan, Burnett, ed., *Letters of Congress*, VII, 151.

state, whence he conducted them to their destination without incident. In no way was he reimbursed for his efforts.[7]

That same year there was gossip that Morgan had purchased depreciated military certificates from former soldiers with the intention of holding them until redeemed by the government at face value. Morgan's biographer, James Graham, argues that Morgan at first encouraged the soldiers to keep their securities, at the same time offering to buy from those men who desperately needed money, his purpose to help them by paying more than certain well-known speculators. According to Graham, the speculators, "disappointed of their prey by the interference of Morgan," hatched the tale that Morgan was reaping a harvest from the woes of his own men. However reliable Graham's account, it is true that Morgan purchased some undeterminable number of certificates. Morgan's only reference to the matter was to acknowledge buying some certificates from a Captain Ambrose Bohanan, who had acquired them from the troops in his own company; but Morgan reported that by 1782 he no longer possessed them. If he had acted with impropriety (such a report reached Washington's ear), substantial proof is lacking. It would indeed appear doubtful that the General who so often displayed a genuine interest in the welfare of enlisted men would take advantage of them. By purchasing their certificates, however, he had placed himself in a position susceptible of criticism.[8]

Morgan in 1782 had written Nathanael Greene that it was "high time to attempt some enterprise." Actually, he started several—first, a grist mill that he and Nathaniel Burwell owned jointly. Burwell, member of the prominent Tidewater family

7. Executive Letter Book 3, 139, Va. State Lib.; Palmer, ed., *Virginia State Papers*, III, 494.

8. Graham, *Morgan*, 408-10; Morgan to Ambrose Bohanan, Nov. 7, 1782, Suit Papers, Packet 5; Fitzpatrick, ed., *Writings of Washington*, XXXI, 509.

from Carter's Grove and a graduate of the College of William and Mary, had extensive land holdings in Frederick County. Each summer he went there for his health, becoming a permanent resident in the 1790's. Within three miles of Saratoga, he built Carter Hall, which was (and is today) one of the most elegant eighteenth-century Virginia mansions. A stone's throw away stands the old Burwell-Morgan mill, managed by Morgan while Burwell looked after a nearby store, which he operated. At times Morgan helped with Burwell's store, and the two men also seem to have run a distillery. Another of Morgan's activities was serving as a middleman for East-West mercantile trade. He often dealt with Baltimore and Philadelphia merchants, including "Old Denmark," Christian Febiger, who had entered business there. Morgan also had transactions with William Allason of Falmouth, Morgan distributing Allason's goods, Allason selling some of Morgan's flour.[9]

Up to his "Head and ears" in his various activities, Morgan in 1785 complained of little time for leisure. As a "Scotsman" would say, he longed to "Keep a loose foot." Particularly bothersome was the task of arraigning men who owed him money. He was still occasionally short on patience, and he said angrily that a John Hooper, who was reluctant to settle his account, deserved "flogging." The scarcity of money constituted a real problem in Virginia; full economic recovery from the conflict with Britain did not come until the 1790's. Many prominent residents

9. Morgan to Greene, July 28, 1782, Graham, *Morgan*, 404-5; Winchester *Gazette*, Mar. 4, 1789; Suit Papers, Packets 9-10; Burwell's Store Ledger, owned by Mr. George Burwell, Millwood, Va.; Morgan-Allason correspondence in Allason Letter Books, 1770-1784, 1770-1787, 1785-1793, Va. State Lib.; Morgan to David Allason, Misc. Coll., Clements Lib., Univ. of Mich.; Samuel Smith to John Fitzgerald, July 14, 1785, Fitzgerald Papers, Lib. Cong.; Febiger to Morgan, May 8, 1784, Myers Coll., N. Y. Pub. Lib.; Febiger to Morgan, Sept. 21, 1786, Febiger Letter Book, Va. State Lib.

of the Valley were debtors in varying degrees, including Isaac Zane, Adam Stephen, Alexander White, Horatio Gates, and Morgan himself. Presumably Morgan, like Gates, was often slow to pay his creditors because he was unable to collect from those who owed him. Though business was thriving in 1787, he told Otho Williams that he had plenty of everything but dollars. Tax officials in the state frequently discovered that people from whom they tried to extract cash had fled "over Allegheny" or to other remote places. While agitation for emissions of new paper money was not forceful enough to sway the legislature, the lawmakers did allow certain levies to be met with flour and hemp, plus warehouse receipts for tobacco.[10]

Since flour mills were all too numerous in the Valley, Morgan and Burwell were anxious to sell their produce in eastern Virginia cities. Morgan at one time thought of taking William Heth, his former rifle officer, into partnership with the idea that Heth would market their flour in Alexandria. To facilitate intercourse with the Tidewater, Morgan and other leading citizens of the back country favored building additional roads, establishing new ferries on the Shenandoah River, and developing inland navigation on the Potomac. In conversation with Washington in 1784, Morgan found him also eager for a Potomac project.[11]

Morgan's interests went beyond internal Virginia trade. He believed that the key to America's economic development and his own future prosperity lay in the West. That it was an area of fertile soil and navigable rivers he knew from his journey into the Ohio country during Dunmore's War. "Kantecoke" [Kentucky]

10. Morgan to Thomas Posey, July 11, 1785, Gratz Coll., Hist. Soc. of Pa.; Morgan to John Dedreck, n. d., Roberts Coll., Haverford College Lib.; Morgan to Williams, Apr. 11, 1787, Etting Coll., Hist. Soc. of Pa.
11. Samuel Beall to Morgan, Mar. 22, 1784, Myers Coll., N. Y. Pub. Lib.; Frederick Legislative Petitions, *passim*, Va. State Lib.; John C. Fitzpatrick, ed., *The Diaries of George Washington* (New York, 1925), II, 280.

drew Morgan's eye as well. In the 1770's and the succeeding decade he watched streams of settlers, many of them his friends and neighbors, tramp westward to pass through the Cumberland Gap and enter "the dark and bloody ground." Morgan saw two factors blocking the way to genuinely successful westward expansion: British maintenance of military posts in the American Northwest and Spanish reluctance to allow American pioneers free access to the mouth of the Mississippi. Were the British removed, Morgan—and Washington—maintained that the Great Lakes fur trade would follow the Potomac waterway, provided a transportation route could be extended across present-day Ohio. Morgan told Washington such a road, running from Winchester toward the Ohio, was under consideration by a group of western Virginians in 1784. Were the Jay-Gardoqui negotiations of 1785-86 fruitful, Morgan felt the Madrid government would open the Mississippi to American barges and flatboats.[12]

The disappearance of these foreign obstacles, plus the linking of East and West by roads, would add to the value of Morgan's extensive lands in the trans-Appalachian region. As early as 1783 Morgan had shown great interest in securing land in the West. By performing an important supervisory role in the surveying of Virginia's grants for her Revolutionary veterans, he gleaned valuable information on choice tracts in Ohio and Kentucky. After receiving 11,666⅔ acres in Kentucky for his own war service, he added to his property there and bought land in Tennessee. Precisely how he continued to increase his holdings is not clear, but by 1795 he owned 100,000 acres in modern West Virginia. His total possessions that year allegedly amounted to 250,000 acres, a large part of which was in the Northwest Territory.[13]

12. Morgan to Posey, July 11, 1785, Gratz Coll., Hist. Soc. of Pa.; Fitzpatrick, ed., *Diaries of Washington*, II, 280.

13. Morgan and others to officers of the Virginia line, Dec. 17, 1783, Emmet Coll., N. Y. Pub. Lib.; W. W. Hening, ed., *The Statutes at*

Busy though he was in the postwar years, and though his health was not always good, he derived considerable pleasure from old army friends. Thomas Posey, Christian Febiger, William Heth, John Eager Howard, Horatio Gates, and Otho Holland Williams were occasional guests at Saratoga. The visitor could expect excellent food served in abundance, delightful summer breezes when sitting on the high front lawn, and plenty of conversation. Morgan loved to talk, particularly about Revolutionary experiences, with a joke and a bit of homespun humor now and then.

With his "old swords," as he called his Revolutionary friends, Morgan carried on a lively correspondence, his letters frequently beginning with "My dear boy" and concluding with apologies for his terrible "scrall." He wrote about his guests, his gardening, his health, and his trips to the Hot Springs of Bath in Augusta County. The Morgan family traveled to Bath at least once each summer to enjoy the mineral waters and mingle with other visitors there. Morgan thought the waters relieved his "rheumatism" (sciatica?). His ailment was one of the curses "laid upon man kind," he told Otho Williams in April 1787. He was troubled by a "touch of it" the preceding winter; "any excess" brought it on again. He warned Isaac Zane that they were both growing old; old age was the "last stake" in life and should be guarded with "care and prudence." [14]

Of his many army friends, Morgan treasured Otho Williams

Large: Being a Collection of all the Laws of Virginia (Richmond, 1809-1823), XI, 556-59; M. H. Dyer, Index to Land Grants in West Virginia (Charleston, 1896), 377; "Locations in Ohio and Kentucky, Military Certificates," Virginia Land Office Papers, Va. State Lib.; Morgan's will, Graham, Morgan, 413.

14. Morgan to Williams, Apr. 11, 1787, Etting Coll., Hist. Soc. of Pa.; Morgan to Zane, June 27, 1794, letter in the possession of Mr. Barry S. Martin, Webster, N. Y.

most. A county clerk before the Revolution, Williams became a Maryland rifle officer in 1775 and later received a serious wound at Fort Washington. At Camden, Guilford Courthouse, and Eutaw Springs, he compiled an impressive combat record. Far from being rough and hearty like Morgan, Williams was a frail man, usually in ill health, whose tastes ran to scholarly subjects, especially classical literature. Each man found the other refreshingly different. Morgan, impressed by Williams's fluent prose, jokingly admitted that he himself hardly wrote like "pope, Voltiere or Shakespear." Williams assured his friend that his "plain Friendly" letters were good enough; education merely gave "polish" to one's sentiments. Williams told the General he was a man of sense and propriety. At least twice in the early 1790's, Williams took time from his post as collector of the port of Baltimore to visit Morgan and then continue to the healing waters at Bath, which Morgan had first recommended to Williams several years earlier.[15]

Williams and other guests at Saratoga found pleasure in the company of Morgan's daughters. Both Nancy and Betsy were described as educated and accomplished. For at least seven years Morgan employed a tutor for them. As he repeatedly said to Otho Williams, he firmly believed in education; and he is reported to have advocated that the Virginia Society of the Cincinnati, of which he was a member, grant a sum of money for the support of Washington Academy at Lexington.[16] Nancy and

15. Morgan's relationship with Williams is best illustrated in the following sources: Merritt, ed., *Calendar of Williams Papers*, 19, 219, 295; Graham, *Morgan*, 244-45, 272, 323; Williams to Morgan, Jan. 13, 1781, Myers Coll., N. Y. Pub. Lib.

16. Brent to Sparks, Sept. 3, 1827, Sparks Papers, Harvard College Lib.; *Western Pennsylvania Historical Magazine*, 24 (1941), 217; Edgar E. Hume, "The Virginia Society of the Cincinnati's Gift to Washington College," *Va. Mag. of Hist. and Biog.*, 42 (1934), 203.

Betsy married Revolutionary officers. Nancy's husband was Presley Neville, son of Morgan's army comrade John Neville. Presley was an aide to Lafayette during the Revolution and later, after taking Nancy as his bride, moved to western Pennsylvania, where his father had previously taken up residence. In 1793, then living in Pittsburgh, he began the first of three consecutive terms in the state House of Representatives. Morgan had the highest regard for young Neville and often wrote to him on business and personal subjects.[17]

Initially Morgan enjoyed excellent relations with James Heard, his other son-in-law. Family tradition has it that Heard, a native of New Jersey, became acquainted with Morgan during the war and accepted an invitation to visit Saratoga. Impressed by economic opportunities in the Valley and the charms of Betsy Morgan, he decided to make his home in Frederick County and take Betsy as his wife. In a very few years Morgan became disillusioned with Heard, who seems to have been a reckless spender and a rowdy, at least under the influence of alcohol. When attending the horse races in Martinsburg, Heard horse-whipped a companion who had handed him a tumbler full of liquor— Heard had asked for it in a mug! Disappointing as Heard's conduct was to Morgan, his main concern was for Betsy, who courageously informed one of her husband's creditors that she would personally pay "any of Major Heard's debts [as] though he was a thousand miles off." [18]

Morgan was able to find escape from personal troubles in the company of his grandchildren. (Nancy gave birth to fifteen children, Betsy to at least four.) A tender and devoted grandparent, he often brought his daughters' children to Saratoga and

17. J. Bernard Hogg, "Presley Neville," *Western Pa. Hist. Mag.*, 19 (1936), 17-26.
18. Graham, *Morgan*, 413n.; Suit Papers, Packet 32; Clarke County Hist. Soc., *Proceedings*, 2 (1942), 30.

entertained them with accounts of his military exploits, using, as one of them recalled afterward, "powerful and graphic" language. At times he presented them with valuable gifts; each of Betsy's daughters received a female slave.[19]

It is not generally known that Morgan also had a son. Born in the mid-1780's, Willoughby Morgan was illegitimate, and his mother's identity remains a mystery. His birth so embarrassed Morgan that he never referred to Willoughby in his surviving letters or in his will. Apparently at a very early age Willoughby was sent to South Carolina, where he grew up and studied law. By 1811 he lived in Winchester and later raised a company of infantry in the War of 1812. Compiling an impressive combat record, he decided to make a career in the army, rising to the rank of lieutenant colonel. A woman who knew Willoughby declared that he possessed considerable formal education, and, like his father, was tall and muscular. After serving at western posts in Indiana and Wisconsin, he died in 1832.[20]

Whether the liaison resulting in Willoughby's birth was Morgan's only lapse while married to Abigail is uncertain. In October 1780, after Morgan had left Hillsboro, North Carolina, to join the state militia, Otho Williams wrote his friend an intriguing letter in which he referred to a smiling little woman who became much distressed to hear that Morgan had departed. How he had wished to be in Morgan's shoes! [21]

19. Graham, *Morgan*, 43; Superior Court Deed Book 4; Presley Neville to Morgan, Mar. 3, 1795, Myers Coll., N. Y. Pub. Lib.

20. Brent to Sparks, Sept. 3, 1827, Sparks Papers, Harvard College Lib.; Draper Papers, 22S215-19, State Hist. Soc. of Wis.; David Holmes Conrad, "Early History of Winchester," Winchester, Virginia Historical Society, *Annual Papers*, 1 (1931), 188, 198-99; Francis B. Heitman, *Historical Register and Dictionary of the United States Army* (Washington, 1903), 726.

21. Williams to Morgan, Nov. 8, 1780, Myers Coll., N. Y. Pub. Lib.

If this incident signified a romantic affair, Abigail was probably unaware of it. In fact, it is not unlikely that she had no knowledge of Willoughby, for Morgan's illegitimate son was a well-kept secret for many years. Whatever Morgan's marital transgressions, he appreciated the good home Abigail made for him and the care she gave him during his sciatic and rheumatic difficulties.

As the years passed, Morgan complained more and more about these ailments. Between 1790 and 1793 he spoke of being confined much of the time. This trying period was momentarily brightened for him by the belated arrival of his Cowpens medal, nine years after Congress had voted to give the award. The Revolutionary medals were made in France and brought to America by Thomas Jefferson in 1789. Morgan's was solid gold. Designed by the prominent artist Augustin Dupré, it bore the likeness of a general leading his troops in battle.[22]

Morgan might have gained new triumphs had he returned to the army at this time. Indian tribes in the Northwest Territory had taken the warpath against American settlers. Two militia armies—one headed by Josiah Harmar, the second by Arthur St. Clair—received thumping defeats while attempting to suppress them. Numerous frontier voices called for Morgan to head an expedition against the Indians. Though Washington and Secretary of War Knox did not offer Morgan the supreme command in the west, they asked the old Indian fighter to accept a commission as brigadier general in 1792. According to Otho Williams, Morgan declined the appointment because of his health; then it was offered to Williams, who also refused because of illness. By the following year, having regained much of his strength, Morgan agreed to become a major general in the state militia. In this capacity he fought no Indians. Yet an unexpected development

22. Graham, *Morgan*, 413-14.

in 1794 brought him into the field once more, this time against fellow American citizens.[23]

23. John Brown to Elias Boudinot, May 10, 1791, Chicago Hist. Soc.; Nicholas Gilman to Josiah Bartlett, Mar. 11, 1792, Bartlett Papers, Dartmouth College Lib.; Sparks, ed., *Correspondence of the Revolution*, IV, 452-53; Fitzpatrick, ed., *Writings of Washington*, XXXII, 77; Merritt, ed., *Calendar of Williams Papers*, 260-61; Morgan's militia commission is in the Myers Coll., N. Y. Pub. Lib.

CHAPTER XII

Upholding the Constitution

I
N THE NINETIES, few frontier Virginians pursued national affairs as avidly as Daniel Morgan. His correspondence contains
repeated pleadings for news of this or that—or any news at all.
People in the East, Morgan enviously wrote Otho Williams, lived
in the "highway" of significant events. Though Morgan read the
newspapers that appeared sporadically in Winchester and more
regularly in Alexandria, letters were his basic source of information. His principal informant was his son-in-law in Pittsburgh,
Presley Neville.[1]

Much of the news created an ominous picture to Morgan: the
growing strength of a political faction intent on undermining
the Constitution. Morgan almost literally worshipped this document which had, at the end of the previous decade, superseded
the weaker Articles of Confederation as America's instrument of
national government. He variously described it as "the best of
constitutions," the "Envy and wonder of the surrounding
world," and the creator of "that beautiful structure the federal
government." [2]

Morgan encountered factionalism earlier at Valley Forge

1. Morgan to Williams, Apr. 11, 1787, Etting Coll., Hist. Soc. of Pa.;
the Morgan-Neville correspondence is in the Myers Coll., N. Y. Pub. Lib.
2. *Columbian Mirror and Alexandria Gazette*, June 7, 1796; Morgan to
Benjamin Biggs, Feb. 12, 1799, Draper Papers, 5NN116-18, State Hist.
Soc. of Wis.

and in the South with Gates and learned to detest it. It had no place in a republic; certainly the Constitution said nothing about political parties. And yet Morgan read of men in Congress who opposed the policies of President Washington. Under the leadership of James Madison, they had given abundant proof of their "wicked design" for "anarchy" by fighting Secretary of the Treasury Hamilton's fiscal measures and by criticizing the government's position of neutrality in the Anglo-French War that began in 1793.[3]

While Madison considered England the enemy, France the friend, and the French Revolution a blow at despotism, men who had gained wealth through the payment of Revolutionary war debts or increasing business feared that the French example might bring democratic excesses in the United States. They saw England as the bulwark of moderately conservative political institutions. They noted, too, that 90 per cent of American imports came from the British, whose tariff payments helped finance the funding of the national and state debts by the Washington administration. Morgan aligned himself with these and other groups behind the President, known as the Federalists, in order to thwart the Republicans, the name given to their opponents.

Morgan thought he saw the dread prospect of anarchy approaching reality as a result of the Republicans' steady stream of fire against the excise on the manufacture of whisky. Enacted by Congress in 1791, the excise law was to produce revenue for Hamilton's economic program by imposing a duty of eight cents a gallon on whisky. There was considerable truth in the Republicans' contention that the tax was discriminatory and extremely high, for it fell principally on Western distillers, who

3. Morgan to Isaac Zane, Dec. 7, 1794, Roberts Coll., Haverford College Lib.

would lose approximately 25 per cent of their product's net value if they paid the duty.

Opposition to the excise was strongest in frontier Pennsylvania, where the only method to dispose of surplus grain was by distilling it into whisky. Strong drink, far from being an occasional pleasure, was an integral part of life; the backwoodsmen said the climate and their rugged existence had given them an abounding thirst. To be sure whisky was almost universally consumed and, in the absence of hard money, circulated as a medium of exchange—more than one minister considered "Monongahela rye" refreshing compensation for preaching hell-fire and damnation.

In the summer of 1794 smouldering resentment turned into violence. Armed men terrorized revenue officials, prevented federal marshals from making arrests, and seized United States mail. On July 13, a band of malcontents destroyed the home of Morgan's friend John Neville, chief excise inspector in western Pennsylvania, who fled to safety in Philadelphia. Opening Philadelphia-bound mail, the rioters discovered letters from Presley Neville to Morgan denouncing the destruction of his father's property. Presley also was forced to flee, leaving his wife and children behind in Pittsburgh for fear they would be mistreated or insulted should they accompany him. On August 1, rebel militia officers drew up their men at Braddock's Field in preparation for an attack on the federal arsenal in Pittsburgh. But a number of the city's leading citizens persuaded David Bradford, fiery head of the assemblage, to call off the assault. After a noisy march through the city, the militiamen went home.[4]

Morgan heard reports of his son-in-law's banishment and grasped for all available news concerning the "dangerous riot over the mountain." The Washington administration believed the situation critical enough to call out a 12,500-man militia army

4. Leland D. Baldwin, *Whiskey Rebels: The Story of a Frontier Uprising* (Pittsburgh, 1939), 76-155.

headed by the President himself. In a letter from Governor Henry (Light-Horse Harry) Lee, Morgan learned that he was to raise and lead part of the Virginia contingent. Though in his late fifties and afflicted by illness in recent years, Morgan assured Lee there was not the slightest danger of his health giving way: "I feel as Hearty as I ever was—and am convinced that I could undergo the fatigues of two or three campaigns." Generating enthusiasm as he wrote, Morgan expressed eagerness to serve his country in the event of any danger, especially a foreign invasion, in which case he would make an "Early stroke" at the aggressor. However, the rebel leaders were "the greatest enemies that we have in America," for the Constitution would be worthless if men violated federal law whenever they chose. He wished to make an example of the Pennsylvanians.[5]

In addition to his devotion to the Constitution, Morgan was concerned about the rebellion because of possible danger to his daughter Nancy's family. Early in September, he heard from Presley Neville, who wrote "to relieve your anxiety" about "Nancy and children." Though he felt certain they were well and unharmed, "no circumstance in life" was worse than going without them. Neville's letter spurred Morgan to raise his force and depart with haste, but the militia were slow in reporting to his camp at Winchester, and guns and ammunition had to be obtained from both federal and state authorities. Moreover, Governor Lee, assuming personal command of all the Virginia forces, asked Morgan to assemble two more troops of cavalry, over two weeks after Morgan's first orders had been issued.[6]

Still at Winchester on September 24, Morgan sent President

5. Morgan to [Lee], misdated Aug. 2, 1794, Emmet Coll., N. Y. Pub. Lib.

6. Neville to Morgan, Sept. 1, 1794, Myers Coll., *ibid.;* Palmer, ed., *Virginia State Papers*, VII, 297, 315-17; Lee to Morgan, Sept. 16, 1794, Draper Papers, 5NN65a, State Hist. Soc. of Wis.

Washington his personal opinion on the rebellion. "For my own part," he wrote, "I think it a very easy matter to bring these people into order." He did not wish to "spill the blood" of a single citizen, but by marching into the disaffected region, the army would demonstrate the government's determination to maintain law and order. Washington replied from Carlisle, Pennsylvania, where the Pennsylvania and New Jersey troops were rendezvousing. He found immense satisfaction in Morgan's serving in the army. The Virginia and Maryland troops were gathering at Fort Cumberland, Maryland, and the President hoped to see Morgan when he visited there.[7]

Morgan was on the way to Fort Cumberland before Washington's message overtook him. After dispatching 2,000 men under Brigadier General William Darke early in the first week of October, he left with a smaller force on October 6, instructing Brigadier General Thomas Mathews to follow with another detachment. When Mathews failed to push forward by the 11th, Morgan wrote urging him to delay no longer, to which the latter replied that Morgan's letter made him "uneasy." The troops to accompany him came in slowly, he complained, and there were no competent officers available to advance with those who had already arrived. At length, Mathews, with 700 men, joined Morgan at Frankfort, Virginia, on October 18. A few days later Morgan's force, having gained another 500 under a Colonel Page, proceeded to Fort Cumberland.[8]

At Washington's suggestion, Lee appointed Morgan head of a special light corps formed to travel in the van of the left wing of the army. Quickly disposing of superfluous baggage

7. Morgan to Washington, Sept. 24, 1794, Graham, *Morgan*, 427-28; Washington to Morgan, Oct. 8, 1794, Fitzpatrick, ed., *Writings of Washington*, XXXIII, 522-24.

8. Palmer, ed., *Virginia State Papers*, VII, 341-42; Mathews to Morgan, Oct. 9, 13, 1794, Myers Coll., N. Y. Pub. Lib.; Fitzpatrick, ed., *Diaries of Washington*, IV, 220.

wagons, Morgan's unit headed northward on October 21, the same day that another light unit set out in front of the right wing of the army. Within a few days Morgan encountered heavy rains that lasted until the end of the month. Over the muddy roads his detachment moved slowly, the horses foundering, the wagons sinking axle-deep in mire. When the mountains were at last to their rear, a soldier in the left wing grandiloquently reported, "No expedition during the last war, nor even that of Hannibal's passage over the Alps, could equal the almost insuperable hardships we have suffered." Yet the men were in high spirits, one of them writing home that "A Military Life is a fine one" with "Plenty to Eat and Drink." [9]

Morgan found no opposition, only sullen, frightened people whose apprehensions increased because many of the troops displayed a vindictive attitude. It was to the General's credit that he was far more successful in keeping down thievery and destruction than the commanders of the right wing of the army. When violence did occur, he promptly paid the citizens for any loss of property. But age had not completely mellowed Morgan's temper, nor had it taken the strength from his arms. At Parkinson's Ferry on the Monongahela, he reprimanded a tavern keeper for selling whisky to the soldiers at an exorbitant price. The man's subsequent failure to reduce his charge made Morgan furious. Grabbing the offender, he "broke his mouth, which closed the business." Though informing Lee of his wish to give the Pennsylvanians good treatment, he would not let them be "impertinent"; the "rebuff" at Parkinson's Ferry would demonstrate his firmness. Even earlier, the whisky rebels had shown respect for Morgan. At Braddock's Field they had voiced con-

9. *Ibid.*; Morgan to Edward Carrington, Oct. 19, 1794, Alexander Hamilton Papers, Lib. Cong.; Baldwin, *Whiskey Rebels*, 230; "A Diary Kept by Dr. Robert Wellford," *Wm. and Mary Qtly.*, 1st Ser., 11 (1902-1903), 10-15; *Va. Mag. of Hist. and Biog.*, 22 (1914), 83.

siderable apprehension because of an unfounded rumor that Morgan, on his own initiative, was leading an army of Virginia frontiersmen over the Alleghenies to protect his daughter Nancy.[10]

Once beyond the Monongahela, Morgan was eager to see his daughter. After making a camp for his troops at Washington, Pennsylvania, he hurried to Pittsburgh, finding Nancy and her children safe. That night, while visiting the Nevilles, Morgan was startled by the entrance of a junior officer, who exclaimed that a group of his soldiers was preparing to assassinate a prominent Pittsburgh lawyer, Hugh Henry Brackenridge, who was said to have played an active role in the rebellion. Coatless and hatless, Morgan rushed out and met the soldiers only twenty yards from the lawyer's door. At Morgan's command they turned back, after being told that Brackenridge would eventually be brought to trial. Morgan detested the lawyer; Brackenridge declared that the General referred to him as a rascal who deserved hanging. In truth, Brackenridge, like most Pittsburgh residents, had mixed feelings about the disturbance. Though believing the tax unfair, he opposed the use of violence. Forced to equivocate because of fear for himself and Pittsburgh, which the back-country rebels viewed as the home of plutocracy, he became unpopular with many opponents of the rebellion. Yet at rebel policy meetings he advised compromise in place of violence.[11]

Washington's army extended its authority throughout the Monongahela country, and the President returned to the East,

10. William Findley, *History of the Insurrection in the Four Western Counties of Pennsylvania* (Philadelphia, 1796), 148; Morgan to Lee, misdated Mar. 6, 1794, Henry Lee, Jr., *The Campaign of 1781 in the Carolinas*, Appendix, xxvi-xxvii; William Bradford to Washington, Aug. 17, 1794, Pennsylvania Insurrection Papers, Lib. Cong.

11. Hugh Henry Brackenridge, *Incidents of the Insurrection in the Western Parts of Pennsylvania* (Philadelphia, 1795), 59-61.

leaving Henry Lee in supreme command. Lee lectured the people on their conduct, ordered them to take an oath of allegiance before a justice of the peace, and called for the arrest of numerous persons accused of an active part in the uprising. Sending some of the Pennsylvanians to Philadelphia for trial, he turned those charged with minor offenses over to state courts or released them after a sharp reprimand. By November 29, nearly all offenders had been pardoned.[12]

When Lee withdrew with most of the troops late in November, Morgan was left in charge in the "Whiskey country." As the Pittsburgh *Gazette* observed, the army had come and gone without firing a shot.[13] People favoring moderation toward the Westerners could be pleased with Morgan's selection. In orders to his troops, he immediately indicated a conciliatory attitude. He announced that they were in the midst of friends, whose good will they should strive to attain. He also declared:

The officers commanding fatigue parties are particularly directed not to suffer the sugar or other trees producing fruit or comfort to the farmers to be cut down for building or any other purpose whatever.

The burning of fencing, where there is such an abundance of fuel easily produced, is strictly forbid and a[ny] violence offered to the person, or depredation on the property of any individual, by the soldiery will be punished in the most exemplary and summary manner.[14]

Morgan notified President Washington that his gentle treatment of the former rebels was bringing him popularity, "for which I am happy." Echoing this report, John Neville told

12. Baldwin, ed., "Orders Issued by General Henry Lee during the Campaign Against the Whiskey Insurrectionists," *Western Pa. Hist. Mag.*, 19 (1936), 79-111.

13. Pittsburgh *Gazette*, Nov. 29, 1794.

14. *Pennsylvania Archives*, 2d Ser., IV, 480-81; Isaac Craig to Morgan, Dec. 2, 1794, Craig Letter Book, Carnegie Lib. of Pittsburgh.

Morgan that high praise for his conduct was reported throughout the western counties. Morgan traveled and mixed with the people; and he gave paroles at his "own risk" to certain men excluded from the general pardon after they agreed to report before the federal court at Philadelphia on the date of their trial. He believed this practice would win "friends" for the government and encourage many rebels to emerge from hiding. Come they did, including John Mitchell, whose robbery of the Philadelphia-Pittsburgh mails had resulted in Presley Neville's banishment from the region. Mitchell's action had disrupted the family of his son-in-law, but Morgan held no grudge against the man, calling him misguided and of low intelligence. Convinced that Mitchell was aware of his mistake, Morgan begged Washington to give the Pennsylvanian a pardon. Though he would "rejoice" if David Bradford and other insurrectionist leaders were arraigned, he had genuine sympathy for the poor and illiterate such as Mitchell, whose "wife and several children depend upon his labor for subsistence alone." As in his appeal for the alleged Tory John Claypool over a decade earlier, Morgan argued from a humane position. Incidentally, he is reported to have sent Mitchell to Philadelphia by himself, hoping he would try to escape. Mitchell arrived there, however, and was one of only two whisky rebels sentenced to death, both of them pardoned by Washington.[15]

Pressing administrative problems were also of concern to Morgan. Left with a small force of 1,200, he had been instructed by Lee to recruit additional men. Though he eventually raised

15. Morgan to Washington, Dec. [?], 1794, Sparks, ed., *Correspondence of the Revolution,* IV, 461-63; John Neville to Morgan, Jan. 28, 1795, and Morgan to Timothy Pickering, Jan. 26, 1795, Myers Coll., N. Y. Pub. Lib.; Morgan to Alexander Addison, Dec. 15, 1794, *Pennsylvania Archives,* 2d Ser., IV, 498-99; Morgan to Washington, Jan. 19, 1795, General Records of the Department of State, Misc. Letters, 1789-1820, National Archives.

four battalions, the work was slow: a dearth of uniforms, meager pay, and a lingering bitterness on the part of many former rebels retarded enlistments. Writing to Secretary of War Knox, Morgan complained that the troops needed overalls, shoes, and stockings. Housing presented still another difficulty. Because Lee had selected a sunken campsite where water often stood for long periods, Morgan decided to erect huts at a higher location, near McFarlin's Ferry, south of Pittsburgh. Heavy rains slowed construction, so that the army was not in its new quarters until the first week in January 1795.[16]

As Morgan gradually procured his supplies, he was able to relax his attention from military matters. Perhaps stimulated by his active participation in national affairs, he decided to undertake a plan he had considered for some time: to run as a Federalist for the United States House of Representatives from Virginia's First Congressional District. He informed Isaac Zane that "No Poppular Motive" had influenced his decision, only a "hearty contempt for the character who now serves us." [17]

The incumbent, Robert Rutherford, was a formidable opponent for Morgan or any other candidate. Born in Scotland and educated at the Royal College of Edinburgh, "Robin" Rutherford had served in the Virginia Senate from 1776 to 1790. An ardent Republican in his political views, he had been elected to the House of Representatives by an overwhelming margin in 1793 and had been a constant opponent of Federalist measures. He railed at Americans who lived in aristocratic elegance instead of republican simplicity. A contemporary anecdote, no doubt of Federalist origin, had it that Rutherford dressed so informally

16. Morgan to Knox, Dec. 18, 24, 1794, Jan. 8, 1795, Myers Coll., N. Y. Pub. Lib.

17. Morgan to Zane, Dec. 7, 1794, Roberts Coll., Haverford College Lib.

that a woman who invited him to dinner thought her servant had ushered in a tramp! [18]

Morgan knew he would have a difficult race because many voters would not think him qualified to hold a legislative position. While admitting a lack of political experience, he declared to Zane his determination to make up for this deficiency by supporting the administration against the anarchists. Writing from Pennsylvania to Zane and other friends in Virginia urging them to speak for him, he also addressed an electioneering letter to the freeholders of the district. "Leave no stone unturned," advised John Neville, for "you are about to Engage in as difficult or worse piece of business than the engagement with Tarleton." More vigorous was the appeal of Presley Neville. "For god's sake," he exclaimed to Morgan, "defeat him, you have been used to conquest, & don't let such a Racoon get the better of you." His spirit aroused, Morgan obtained a leave of absence and hurried home to make a last-minute plea to the voters. Despite the support of a number of important citizens and the affection— "stupid veneration," a Republican called it—of many former soldiers, Morgan's efforts were not enough; Rutherford won another term.[19]

Resuming his military duties in Pennsylvania after over a month's absence, he began preparations to disband most of the army and to leave a skeleton detachment under a junior officer.

18. *Biographical Directory of the American Congress* (Washington, 1950), 1768-69; Henry Bedinger II to George M. Bedinger, "Henry Bedinger and Old Shepherdstown," unpublished MS, Danske Dandridge Papers, Duke Univ. Lib. During the Third Congress, Rutherford voted with Madison on 38 of 42 roll calls. *Annals of Congress* (Washington, 1834-1856).

19. Morgan to Zane, Dec. 7, 1794, Roberts Coll., Haverford College Lib.; John Neville to Morgan, Jan. 28, 1795, and Presley Neville to Morgan, Mar. 3, 1795, Myers Coll., N. Y. Pub. Lib.; Daniel Bedinger to Henry Bedinger II, misdated Nov. 22, 1795, "Henry Bedinger and Old Shepherdstown," Dandridge Papers, Duke Univ. Lib.

A more unpleasant task arose from trouble occurring between certain officers and Pittsburghers during his stay in Virginia. Disregarding Morgan's order that the residents be treated with respect, these officers made themselves obnoxious by carousing in the taverns, roaming the streets at late hours, and brawling with the townspeople. The Pittsburghers retaliated with numerous lawsuits. Hugh Brackenridge, already suspected by Morgan and others of having engaged in traitorous activity, did not endear himself to the army by frequently acting as prosecutor for the plaintiffs. When Morgan returned, he heard only the officers' version of the controversy with the townspeople. On the other hand, several traders had caused a good deal of ill will by charging excessive prices for goods while the General was away. Though viewing the recent happenings as unfortunate, Morgan wrongly concluded that Brackenridge had instigated most of the disturbance, particularly the suits. As he explained to Washington, "Mr. B[rackenridge], I am informed, was the person who advised, nay, urged, those suits to be brought. This man I consider a bad member of society, and who will, I fear, do all in his power to foment disturbances in this country." Even so, Morgan realized that the officers were not without fault, and he assured Washington of his wish to settle all disputes as fairly as possible and to avoid misunderstandings in the future. In the opinion of one of Morgan's aides, the General's presence in the frontier counties had been essential to the maintenance of tranquility because he had the respect of all—"some from fear and others from affection." [20]

Sometime in June, just before breaking camp, Morgan ad-

20. Morgan to Benjamin Biggs, Apr. 2, 1795, Darlington Memorial Lib., Univ. of Pittsburgh; John Neville to Morgan, Apr. 12, 1795, and "Office at Camp" to Pickering, Mar. [?], 1795, Myers Coll., N. Y. Pub. Lib.; Morgan to Washington, Apr. 9, 1795, Sparks, ed., *Correspondence of the Revolution*, IV, 472-73.

dressed an open letter to the western Pennsylvanians, warning them never again to follow men who advocated forceful resistance to law and order. Such "enemies of government" would lead them to destruction and then forsake them, he concluded. It is true that certain hotheads had set off the Whisky Rebellion and that many of them had fled at the approach of Washington's army. Without the leaders there would probably have been no rebellion; nevertheless, the back-country people were deeply angered by the whisky excise, which, to them, was merely an example of the federal government's lack of concern for the West. Apparently Morgan never admitted that the Pennsylvanians might have legitimate grievances.[21]

For lack of information, conclusions concerning Morgan's performance as a military administrator must be limited. The General himself was convinced that he had provided well for his soldiers after their early difficulties. Most of the disaffected people, he felt, were now aware that they had been in error in opposing the whisky excise with force, while others were quiescent only because of the military strength that the government had brought to bear upon them. He seems to have been accurate in thinking himself popular with many of the people. While certain bitter elements disliked him, their feeling would likely have been the same toward any commanding officer. Yet Morgan made mistakes: he falsely accused Brackenridge of fomenting disturbances, and he failed to see that the rebels were genuinely against the excise tax. Even though he misjudged the Pennsylvanians, he was right in adhering to a moderate policy; they had acknowledged the central government's power and determination to enforce its laws.

Following his military service, Morgan remained active in

21. For Morgan's address, see Neville B. Craig, *Exposure of a Few of the Many Misstatements in H. M. Brackenridge's History of the Whiskey Insurrection* (Pittsburgh, 1859), 66.

politics, devoting his energies to enlisting support for the Jay Treaty. Chief Justice John Jay, sent to London to settle outstanding differences between the United States and Britain, came back with less favorable terms than his country expected. Washington, believing the treaty better than none at all, was instrumental in securing Senate ratification, despite strong Republican opposition. Morgan is said to have admitted to Aaron Burr that he had opposed the pact until he heard the "old horse," Washington, was for it; then "I shut my pan." Such familiarities did not enter a letter that Morgan and other leading citizens of Frederick County addressed to the President expressing their approval of his signing the treaty.[22]

The Senate's acceptance, however, would not insure the terms being carried out. Should the Republicans in the House marshal enough votes to defeat the appropriation needed to put the treaty into effect, Jay's efforts would be undone. Morgan circulated several petitions in favor of the measure and sent them to Congressman Rutherford. The General wrote William Loughton Smith, a Federalist representative from South Carolina, that many intelligent men had signed their names to the petitions and that Frederick County's *"General Wish"* was for the House to support the treaty. On April 30, 1796, following a heated two months' debate, the House passed the necessary appropriation by a narrow margin. Rutherford cast his vote against it.[23]

Rutherford's stand infuriated Morgan, who had already decided to try again for the House. Morgan felt his chances of

22. Charles Carter Lee Notes, Lib. Cong.; *Virginia Journal and Alexandria Advertiser*, Jan. 19, 1796. Washington thanked the Frederick County men for their support. Fitzpatrick, ed., *Writings of Washington*, XXXIV, 395-96.

23. Morgan to William Loughton Smith, Apr. 21, 1796, Smith Papers, Lib. Cong.; *Columbian Mirror and Alexandria Advertiser*, May 3, 1796; *Annals of Congress*, Apr. 30, 1796 (customarily cited by date instead of by volume).

winning were better than in 1795, when he had been able to campaign only a short time. But Rutherford, while still in Philadelphia, had learned from a friend in Shepherdstown, Virginia, that his prospect of victory was excellent. Federalist Fisher Ames of Massachusetts, visiting in western Virginia, complained to Secretary of the Treasury Oliver Walcott that "Mr. Rutherford is as little respected here as in Philadelphia, and yet the many whom he flatters and deceives, will support him against General Morgan. This is the opinion of federal men." [24]

Campaigns and elections in eighteenth-century Virginia were usually lively and exciting; the Morgan-Rutherford contest was no exception. The candidates traveled throughout Berkeley and Frederick counties, which comprised the district, explaining their views and appealing for votes. Rutherford attacked the Jay Treaty as a sign of America's subservience to England and a slap at her old benefactor France. Though the Paris government, believing the treaty meant her former ally was moving toward an alliance with Britain, broke off diplomatic relations with the United States, Rutherford promised his constituents that France would not declare war. Morgan defended Jay's agreement and criticized the French for retaliating by seizing American merchantmen on the high seas; their conduct was "imperious and oppressive." [25]

On election day, March 20, 1797, Morgan was in the courthouse at Winchester, watching intently as each freeholder ar-

24. Robert Rutherford to Henry Bedinger II, Dec. 22, 1796, "Henry Bedinger and Old Shepherdstown," Dandridge Papers, Duke Univ. Lib.; George Gibbs, *Memoirs of the Administrations of Washington and Adams from the Papers of Oliver Walcott* (New York, 1856), II, 372-73.

25. *Columbian Mirror and Alexandria Advertiser*, Jan. 2, 1797; Richmond *Virginia Gazette and General Advertiser*, Jan. 16, 1797; Daniel Bedinger to Henry Bedinger II, May 16, 1797, "Henry Bedinger and Old Shepherdstown," Dandridge Papers, Duke Univ. Lib.; *The Time Peace*, 1 (Apr. 7, 1797), 47.

rived. (Rutherford was at Shepherdstown, seat of Berkeley County.) The scene was probably similar to those at most polling places in Virginia. In the center of the courtroom stood a long table behind which sat the sheriff and the ranking justices. Morgan sat at one end of the table. Each freeholder stopped in front of the sheriff, who called his name in a loud voice and asked how he would vote. If the voter replied that Morgan were his preference, it would not have been uncommon for the General to have bowed and publicly thanked the man.[26]

A count of the votes at Winchester and Shepherdstown revealed Morgan as the victor. The old General who could be arrogant and bombastic exposed a very humble side in thanking the freeholders. Admitting his lack of an "early education," an acquaintance with legislative procedure, and a knowledge of the "history of government," he had not the "vanity" to think he would distinguish himself in the higher councils of his country; his forte lay in the "rugged duties of the Field." But he would support the Constitution and the laws of the United States to the best of his ability, affiliating himself with no political party. The Federalists were not a party, according to Morgan; they were the government.[27]

Rutherford complained to the House Committee of Privileges and Elections that irregularities had taken place at the polls in Winchester. He charged that men from other counties stepped up to cast illegal votes for Morgan and that the General rented wagons to bring freeholders there. He also claimed that meat and drink were supplied to Morgan's friends, who became rowdy in front of the courthouse, and that the sight of the turbulent mob discouraged many of his own supporters from voting.[28]

26. Charles S. Sydnor, *Gentlemen Freeholders: Political Practices in Washington's Virginia* (Chapel Hill, 1952), 19-21.
27. *The Time Peace*, 1 (Apr. 7, 1797), 47.
28. *American State Papers, Miscellaneous* (Washington, 1834), I, 158.

In a letter published in the Alexandria newspaper, Morgan replied to Rutherford's accusations. His opponent's conduct, he declared, had been "illiberal and indecent" toward him throughout the election campaign, whereas he had avoided "personal and ill natured reflections," concentrating instead upon issues. Now Rutherford attempted further to defame his reputation. If fraudulent votes were given, he did not know about them, and he certainly had not encouraged them. He had promised to rent wagons for some of his friends who seemingly had no other way to reach Winchester, but they had not availed themselves of this opportunity. It was also true that some of his backers had wished to pass out meat, bread, and grog during the campaign, an offer which he had rejected, "having always determined, and repeatedly declared, that my election should rest upon the unbought and uninfluenced suffrages of my fellow citizens." To the charge of disorderly conduct by his friends at Winchester, the General remarked that he had never heard of it except from Rutherford; and if there had been trouble, he could not have been an instigator, since he had remained in the courthouse throughout the voting period. Any turbulence must have come after the election as the result of Rutherford's "ill natured petulant language, which he dealt out so profusely to many of the electors who voted against him." In short, the tone of Morgan's letter was one of confidence. Rutherford had made grave charges, and he must prove them or no longer have the reputation of a "man of truth." [29]

Later in the year the Committee of Privileges and Elections reported to the House a lack of evidence to substantiate Rutherford's claim, thus closing the matter. The outcome did not necessarily indicate an absence of truth in Rutherford's accusations, for wrongdoings were difficult to prove. But if Morgan (or

29. *Columbian Mirror and Alexandria Advertiser*, Aug. 29, 1797.

his friends) passed out favors, he only followed the pattern of other candidates for legislative office in Virginia; in 1798 John Marshall reputedly spent several thousand dollars on barbecues. Even Rutherford, according to Morgan, had previously offered his voters free transportation to the polling places.[30]

Early in May 1797 Morgan journeyed to Philadelphia to take his seat in Congress, called into special session by President Adams to review the critical state of American relations with France. Whether Morgan was in awe of his more learned colleagues is not clear, but he seldom, if ever, spoke during the debates.[31] Addressing Congress on the French crisis, Adams stressed that American prestige must be increased by enacting measures for national defense, although he assured the lawmakers that war was not his purpose. Accordingly, William Loughton Smith in the House introduced a series of resolutions which included purchasing new warships, authorizing the President to use the navy for convoy duty, and increasing the regular army. To the Republicans, Adams's program seemed designed for war, and with some Federalist support they succeeded in reducing Adams's measures. In July Congress adjourned until November.

If Morgan failed to take an active part in the debates between Federalists and Republicans in Philadelphia, he was not reluctant to speak out against the government's critics after reaching Virginia. He did so in orders to the brigadier generals of his militia

30. *American State Papers, Miscellaneous*, I, 158; *Journal of the House of Representatives*, [*Fifth Congress*] (Washington, 1826), 99. In 1791 a Frenchman in Winchester recorded his impressions of Virginia elections: "Your election days are days of reveling, of brawls; and the candidates offer drunkeness openly to anyone who is willing to give them his votes. The taverns are occupied by the parties. The citizens flock to the standard of the candidates; and the voting place is often surrounded by men armed with clubs, who drive back and intimidate the citizens of the other party." Ferdinand M. Bayard, *Travels of a Frenchman in Maryland and Virginia*, ed. Ben C. McCary (Williamsburg, 1950), 65-66.

31. No remarks by Morgan are recorded in the *Annals of Congress*.

division published in the Alexandria newspaper, orders evidently issued only for political reasons. These officers were to establish regular patrols throughout their districts, a strange procedure in peacetime. General William Darke, commanding in the northwestern part of the state, was to be especially prompt because Negroes in that area were becoming restless under their masters, numerous ones having run away. Morgan said reports reaching him indicated that "different self created societies" were guilty of arousing the slaves to try for their freedom, and he sternly announced that those who excited disorder, black or white, were "very wrong and ought to be checked." [32]

There was no reason for Morgan to communicate with his generals through a newspaper; previously he had written them of their instructions. The orders were extremely vague and, except in the case of Darke's area, did not state why there should be militia patrols. Probably Morgan meant to frighten the Virginia Republicans into ceasing their attacks against the Adams administration. The reference to "self created societies," an expression borrowed from Washington and other Federalists, was directed at the Democratic Societies and meant as a blow to the Republicans. Named for the Jacobin Society of Paris, these organizations, in sympathy with the French Revolution, detested England and generally worked to elect Republicans to office. They were unmerciful critics of Washington, who falsely accused them of fomenting the Whisky Rebellion. Whether or not Morgan's patrols were ever formed is unknown.

The orders soon brought repercussions. Henry Bedinger II of Norfolk, a Republican, thought that Morgan wrote with the modesty of an "Eastern Bashaw," and he begged his brother Daniel of Shepherdstown to compose a stinging reply. Henry, considering Morgan a "vindictive scoundrel," felt it best that

32. *Columbian Mirror and Alexandria Advertiser*, Sept. 13, 1797.

his brother should throw the General on the wrong track by dating his communication Alexandria or Fredericksburg. Personal as well as political reasons probably encouraged Henry Bedinger to wish a blow at Morgan; the Bedinger and Rutherford families were intermarried, and Henry and Daniel Bedinger were intimate friends of Robert Rutherford.[33]

On October 13, 1797, the *Columbian Mirror and Alexandria Advertiser* carried a letter entitled, "What an Age of Prodigies do we live in," dated Alexandria and signed *Philanthropos;* it was obviously written by Daniel Bedinger. There was a new phenomenon in western Virginia, declared the author, an aged major general turned writer—his "unparallel lubrications" clothed in "all the majesty of pomp." Under what law or by whose authority could a militia general call upon his subordinates to control the state in time of peace, asked *Philanthropos*. General Morgan was clearly trying to take over the duty of civil officials, either to gratify his spleen or to promote his re-election. *Philanthropos* could not fathom the attack on the Democratic Societies, arguing that the members had the right to organize such groups and express their views, even though they were not major generals. Charging "arrogance and presumption," he asked the General to make a reply, if he had the *"capacity."* A last request was for the answer to avoid the words "self created societies"; they were now too hackneyed to arouse the least attention. When Morgan read the *Advertiser*, his anger may be imagined, but he made no reply. *Philanthropos* had the better of him, and the General must have realized it.[34]

When Morgan resumed his seat in Congress that October, he found little business before that body. The lawmakers awaited news from three commissioners (Charles C. Pinckney, Elbridge

33. Daniel Bedinger to Henry Bedinger II, Oct. 3, 1797, Henry Bedinger Davenport Letters, Dandridge Papers, Duke Univ. Lib.
34. *Columbian Mirror and Alexandria Advertiser*, Oct. 13, 1797.

Gerry, and John Marshall) whom President Adams had sent to Paris in an attempt to ease America's strained relations with France. In the spring of 1798 Congress learned that three mysterious Frenchmen, referred to as X, Y, and Z in the diplomatic dispatches, had demanded a bribe, a loan, and other concessions from the American representatives merely for the privilege of speaking to Foreign Minister Talleyrand. The spirit for war grew strong as Americans shouted "Millions for defense but not one cent for tribute." With France discredited, the Republicans were on the defensive, and Federalist leaders in Congress pushed through bills providing for a navy department, organizing a provisional army of 10,000 men to be headed by Washington, authorizing the capture of French ships, suspending commercial intercourse with France, and abrogating the Revolutionary War treaties with the old ally.

Morgan had supported the Federalist program with enthusiasm and also favored passage of a sedition measure then under debate. He hoped to remain in the House until adjournment in July to vote for this bill, but a recurrence of rheumatism forced his return to Virginia. The Federalists designed the Sedition Act, as it became known, to silence the Republicans by providing that those who obstructed the policies of the government or wrote maliciously about its officials were subject to fines and imprisonment. Though a blow to freedom of the press, Federalists believed it necessary because of the viciousness of the opposition.[35]

The passage of the Sedition Act led Morgan to believe the Federalist victory nearly complete. It was his "consolation" for time spent away from home, he wrote Presley Neville. The

35. Morgan's voting record is in the *Annals of Congress*, Apr. 25, May 18, 26, June 1, 1798. The vote on the French treaties took place after Morgan's return to Virginia. In Appendix III, Manning J. Dauer, *The Adams Federalists* (Baltimore, 1953), provides charts showing the votes in the House on what he considers party measures during the Fourth, Fifth, and Sixth Congresses.

Republicans, many of whom were sorely embarrassed because of the XYZ affair, resembled "a parsell of Egg sucking Dogs that had been caught breaking up Hens Nests." He expected to see the Republicans helpless when Congress met again; the Federalists would "crush them to attoms."

For the remainder of the summer Morgan battled to regain his strength, finding that an old man, like an "old horse," recovered slowly. He was too weak, he informed Neville, to give his land agent in Kentucky the whipping he deserved for improperly handling his grants there. Were he ten years younger, he would ride all the way to Kentucky to thrash the agent from "post to gunfiring." [36]

What energy Morgan had left, he saved for use against the Republicans when Congress convened in November. Though still refraining from speaking in the debates, he voted with his Federalist colleagues for a bill to increase the navy and for approving a committee report opposing repeal of the Alien and Sedition Acts. Outside Congress, however, opposition to the Federalists was growing. Madison and Jefferson assailed the Alien and Sedition laws through the Virginia and Kentucky Resolutions, arguing that under the Constitution the states had the right to decide when Congress exceeded its authority. Designed in large part as a political measure, these resolutions, by focusing attention on the danger to personal freedom, gave Jefferson an issue for the election of 1800. [37]

As Morgan saw party lines tighten, he felt forebodings of doom for the nation. In his opinion the Republicans were dividing the country and threatening to destroy it. Even the legislature of his own state, supposedly the "most respectable" one in the union, had adopted the Virginia Resolutions. "My God!

36. Morgan to Neville, July 26, 1798, Myers Coll., N. Y. Pub. Lib.
37. *Annals of Congress*, Feb. 11, 25, 1799. The navy bill was defeated in the House.

Who would have thought it," he cried to General Benjamin Biggs. Today was the time for friends of a united America to speak out; tomorrow might be too late.[38]

The General's health continued to decline; he now complained of a severe pain recurring frequently in his chest. Toward the end of February 1799, he departed for home, approximately a week before the end of the Fifth Congress. Too ill to run again for the House, he fired a parting shot at the enemy in a letter to his constituents, saying "Rouse yourselves" and turn back the Francophiles.[39]

38. Morgan to Biggs, Feb. 12, 1799, Draper Papers, 5NN116-18, State Hist. Soc. of Wis.

39. *Columbian Mirror and Alexandria Advertiser*, Apr. 18, 1799. Timothy Pickering recalled later that Morgan was "a very sick man—with one foot in the grave." Pickering to James A. Hamilton, Jan. 4, 1821, Pickering Papers, Mass. Hist. Soc.

CHAPTER XIII

Reckoning

A YEAR BEFORE he retired from Congress, Morgan's lameness had made it so difficult for him to look after Saratoga that he had moved to "Soldier's Rest," one of his smaller farms. But at the conclusion of his term, feeling the need of regular medical attention, he and his wife took up residence with Betsy Heard's family in Winchester.

The veteran of many grueling military campaigns received countless visitors. He was a famous man, one of the few first-rate American generals in the Revolution. Who had bettered his record as a battlefield tactician? His achievements against Burgoyne and Tarleton spoke for themselves. Who, with the possible exception of Arnold, had performed more spectacularly in leading men in action? If Arnold's personal magnetism had electrified the Americans at Bemis Heights and Valcour Island, so Morgan's drive and zeal had elicited a similar response at Quebec and at the Cowpens. Who had accomplished more with riflemen? And who had excelled Morgan in combining the peculiar talents of militiamen and partisans with Continentals?

Perhaps Morgan more than any other patriot officer typified the difference between British and American military practices during the Revolution. With a tradition of frontier combat behind him, he emphasized the thin skirmish line and individual marksmanship; the British, the bulky linear formation and volley fire. Morgan encouraged his sharpshooters to pick off enemy officers, whereas a kind of gentlemen's agreement existed in European wars to spare the opposing leaders. As an Indian fighter, Morgan had concluded that there was nothing cavalier about war; it was an ugly business, with one's chances of winning enhanced by crippling an opponent in any way possible, not by following time-honored rules and customs. Furthermore, Morgan was quick to recognize the value of light infantry. The Revolutionary contest was fought over vast distances and on rough, forested, and swampy terrain; units that could range widely, move swiftly, and strike suddenly, as Morgan's riflemen did in the Saratoga campaign, were of tremendous advantage. His accumulative success with light troops exceeded that of any other American commander, although Wayne, Pickens, Sumter, Marion, Elijah Clarke, Richard Butler, Henry Lee, and Charles Scott also headed troops that performed well as light infantry. The British, despite the creation of light regiments under Simcoe, Tarleton, and Ferguson, were slow to understand the importance of mobile forces. Not until too late did most royal officials realize that America was ill-suited for the conventional warfare of the Old World.

In other respects Morgan exemplified the contrasting procedures of the two armies. Like most American officers, he treated enlisted men with more sympathy and understanding than they received in the King's army. Washington thought the degree of fraternization between officers and men often went beyond propriety, causing the officers' authority and prestige to be severely shaken. On the other hand, the fact that the American soldier was acknowledged by such officers as Morgan and was encouraged to believe that he had a personal stake in the war meant that, given adequate training, he could more than hold his own against the redcoat or Hessian who performed merely for pay and in response to orders. Morgan, by virtue of his strong personality and commanding presence, could mix freely with his soldiers and acquire their good will without losing their respect. A contemporary wrote that no officer "knew better how to gain the love and esteem of his men. . . ." For that matter, Morgan's relations with his principal subordinates was almost uniformly good, just as he had demonstrated the ability to work well with Gates, Greene, Arnold, and his other superiors.[1]

Finally, Morgan's very rise through the officer ranks was remarkable for the eighteenth century. Performance was no touchstone to preferment in British and other European armies. In England, commissions to the rank of colonel were usually purchased, going to young men, and sometimes boys, whose families possessed money and influence; as a yeoman farmer before the Revolution, Morgan's chance of entering the officer class would have been remote indeed. But the American service was different. Morgan's advancement, to say nothing of his increasing social and economic stature and his election to Congress, forcefully testified to the democratic spirit already beginning to permeate America.

That Morgan saw the broad liberal implications of the Revolution in general and the Declaration of Independence in particular may be doubted. He was an activist and seldom revealed an intellectual bent. No doubt he had taken to arms in 1775 partly because he loved the excitement and drama of warfare with its opportunity for glory. Yet it is difficult to imagine that he left home a sick man in 1780 and painfully rode over two hundred miles to join the Southern army simply to gain laurels in the field. In reality, he fought foremost for "my country." If as a Federalist Morgan's efforts to silence the Republicans struck at the freedom he had helped to win for his countrymen in the Revolution, it was equally true that his activities and utter-

1. Fredericksburg *Virginia Herald*, July 20, 1802.

ances were no worse than many other Federalists'. The 1790's were filled with political turmoil and controversy, an illusion of the decade being that organized political opposition had no place in the American form of government.[2]

Leaving the political battles to Federalists in Congress, Morgan in Winchester displayed a new abiding interest: religion. He embraced it with all the enthusiasm he had thrown into his assaults on Tarleton and Rutherford. Deism, then popular with many French Revolutionaries, was to Morgan incompatible with the Lord's way and the ruination of responsible government. The "first and best" support of stable political institutions was orthodox religion without which anarchy "fixes a Compleat hell" upon earth. Morgan, who said his faith was based on "fundamental principles," joined the Winchester Presbyterian church and attended services whenever able.[3]

For the most part the General stayed at home, his health at times better, at times worse. Occasionally he reminisced with six Winchester men who had gone with him to Quebec in 1775. All Germans, these veterans formed a kind of club called the Dutch Mess which met to recount Revolutionary days.[4]

In the spring of 1799, George Washington read a newspaper account of Morgan's death, discovering later that the story was

2. Julian P. Boyd, editor of *The Papers of Thomas Jefferson*, having read numerous Morgan letters during the crucial days of Greene's Southern campaign, has appropriately called them so heart-warming in their expression of patriotism as to make objective analysis difficult. *Jefferson Papers*, IV, 564n.

3. Morgan to Files Fisher, Jan. 11, 1798, *Historical Magazine*, 1st Ser., 2 (1858), 166; Hill's Notes.

4. There appear to have been occasional reunions of all Morgan's former Winchester riflemen with the community participating. Winchester *Gazette*, July 28, 1822; Winchester *Virginian*, Sept. 27, 1843; William G. Russell, *What I Know About Winchester*, Winchester-Frederick County Historical Society, *Papers*, eds. Garland R. Quarles and Lewis N. Barton, II (Staunton, 1953), 34, 43n., 62n., 64n.

untrue. He wrote Morgan of his pleasure to learn his old comrade still lived, and he wished him a complete recovery and a long life. But Washington himself did not live out the new year. Gone too were many of Morgan's other Revolutionary associates, including Greene, Febiger, Butler, and Williams. Arnold, the traitor, was in England. Gates was still alive, but after he moved to New York City in 1790, the warmth between the two Saratoga veterans melted; the reason is obscure but may well have been because of politics, since Gates was as ardent a Republican as Morgan was a Federalist.[5]

Certain that death was at hand, Morgan drew up his final will in March 1801, dividing his estate between his daughters, after leaving his wife a large farm. Fearing that his son-in-law James Heard might create "sad Havock" with Betsy's inheritance, Morgan provided that Heard could never dispose of it without her permission. Betsy acquired Saratoga through her father's will, eventually selling it to a son of Nathaniel Burwell, whose descendants have retained it to the present.[6]

The end came for Morgan early in July 1802. For the past six weeks or more he had been so uncomfortable in his bed that friends felt compelled to remain up with him at night. None was more dedicated to the old soldier than the Reverend William Hill, Morgan's pastor. Henry Lee reported that as a younger man Morgan had expressed a great dread of death, saying he would be content to spend part of his life as a galley slave rather than exchange it for the "unknown" world. But Hill and Lemuel Brent, another Winchester friend, observed that Morgan believed God had forgiven him for his follies of earlier years and that he faced death with the same courage he had displayed

5. Washington to Morgan, Apr. 10, 1799, Fitzpatrick, ed., *Writings of Washington*, XXXVII, 182-83.

6. Morgan's will, Graham, *Morgan*, 460-62; Morgan to Presley Neville, July 26, 1798, Myers Coll., N. Y. Pub. Lib.

throughout life. Mentally he retained his old vigor. Subsequently a neighbor remembered "verbatim" a conversation between the patient and his physician during the last days. "Doctor," said the General, "if I could be the man I was when I was twenty-one years of age, I would be willing to be stripped stark naked on the top of the Allegheny Mountain, to run for my life with a pack of dogs at my heels." But the past was gone. Morgan died on the morning of July 6, 1802, at the age of sixty-six.[7]

William Hill preached Morgan's funeral address. He described the major events of the General's life, even calling attention to Morgan's wild escapades as a young man. Hill himself had found Morgan "a steady friend, and one whose heart could not stand the face of distress or the tale of woe." He knew that Winchester would always remember its "Beloved Patriot and Hero."[8]

But within 100 years, visitors might have wondered whether the local citizens had ever heard of their old hero. Morgan's remains had been removed from the original burial location, the local Presbyterian graveyard, for fear Yankee soldiers would carry them away during the Civil War; they were reinterred in Mount Hebron Cemetery in 1868. His gravestone, already chipped and blurred, became more difficult to read. And as the cemetery expanded, the older part where Morgan's casket lay was no longer properly attended; grass grew up around the General's marker. Then, in July 1951, Winchester was rudely awakened. At Spartanburg, South Carolina, a city near the Cowpens battlefield, the chapter of the Daughters of the American Revolution enlisted the aid of other civic groups to remove the General's

7. Henry Lee, *Memoirs of the War in the Southern Department*, 393; Brent to Sparks, Sept. 3, 1827, Sparks Papers, Harvard College Lib.; David H. Conrad, "Early History of Winchester," Winchester, Va. Hist. Soc., *Annual Papers*, 1 (1931), 172; Graham, *Morgan*, 448-49; Fredericksburg *Virginia Herald*, July 20, 1802.

8. The sermon is in Hill's Notes.

remains to their community, where they would be accorded more respect than at Winchester. But when a Spartanburg delegation with picks and shovels appeared at Mount Hebron Cemetery in Winchester, a startled caretaker called the police. Soon a crowd of Winchester "patriots" gathered at the cemetery, determined to keep what was rightfully theirs. Outnumbered, the South Carolinians retreated home. *Life* magazine described the incident in a lively article entitled, "Who Gets the General's Body?"

In the end, Morgan's memory was the victor, for the Winchester-Frederick County Historical Society erected an impressive granite monument bearing the General's likeness over the grave. Unveiled by children descended from members of Morgan's first rifle company, it was dedicated by Congressman Burr P. Harrison. Even in death, Morgan was the center of activity and not a little controversy.[9]

9. *Life*, 31 (Sept. 3, 1951), 53-54.

BIBLIOGRAPHICAL ESSAY

Bibliographical Essay

O F ALL THE sources pertinent to Morgan's story, four may be called indispensable; without them the General's biography could not be written. This essay perforce must begin with the materials of Reverend William Hill of Winchester, Morgan's pastor and intimate friend, who first had in mind a life of Morgan. Encouraging the General to reminisce and taking down his remarks, Hill thus gathered valuable data for a book which, for some reason, he never wrote, although he lived in Winchester until his death in 1852. That Morgan's memory was fairly accurate and that Hill usually recorded precisely what he heard are indicated by the fact that many of Hill's statements can be corroborated elsewhere. The major exception to this generalization is Hill's contention that Gates tried to draw Morgan into a plot against Washington after Saratoga, that Gates failed to acknowledge Morgan's valuable services against Burgoyne, and that Morgan initially refused to join Gates in the South in 1780. Contemporary documents fail to reveal any substance to Hill's claim. Yet Hill, by giving his "Morgan-Gates controversy" to Henry Lee (*A History of the War in the Southern Department*), has kept it alive; almost every anti-Gates historian includes it in his writings.

As for Hill's recorded remarks on Morgan, they consist of biographical data ("Hill's Notes" in my footnotes) in the Virginia Historical Society's Ludwell-Lee Papers, and an outline of his proposed biography in the Union Theological Seminary Library in Richmond, Virginia. Hill also wrote a brief, unpublished sketch of Morgan used by James Graham in his full biography of Morgan. Graham's *The Life of General Daniel Morgan* ... (1856) is even more valuable than Hill's material. My over-all reaction to Graham's labors is one of admiration. Without the advantages of our modern, well-ordered research libraries with their rich manuscript collections, not to mention the wealth of printed matter to roll from the presses in recent times, this congressman from New Orleans collected no small amount of information in preparing Morgan's biography. He saw many of the published works available in his day, such as Jared Sparks's edition of Washington's Papers and Tarleton's memoirs; and he gained access to part of the Nathanael Greene Papers.

Since Graham married one of Morgan's great granddaughters, he had certain unique advantages—a good deal of family information, an essay on Morgan by his grandson Morgan Neville, and, most important, the General's own Papers which were still in the family. For the most part Graham was judicious in his analysis of this material, displaying far more objectivity than many mid-nineteenth-century biographers. The rub is that Graham failed to emphasize Morgan's unique contributions with light troops and he showed no inclination to picture the whole man—his book in reality is the study of a public figure and his times.

These deficiencies can in part be remedied by a careful reading of the General's Papers, which now reside in the New York Public Library's Theodorous B. Myers Collection, Myers having purchased them in New Orleans late in the last century and subsequently donating them to this magnificent repository. Actually, Graham printed most of the pertinent military correspondence in toto in his book. Since he was generally careful in transcribing the letters, I have often cited his work instead of the manuscripts themselves. For the purposes of greater accessibility, I have also followed this procedure for copies of letters in this book, although attempting to check the originals whenever it seemed feasible or desirable.

Though much of the Myers Collection appears in print, there are many valuable unpublished documents, military and non-military in nature. Some items bearing on the Revolutionary War, which Graham considered unimportant, show Morgan's thoughts on tactics, supply problems, his fellow officers, and other matters. Then, too, there are many revealing letters on Morgan's personal life and his post-Revolutionary business ventures; especially worthwhile in these respects is the Morgan-Presley Neville correspondence.

BIBLIOGRAPHICAL ESSAY

The fourth category of material warranting the designation "indispensable" consists of the Virginia records preserved in the Frederick County Clerk's Office and the Virginia State Library. Frederick County has availed itself of the state law to deposit valuable papers in the State Library to insure their preservation. Here the Frederick Legislative Petitions and Personal Property Tax Books were of immense value, as were the microfilm copies of the Frederick Superior Court Deed Books, Deed Books, Will Books, and Order Books. Using most of these records, along with Morgan's Suit Papers in the Clerk's Office in Winchester, I was able to piece together the story of Morgan's life before the Revolution as well as to unravel some problems concerning his postwar activities. The William Allason Papers, also in the State Library, threw light on Morgan's social diversions and his indebtedness.

A special word about the Order Books and Suit Papers is appropriate. They are a mine of information on social and economic history. Fascinating reading, they demonstrate that Morgan's rowdy conduct and his numerous debts were far from being odd or unusual in the two decades before Lexington and Concord.

Numerous repositories in this country shelter Morgan letters or other documents that illuminate various portions of his life. These include the William L. Clements Library, University of Michigan: Nathanael Greene Papers (particularly the Southern campaign of 1781); Duke University Library: Danske Dandridge Papers (strong on Morgan as a Federalist politician); Harvard College Library: Jared Sparks Papers (especially a lengthy Morgan biographical letter from Lemuel Brent of Winchester to Sparks, Sept. 3, 1827); Haverford College Library: Charles Roberts Autograph Collection; Historical Society of Pennsylvania: Ferdinand J. Dreer, Frank M. Etting, and Simon Gratz collections; Library of Congress: George Washington Papers; National Archives: Papers of the Continental Congress; New-York Historical Society: Horatio Gates Papers (contain more significant hitherto unpublished information on Morgan's military service than any other except the New York Public Library's Myers Collection); State Historical Society of Wisconsin: Lyman C. Draper Papers. Additional collections in these and other locations also illustrate some of Morgan's activities.

Turning to contemporary newspapers and magazines, I was disappointed to find them far less valuable than I had foreseen. For the years of the war with England, the Williamsburg *Virginia Gazette* provided some information on Morgan, although the data is not extremely significant. By far the most rewarding newspapers were the *Virginia Journal and Alexandria Advertiser* and the *Columbian Mirror and Alexandria Advertiser* containing electioneering and other letters on politics in the 'nineties by Morgan and his Republican antagonist, Robert Rutherford. From newspapers I went to periodicals. Recalling the spate of Civil War reminiscences in late nineteenth-century magazines, I hoped to see something remotely comparable in the periodical literature during the thirty years after the Revolutionary War. Judging from the twenty or so journals I was able to examine, very little material of that kind exists. One Morgan letter came to light in the *Time Peace*, 1 (1797).

Certain key federal and state documentary publications help fill in Morgan's story: *American State Papers; Annals of Congress; American Archives; Calendar of Virginia State Papers and Other Manuscripts; Journals of the Continental Congress; Journals of the House of Delegates; Journals ... of the ... Council of State of Virginia; Letters of Members of the Continental Congress; Official Letters of the Governors of the State of Virginia; State Records of North Carolina.*

Further invaluable edited works are the published papers of Morgan's contemporaries. Particularly worthy of note are Julian P. Boyd's edition of the Jefferson Papers (still in progress); John C. Fitzpatrick's Washington Papers; Jared Sparks's letters to Washington; Charles Lee Papers (no editor mentioned); Elizabeth Merritt's Williams Papers. All of these have letters to or from Morgan. It is entirely possible that Morgan material will come forth in one or more of the editorial projects being planned or already under way; these include the Papers of Franklin, Madison, and Hamilton.

Just as I have benefited from the labors of many editors, so have I profited from the books and articles of innumerable scholars who have worked the field before me. Fortunately, the past dozen years have witnessed a great revival of interest in the military side of the Revolution, not to be compared with the Civil War mania but still impressive. In this period our best general histories have come forth —by John C. Miller, Willard Wallace, Christopher Ward, Lynn

BIBLIOGRAPHICAL ESSAY

Montross, John R. Alden, George F. Scheer and Hugh Rankin, and Howard Peckham. Their excellent bibliographies, and to a limited extent my footnotes, point out the major diaries, memoirs, monographs, and other special studies of the War for Independence.

A number of fairly recent biographies have also broadened my perspective on Morgan and his comrades in arms. Louis Gottschalk's two volumes on Lafayette in America, appearing in 1937 and 1942, bear the marks of first-rate scholarship. In 1941 Samuel W. Patterson brought forth a study of Horatio Gates, corrective in some ways but nevertheless much too laudatory. That same year Harry E. Wildes came out with his *Anthony Wayne*. Seven years later, with the Revolutionary "renaissance" just beginning, Douglas S. Freeman presented the first two volumes of his exhaustive biography of Washington; if there is any merit in the contention of some critics that Washington himself is partially obscured by a mountain of detail, it is also true that Freeman's work contains one of the most valuable bibliographies of the Revolutionary War to date. John R. Alden in 1951 wrote a biography of Washington's antagonist, Charles Lee, whose conduct at Monmouth was viewed somewhat favorably. This was followed in 1954 by Willard M. Wallace's splendid *Traitorous Hero*, a life of Benedict Arnold, suggestive and revealing to me since Arnold and Morgan displayed many of the same soldierly qualities. Finally, the year 1960 brought Theodore Thayer's biography of Nathanael Greene, Thayer being the first of several Greene scholars to reach publication. Along with these generals on the shelf of Revolutionary biography, Daniel Morgan deserves a place.

INDEX

Index

A

Acland, Maj. John, 72
Adams, Abigail, 142
Adams, John, 22, 63, 99, 203, 206
Albany, N. Y., 61, 63, 64, 71
Alexandria, Va., 178, 186
Allason, David, 8, 10
Allason, William, 8, 9, 177
Allentown, N. J., 87
Amboy, N. J., 58, 59, 60
Ames, Fisher, 200
Anderson, Lt. Thomas, 141, 151
Andrews, Lt., 53
Annapolis, Md., 119
Arnold, Benedict, 98, 173, 211, 213; Quebec expedition, 27-44; wounded, 44-45; spends winter outside Quebec, 50; praises Morgan, 54; joins Northern army, 61, 63, 64; plans attack on Burgoyne, 65; supports Morgan at Freeman's farm, 67-69; disputes report, 70-71, 76; joins Morgan at Bemis Heights battle, 73, 75; contribution to Saratoga victory, 75-76
Ashby, John, 3, 6, 7

B

Balcarres, Lord, 72-73
Bateaux, 29-35 *passim*
Bath, Va., 181
Battletown (Berryville, Va.), 9, 10, 12*n.*
Bedinger, Daniel, 204, 205
Bedinger, Henry II, 204, 205
Bemis Heights, description of, 64; battle of, 71-75, 209
Bennington, battle of, 63
Berkeley County, 22, 101, 201
Bigelow, Maj. Timothy, 27, 48, 49, 53
Biggs, Gen. Benjamin, 208
Blackburn, Samuel, 13
Board of War, 83, 117, 158
Bohanan, Capt. Ambrose, 176
Brackenridge, Hugh H., 192, 197, 198
Braddock, Gen. Edward, 3, 4, 5, 6
Bradford, David, 188, 194
Brandywine, 78, 79
Brent, Lemuel, 213
Breymann, Lt. Col. Heinrich von, 75

227

INDEX

Lincoln, Gen. Benjamin, 101, 102, 116
Livingston, Col. James, 41, 43, 46, 47
Long Canes, battle of, 125
Loring, Betsy, 85
Loring, Joshua, Jr., 85

M

McDonald, Maj. Angus, 14, 16, 17, 22
McDowell, Maj. Charles, 133
Mackenzie, Roderick, 154
Maclean, Col. Allan, 38
Madison, James, 187
Marion, Francis, 108, 121, 210
Marshall, John, 203, 206
Mathews, Gen. Thomas, 190
Maxwell, Gen. William, 78, 79, 86
Meigs, Maj. Return J., 28, 30, 32, 33, 35, 47, 48, 49
Mercer, John F., 174, 175
Merchant, George, 39, 39n.
Militia in the Southern campaigns. See Gates; Greene; Morgan; Marion; Pickens; Sumter
Mingo Indians, 17
Mitchell, John, 194
Monmouth campaign, 86-91
Monongahela River, 191, 192
Montgomery, Gen. Richard, 40-44 passim, 53, 54
Montreal, 27, 40, 54, 63
Morgan, Abigail Curry, 15, 56, 100, 183, 184; background and character, 11

Morgan, Betsy, 11, 181, 182, 183, 209, 213
Morgan, Daniel, arrives in Winchester, 1; general characteristics, 1, 9, 11, 88, 169, 170, 171; parents and early life, 2; journeys to Virginia, 2-3; works at various jobs, 3; an independent teamster, 3, 8, 12; joins Braddock's expedition, 4; physical strength and stamina, 4-5, 9, 34, 35, 47-48, 53, 145, 149, 152, 191; whipped for striking British soldier, 4-5; temperament, 4, 9, 38, 39, 40, 52-53, 109, 157, 158, 169, 172, 174, 191; stays with Dunbar's command, 5, 6; becomes a ranger, 6; wounded by Indians, 7; drinking and card playing, 7-8; pride, 9, 96-100 passim, 170, 171; alleged misdemeanors, 10; early relationship and eventual marriage to Abigail Curry, 10-11, 15; rents farm, 12; financial difficulties, 12-13, 106, 157, 158, 165-66, 177-78; buys land, 13; holds minor county positions, 13-14; gains respect of important county leaders, 14; militia captain in Dunmore's War, 16, 17, 18; opposes Boston Port Act, 19; raises rifle company, 22-23; march to Cambridge, 24-25, 25n.; employs sharpshooters against British, 25; renews acquaintance with Gates, 25; joins Arnold's Canadian expedition, 26; commands

232

mands troops left in whisky country, 193-95, 196-98; defeated for House of Representatives, 195-96; performance in whisky country summarized, 198; supports Jay's Treaty, 199; elected to House of Representatives, 199-201; Morgan's opponent unsuccessfully contests election, 201-3; encounter with *Philanthropos*, 203-5; supports Federalist measures, 203, 206, 207; on Virginia Resolutions, 204-5; "Soldier's Rest," Morgan's home, 209; significance as a Revolutionary leader, 209-12; religious views, 212, 213; final will and death, 213-14; funeral address, 214; controversy over Morgan's remains, 214-15

Morgan, Nancy, 11, 181, 182, 183, 189

Morgan, Willoughby, 183, 184, 185

Morgan's rifle company, 34, 44, 50; composition, 23; march to Boston, 24-25; losses at Quebec, 55

Morgan's rifle corps, 62, 66, 67, 68, 72-75 *passim;* formed, 57; skirmishes in N. J., 58, 59, 60; searches for Howe, 60; skilled in Indian methods, 61; harasses Burgoyne's scouts, 64-65; accomplishments at Freeman's farm, 69-70; subject of Arnold-Gates quarrel, 70-71; needed in Pennsylvania, 78; some men

without shoes, 79; acclaimed by Lafayette, 79; stops Grey's thrust, 81; occupies Philadelphia, 86; harasses Clinton through N. J., 86-89, 92; disbanded, 92

Morison, George, 48

Morris, Maj. Jacob, 66-67

Morristown, N. J., 56

Muhlenberg, Gen. Peter, 100

Murphy, Timothy, 73-74, 170-71

N

Nelson, Gov. Thomas, 162, 163, 165, 166, 169

Nelson, Maj. William, 162, 163, 165

Neville, Col. John, 94, 182, 188, 193, 196

Neville, Presley, 182, 186, 188, 189, 196, 206

New Brunswick, N. J., 58, 59

Newburgh Addresses, 175

Newburyport, Mass., 28

New Providence, N. C., 112, 113

New Windsor, N. Y., 79

New York City, 54, 60, 86, 92, 213

Ninety-Six, S. C., 111, 124, 126, 130, 146, 149, 167

Nixon, John, 75

North Carolina Board of War, 109, 110

Northern army, Ar..erican. *See* Burgoyne; Gates; Morgan

Northwest Territory, 179, 184

INDEX

O

Ogden, Matthias, 28
Ohio country, 16
Oriskany, N. Y., 63

P

Pacolet River, 122, 124, 126, 129, 130
Partisan warfare in South. *See* Marion; Pickens; Sumter; Morgan
Paterson, John, 75
Pee Dee River, 121, 130, 149, 150, 153
Peekskill, N. Y., 61
Pemberton, James, 84
Pennsylvania riflemen, 22, 25, 26, 28, 32, 34
Peters, Richard, 83
Philadelphia, Pa., 60, 80, 86, 119, 193, 194, 203
Phillips, Gen. William, 65, 68, 148
Pickens, Col. Andrew, 122, 125, 129, 133, 136-44 *passim*, 146, 210
Pinckney, Charles C., 205
Pindell, Dr. Richard, 145, 146
Pittsburgh, Pa., 186, 192-97 *passim*
Plains of Abraham, 38, 41
Point aux Trembles, 40
Pompton, N. J., 93
Poor, Gen. Enoch, 72
Porterfield, Charles, 52
Posey, Thomas, 180
Princeton, N. J., 56
Proclamation of 1763, 16

Province Island, 80
Putnam, Gen. Israel, 61, 79

Q

Quebec, 27, 36-41 *passim*, 53, 54, 209, 212

R

Radnor Meeting House, 81
Ramsour's Mill, N. C., 148
Rawdon, Lord, 143, 167
Read, Dr. William, 152
Republican party, 187, 203, 206, 207
Richmond, Va., 119, 157, 161, 164, 165, 175
Riedesel, Maj. Gen. Baron von, 65, 69, 73
Riedesel, Mrs. von, 74
Riflemen. *See* Kentucky rifle; Morgan's rifle company; Morgan's rifle corps
Rose, Duncan, 158
Roxbury, Mass., 25
Rugeley, Col. Roland, 113
Rutherford, Robert, 195, 199-203 *passim*, 205, 212
Rutledge, John, 118, 127, 146

S

St. Clair, Gen. Arthur, 95, 184
St. Lawrence River, 36, 44
St. Leger, Col. Barry, 63
Salisbury, N. C., 148, 150, 151
Saratoga, N. Y., 63, 75
Sault au Matelot, 42, 46, 47
Savannah, Ga., 126, 169
Schuyler, Gen. Philip, 27, 40, 41*n.*, 62

INDEX

X

XYZ affair, 206, 207

Y

Yadkin River, 111, 148, 150, 151, 152

DATE DUE
